are they not all

ministering spirits

sent forth

to minister for them

who shall be

heirs of salvation

# DORSET'S BEST CHURCHES

BRENDAN LEHANE

*Photographs by David Bailey*

THE DOVECOTE PRESS

*To Joanna, who shared it all, with love and thanks.*

All Persons are requested to take off, Pattens and Clogs before entering ---➤the Church ◄←

*Trent, notice in the porch.*

First published in 2006 by The Dovecote Press Ltd
Stanbridge, Wimborne Minster, Dorset BH21 4JD

HARDBACK ISBN 1 904349 49 8
PAPERBACK ISBN 1 904349 41 2

Text © Brendan Lehane 2006
All Photographs are © David Bailey 2006,
except the interior of St Mary, East Lulworth,
which is © The Weld Estate/photographer David Bailey

The author has asserted his rights under the Copyright, Designs
and Patent Act 1988 to be identified as author of this work

Designed by The Dovecote Press
Printed and bound in Singapore

All papers used by The Dovecote Press are natural, recyclable products
made from wood grown in sustainable, well-managed forests

A CIP catalogue record for this book is available
from the British Library

1 3 5 7 9 8 6 4 2

# CONTENTS

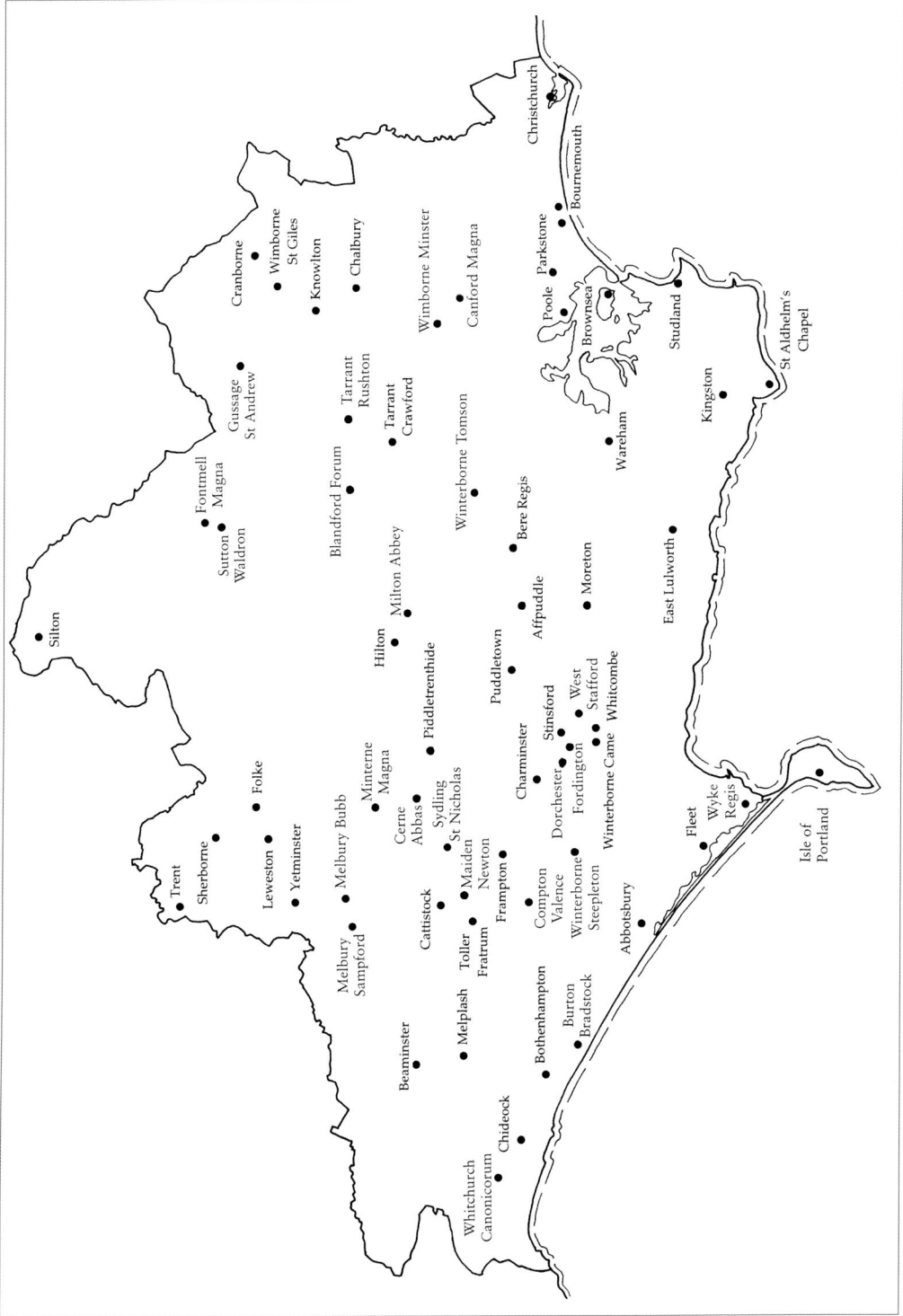

Christchurch

Bournemouth

Cranborne

Wimborne St Giles

Knowlton

Chalbury

Wimborne Minster

Canford Magna

Parkstone

Poole

Brownsea

Studland

St Aldhelm's Chapel

Gussage St Andrew

Tarrant Rushton

Tarrant Crawford

Winterborne Tomson

Kingston

Wareham

Fontmell Magna

Blandford Forum

Bere Regis

Sutton Waldron

Silton

Milton Abbey

Hilton

Piddletrenthide

Affpuddle

Moreton

East Lulworth

Puddletown

Folke

Minterne Magna

Stinsford

West Stafford

Whitcombe

Melbury Bubb

Cerne Abbas

Sydling St Nicholas

Charminster

Dorchester

Fordington

Winterborne Came

Lewestton

Yetminster

Maiden Newton

Fleet

Wyke Regis

Trent

Sherborne

Cattistock

Frampton

Compton Valence

Winterborne Steepleton

Abbotsbury

Isle of Portland

Melbury Sampford

Toller Fratrum

Beaminster

Melplash

Bothenhampton

Burton Bradstock

Whitchurch Canonicorum

Chideock

# INTRODUCTION

Dorset churches, like those of other counties, are generally at the centre of a village, open during daylight hours and free. They offer space to pray, meditate, introspect, repent, forgive, resolve, shelter from rain. They still house religious services, but these, since a diminishing number of us attend, can be rare. Why do we go in? Well, they have – whether you go for such things or not – strong links with matters thought to be as on a higher plane than the daily round, momentous events like birth, marriage and death. Most Dorset churches have been the custodians of such concerns for hundreds of years. Many of us were as children brought to services on Sundays whether we liked it or not, and have with the years, even if we are not believers, developed some nostalgia for the music and words we grew accustomed to then. Some of us feel we can keep in touch with the beloved dead, the parents or grandparents who accompanied us, or with ancestors we never met, or, in some unspoken way, with a human hope that may go back to the beginning of human existence.

What about people, especially younger people, who do not feel the same draw, who were never encouraged to think of churches as theirs or as holding out a welcome to them? Why should they bother? More than anything, the church is usually the only accessible building in the village whose walls remember a thousand years of colourful history and personal dramas. Most Dorset country churches have supplied the central threads in the lives of twenty, thirty, even forty generations, and here they still stand, patched, propped, leaning in places, heavily reconstructed in others, but still – many of them – essentially the churches that have stood for five and more centuries, often beautiful, sometimes moving, usually packed with character and more tangible legacies from the distant past. You can be fairly sure when you stand in a mainly Perpendicular, fifteenth century church (which most in the county are) that the serene space before you has witnessed erring villagers publicly disgraced, the fear evoked by hellfire homilies, criminals taking sanctuary from the law, wall paintings depicting the naked damned hauled hellwards by demons, parsons evicted for being Catholic, or not Catholic, or High Church, or Low Church, or drunk, or dishonest, numerous religious statues hooked down and smashed on the flagstone floor, yards of exquisite stained glass shattered by government officials with poles and bars, devils exorcised, horses stabled (a familiar practice during the Civil War), ghosts appearing to the susceptible, two-hour sermons preached to congregations kept wakeful by vergers with prods, thanks given for victories over French fleets, Algerian pirates, the Spanish Armada, Napoleon, Hitler (all of whom at times threatened the harbours of Dorset) and thousands more cameos of the county's history. At times, war has been waged in the church itself, as when one faction set fire to the part of Sherborne occupied by the other, or Cromwell turned Shroton church into a temporary prison.

But not many of these things have left visible traces. We have to be told, or to read about them. All too often, though we know they must have happened, the scarcity of records means there is absolutely nothing with which to conjure up or describe the notable incidents of long ago. To make things rather more difficult, people who have in the past embraced a new building style have very often disliked and, if they could afford to, destroyed as much as they could of

*Hilton, medieval carving of a bagpipe player* (see page 73). *Others can be found at Piddletrenthide and Stinsford.*

the styles that preceded them. Normans seem to have left few Saxon churches standing, certainly no wooden ones in Dorset. Large parts of our Perpendicular churches replaced earlier bits which offended the new builders' taste: central towers gave place to west towers, and the curvy window tracery of former times to stiffly upright patterns. Seventeenth century architects were happy to demolish Tudor buildings. Georgians hated Gothic. Victorians despised Georgian, but for a long time, instead of introducing styles of their own, they went back to medieval

*West Stafford, the royal arms of James I* (see page 138). *Displaying royal arms was made compulsory after Charles II's Restoration.*

Gothic – or rather to very limited snatches of the Gothic era. In their turn Victorian styles were vilified until in the mid-20th century John Betjeman opened a whole generation's eyes to the attractions of much that survived. We of today are a uniquely eclectic age, keen – officially anyway – to preserve almost any building representative of the past.

A happy result of the chopped, chequered architectural history of many English churches is the way many have come down to us in a delightful jumble of style, shape, ornament and texture. They look marvellous, those archetypal village shapes, with their crenellated towers, turrets and aisles, their arched doors and windows, their blotchy accretions of moss, lichens, cracks and warts, as full of character as a carbuncled Rembrandt face. There will usually be much more inside: not just architectural features and standard furniture like pews, pulpits and altar, not only dignified monuments, effigies, shrines, screens as tall as the ceiling, statues of saints and heroes. Many Dorset churches offer whimsy and humour too. Strange scenes stare at us from the tops of columns, from the underneaths of ancient fold-up seats, or from the beams of ceilings. There are geese hanging foxes, foxes preaching sermons, a boy being caned on his bared bottom, the swollen cheek of a sufferer from toothache, an effigy with two left feet, medieval bagpipes, pictorial riddles, a mermaid, tortoises, pomegranates, three hares with but three ears between them, the teasing Green Men with leaves for hair and twigs growing from their nostrils – and so on and so on.

This random pageant of congruous and incongruous survivals arouses in many a wish – sometimes a consuming wish – to find where every enduring component fits into the pattern of the past and how any particular church comes to be in its present state. Why do steps lead up one side of the chancel arch and nothing emerge on the other? Why are half the nave's columns round and the rest eight-sided? Why does this buttress clasp the outside wall like a limpet and that one curve gracefully away to plant its vertical pillar yards from the wall? Why is one church so dark and another so light? What explains the outward lean of so many nave and chancel walls? Why is the organ of one church set on the west-end gallery and that of another tucked into a chapel off the chancel? What led to doors being bricked up? Why are some altars placed among the congregation's pews and some far away, up steps and flush against the east wall? How have murals or box pews or old stained glass survived in at least fragmentary form in one church and left no trace in another? Why are the interiors of most churches plastered but a few of bare, cold stone? Why do wall marks show a nave's or chancel's roof was once several feet higher or lower?

In almost every case, what appears a mystery turns out to be a clue, an often cryptic pointer to some aspect of the church's past. Considered together, the clues may disclose some of the church's history, periods of extravagance or cutting back, some fashion in ornament or design, a local school of craftsmen, a time when civil war or epidemic meant the rapid succession of parsons and perhaps lasting damage to the structure, a shift towards Puritanism, or – the other way – to High Church practices, a pushy family in the neighbouring manor or the influence of a particularly long-lived parson. Often, we can see where in that history a surviving piece fits: the Tudor couple recumbent under a carved canopy, the crusader's helmet, the martyr's wonder-working tomb, seventeenth century stained glass from Holland, the twentieth century archbishop's vestments, the Saxon rock carved into the crude likeness of a winged angel, a Latin tribute to some 18th century grandee.

Many people of course ask no more of churches than the chance to go in, admire, wonder or disparage, feel akin or alien,

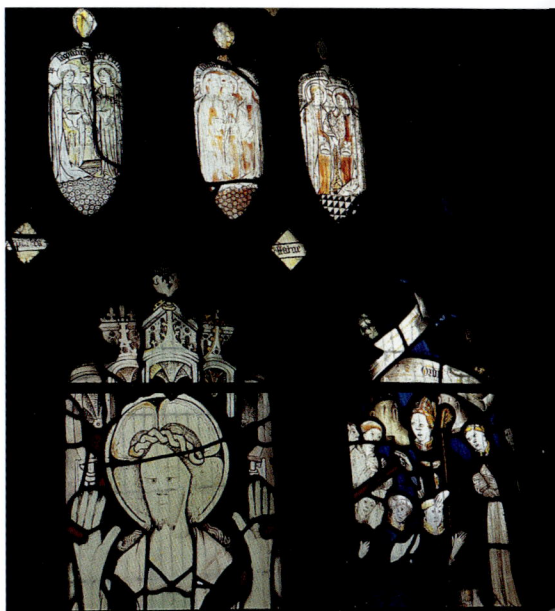

*Stained glass at Melbury Bubb* (see page 83). *Three different stories in a single panel.*

ponder awhile and leave. Others prefer to read, mark and learn, to work out who built when, or the source of a style, or how new fashion was made possible by new technology, discover the progress of construction, spot signs of puritan wrecking, 18th century neglect or Victorian glossing. Their interest may grow in one or other category of things. One day a pillar comes across as no more than a staff of stone, holding something up. The next it may be seen to possess texture, shape, ornament, a stylish capital and base, wear, character, the marks of a particular period. It has grown a biography, and a context. So too with stained glass, the tracery of a window, gravestone lettering, a medieval mural, royal arms, misericords, screens, bosses and bench-ends. Gradually the timeless parish church, taken for granted for half a lifetime, discloses innumerable quests that will take the searcher into history's recesses and, if he or she chooses, to other churches throughout Dorset and far beyond.

# THE CHURCHES

## ABBOTSBURY

*St Nicholas*

In evening sunlight the terraces worn by medieval tillage into the slope of St Catherine's Hill are shown up by the alternation of bright green and shadowy stripes. The sun's rays also show up the bumpy protuberances and uneven dips of the adjacent hills and valleys. These are the kind of contours not fashioned by nature but by human use: sites of buildings, farm works, tracks, a whole village, but most dramatically and best recorded – a whole monastery.

From a few years before the Norman Conquest to the immediate aftermath of Henry VIII's dissolution of the monasteries, covering what is now the southern part of St Nicholas' churchyard and some land beyond, there stood the massive structures of a Benedictine abbey: the palatial chamber of the abbey church, the broad arcaded square of the cloisters, refectory, dormitories, libraries, reading-rooms, kitchens, abbot's quarters, estate offices for the management of the surrounding farms and manors – all of these alive with the comings and goings of monks, priests, clerks, reeves, pardoners and nuns, with the crunch of hooves and carriage wheels, the hum and resonant chant of worship, the buzz of conversation, greeting and conspiracy, and the turbulent colours, the reds, golds, greens and blues of cloaks, and rich weaves and embroideries of clerical vestments. The abbey's wealth is still evidenced by the tithe barn and the late 14th century chapel of St Catherine, solidly intact on Chapel Hill nearby, with bulky buttresses

TOP *St Catherine's Chapel, with the Fleet and Chesil Beach beyond, and Portland in the distance.*

BOTTOM *Abbotsbury; the nave, reredos and bullet-scarred pulpit.*

supporting a fine stone barrel vault. That buoyant medieval world of perpetual and colourful commotion is hard to conjure from today's tame sward, gravestones and the few lonely ruined fragments that still stand.

Abruptly, after 500 years, almost everything was gone. In 1505 the local magnate, Thomas Strangways, endowed a chantry chapel and the requital of priests who would, in perpetuity, pray for his own and his family's salvation. Perpetuity had not lasted forty years before Thomas's son Giles was among the leaders of a fundamental reversal. He was appointed agent for the disposition of monastic lands, allotted himself the plum estates of Abbotsbury and agreed to the terms; all edifices 'within the site and precinct of the late monastery' were to be 'thrown down and removed'. Only a half of the tithe barn and the church built for the secular community were allowed to remain. Both remain today. So too do the descendants of those swans the early monks introduced as a food supply to the brackish waters of the Fleet lagoon, down at the end of the lane the churchyard fronts.

Though it is made of local rubble, the outside of the church has the honey colour of Ham-stone. The crumbly look of its surface makes it, and particularly the tower, a bit reminiscent of the battered sea cliff further along the coast at Burton Bradstock. The tower is at the west end, but placed a few feet north of its centre. Apart from the porch, the church forms a plain rectangle in shape. The list of vicars dates from 1312, and the porch and much of the north wall, which has battlements, was built in the 14th century. The tower came early in the 15th century. It was then, presumably, fairly central to the west wall. A rebuilding later in the century produced the present chancel's east wall and the north aisle's east end, or north chapel

*Abbotsbury. Only the church and tithe barn survive from the great Benedictine abbey.*

(which now contains the organ). Then, early in the 16th century, the two nave arcades and a new south aisle (lacking battlements) were built, rendering the tower off-centre. The position of the old east window, now blocked up but easy to locate from the outside, seems to have been off-centre in both arrangements. The six identical Perpendicular windows of the south aisle make an impressive front, but the round arches above them are very unperpendicular, perhaps an unusual personal whim. Gargoyles around the church are well preserved and not very ferocious.

Inside the two-storey porch an archbishop greets us. He is of Purbeck marble and dates to about 1200. The personality of the interior is unusual. Under a flat white roof it is not by and large richly furnished, and then again not poorly. It is not markedly spacious but certainly not cramped. It is not dirty or neglected, but not pampered or burnished either. It has an easy-going, comfortable, agreeable feel and look. The east end, led up to by the grand avenue of arcade pillars and

seeming, under its plaster barrel-vault, to keep the best contents to itself, exercises a strong draw as you wander round the west end and middle. Still, there is plenty to catch the eye elsewhere. Above the sadly inaccessible west gallery it is possible to glimpse, but only glimpse, tantalising wall memorials and a hatchment. The octagonal font, probably 15th century, has two deep trefoil arches carved on each face. The royal arms attached to the gallery front, including the white horse of Hanover, blue lion of Lüneburg and two gold lions of Brunswick, but excluding the French fleur-de-lis, which was finally removed in 1801 (250 years or so after England's loss of its last scrap of French territory), and lacking the identifying initials of a king, must date to the reign of George I, II or III. Among the ordinary plant themes of the arcade capitals is one, on the second column from the east in the south arcade, which shows an animal with a doglike face, collar and beefy tapering tail swallowing a chicken whose head is already devoured. There is an original stained glass head, shoulders and clasped hands of the Virgin Mary and some other fragments in a south aisle window two from the east end. The east window of the south aisle, in memory of the fifth Earl of Ilchester, direct descendant of the first owner Sir Giles Strangways and ancestor of the present one, shows Saints Nicholas, Catherine and Andrew and some very Art Nouveau heads of children in the tracery and tops of the main lights. The beautiful pulpit, with its echoing tester, is early 17th century and richly carved. Two holes in the back of the canopy are supposed to have been caused by bullets fired by a Parliamentary army in 1646.

At the east end, two steps and the beginning of the barrel vault mark the entrance to the chancel. Ahead is the wood and plaster reredos, made and installed in mid 18th century at the expense of the original east window, a fine classical configuration carrying the timeless ten injunctions from Exodus, between

Corinthian columns, under a frieze of vine fruits and leaves and a pediment bearing two pitchers and a central bowl. Above, the white plaster curved roof of 1638 closes the view with a pattern of squares and half squares framing a variety of angels and six-winged seraphim. 'Glory to God in the Highest . . .' runs a text running through in unfurled scrolls. Masks, lotus leaves and lilies decorate the corners, while in the centre the heads of four inward-looking tortoises or turtles meet at a junction of lines. Along the lower level appear the names, dates and arms, contained in strapwork, of various 17th century members of the Strangways family. The fox that appears in some of the heraldic devices is owed to a profitable marriage into the Fox family, whose name was added to their own. More about this family appears under Melbury Sampford, their main home.

## AFFPUDDLE
### St Laurence

The river Piddle or Puddle careers down the chalk hills of central Dorset, frisking and frothing with young energy as it passes the churches of Alton Pancras, Piddlehinton, Piddletrenthide, Puddletown, and Tolpuddle. At Affpuddle, overhung by willows, it runs beside the churchyard within a landscape of trees and lush hedged meadows. The large straight-sided churchyard is lush too and far from overcrowded. Few tombstones date from before 1800. There is an avenue of eight yews that lead from nowhere special to nowhere in particular.

The tower, at the western end, is bright, tall, angular (the square-cut stair turret stresses the look), rather neat, unadulterated Perpendicular and very handsome. The trim, groomed look pervades the place, outside and in. The brightness of Portland stone is toned down by a patina of lichens, patches and stripes of flint and dark heathstone, and the warm honey-tones of the Ham-stone which was used, as often, for conspicuous details: the tower's battlements, the spruce

*Affpuddle. St Laurence.*

pinnacles sprouting from them, belfry windows and so on. Right-angled buttresses are a little set back from the corners. Gargoyles are well worn but some of the depicted monsters are recognisable. Most windows of the nave and north aisle are Perpendicular, but two in the chancel may go back to the first building in about 1230. One is the east window itself – three slightly pointed lancets, the middle one taller than those that flank it; the other the smaller window in the chancel's south wall. A third survival is the fine doorway within the south porch, with its broad, point-topped trefoil and carved plant design in the spandrels. These three features have, doubtless, over the centuries, been removed, restored and replaced in new-built walls, but their shapes and mouldings put them firmly back in the early 13th century, high point of the Early English style.

Inside, the eye is caught at once by the lumpy, glinting turbulence of carved wooden bench-ends: flowers and leaves, beads and bands, swirls and swathes and splaying inflorescences, some linenfold panels and, on the eastmost bench of the north aisle, an inscription explaining 'These seatys were made in the yere of our Lord God MCCCCCXLVII. The tyme of Thomas Lylinton, vicar of this Cherche'. (The Roman numerals for the year 1547 would normally be MDXLVII). Lylinton, or Lillington, had been a monk of Cerne Abbey, which had owned the Affpuddle estate since Saxon times. The abbot appointed him vicar in 1534, the year made ominous by Henry VIII's Act of Supremacy, whereby he created himself supreme head of the Church of England. For several years the heads of the great rolled – Thomas More's, Anne Boleyn's, Thomas Cromwell's. Colour, incense, sound, idols, some furniture were excluded from the church. Chancels, considered chambers of Romish hocus-pocus, were blocked off. The English bible and prayer book came in, frightening simple souls since Latin sounded to the rustic ear both inscrutable and just right. From 1539 the monasteries went, Cerne Abbey and about 3000 others, sold off to highest bidders or useful favourites. Sir Oliver Laurence bought Affpuddle. But Lillington, remarkably, was still vicar in 1552, commissioning these carvings while the Reformation shook the land. He may have ordered the pulpit and its carvings too, though most of Dorset's carved pulpits have come down from the early 17th century. (Not many pre-Reformation rural churches have pulpits at all. It was Protestantism which made the sermon central to the service). The roundels on the carved pulpit panels contain in four cases the symbols of the Evangelists, all given wings, and in the fifth a pelican, revered for its supposed Christian virtue in giving its own blood to restore its young to life. The human figures above, often wrongly said to be the Evangelists, are a puzzle. One looks like a crowned king, three others half-

*Affpuddle. Carved bench-end inscribed, 'These seatys were made in the yere of our Lord God mccccxlvii [1547]. The tyme of Thomas Lylinton, vicar of this Cherche'.*

monk half-clown, and the fifth a wild man, possibly John the Baptist.

The Laurence family may be assumed to have given the church its dedication to St Laurence, a 3rd century Roman priest who, told to hand over his church's treasures, gathered the local poor and presented them. For this, naturally, he was roasted on a gridiron. There is a memorial in the chancel to Edward Laurence, who died aged seventeen in 1751, a descendant of Sir Oliver.

One of the family became through marriage an ancestor of George Washington, and the claim is made that the bars and stars in the Laurence family arms became the stars and stripes of the American flag. The same family and claim are associated with the church at Steeple.

There are two fonts, both Norman, one square, one round, at either end of the north aisle. The round one, with tapering sides, is from Turnerspuddle, moved when the church became redundant. Bits of the original rood screen are included in the screen which divides the so-called Lady Chapel, at the aisle's east end, from the nave. The rood screen is also starkly recalled by the functionless gap in the wall beside the pulpit which once led to it from the stairs below. The tower arch is panelled on the inner, or soffit, side, as is the local way. The colourful reredos was made – as was the Crucifixion sculpture in the churchyard – by Loughnan Pendred. These and other ornaments were the gifts of Sir Ernest Debenham, founder of the great London drapery store. A very practical tycoon, he bought the Briantspuddle estate in 1914, and created the Arts-and-Crafts village of the same name, complete with milk factory, a mile downstream from Affpuddle. After his death in 1952 the estate was sold off in small lots.

# BEAMINSTER
*St Mary*

Binoculars, often useful in churches, are particularly so for the external tower sculptures here.

To anyone standing on the rim of hills that surrounds Beaminster, the town can look like a heavy object which, placed on a vast sheet of countryside, weighs it down in the middle. St Mary's stands at one edge of the town, and at the church's western end rises what is perhaps the most delectable church tower in Dorset. Slender, of warm, rich Ham-stone, with set-back buttresses (at right angles to the wall but away from the corner of the

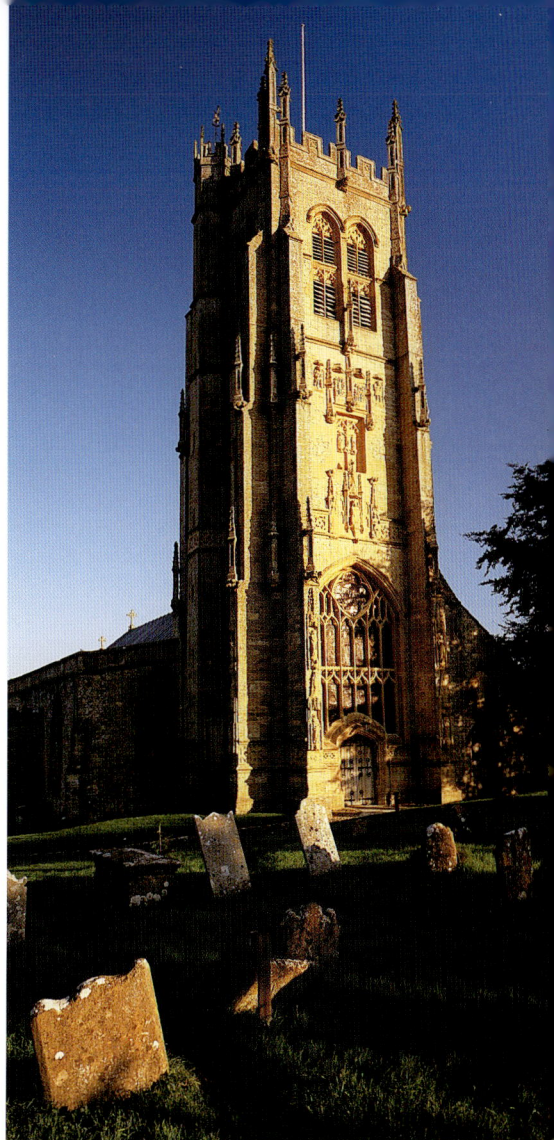

*Beaminster, perhaps the finest church tower in Dorset.*

building), battlemented on top, it jangles with pinnacles like a generalissimo's chest with decorations. Tufted with leaflike crockets, these slender little lances – over forty of them – point heavenward from battlements and stair turret, or sprout from malign gargoyles way below. More importantly, the central stage of the western face is a glorious, orderly mustering of heavily restored or replaced medieval sculpture.

The rest of the church's exterior does not

*Beaminster. Detail from the west tower showing the Crucifixion, with the Resurrection and Ascension of Christ above.*

which is a canopied figure of the crowned Virgin and Child. In the niche to the left is a badly eroded figure of St James the Less, held to be Christ's brother. That to the right is St George. On a smaller scale above is a relief carving of Christ's Crucifixion. As in most portrayals, the Virgin Mary and St John stand to left and right of the cross. Above are two detailed scenes: on the left the Resurrection – Christ rising from the dead; and on the right the Ascension of Christ into heaven. This is by no means the only version of the subject that shows a marvelling crowd and, above them, two splayed feet and the hem of an ankle-length garment rising into the ether. The figure to the left of these seems to be a journeyman with a pack strapped to his back, that to the right a fuller with his tools. The faces of both may have been recognisable when made, being perhaps likenesses of benefactors. Within the tower, pipistrelle bats make their winter home.

Though its west tower was unaccountably spared, St Mary's has seen its fair share of destruction, and not only from external enemies. There had of course been Reformation, iconoclasts, fire caused by royalists, breakage by Cromwellians, further fires, changes of fashion, the need to accommodate larger congregations, erosion by acid rain and industrial fumes, and Canon Codd. In 1862 this parson, after a period of much debate and dither, instituted a programme of repair and reorganisation. Roof, corbels, much timber, the flagstones that covered the floor, window tracery, organ, pulpit, altar rails, reading desk, box pews, wooden panels painted with Lord's Prayer, Creed, Ten Commandments and Royal Arms, the upper floor of the Mort House, were in some cases repaired and restored (not always well) or, in many cases, swept away. Railway and main road had avoided Beaminster, and lacking these links with modernity it was losing population and the need of as much seating as it had. So the galleries, which ran not only along the west end but the north and south aisles as well,

match up. Windows are mainly tall, three-light, 15th century Perpendicular. The north chapel, originally of the same period but much restored in the late 18th century, has two four-light windows with tracery. The chancel's east window has five, with very simple Perpendicular tracery. There is no chapel south of the chancel, though there was once a 15th century chantry chapel. Tucked into the south-west corner of the church is the modern rebuild of an early 16th century vestry. The original was of two storeys, comprising a mort-house, or ossuary – for storing bones dug out of the churchyard to make space for new burials – and above what served among other things as a schoolroom. But the tower is the main thing, not helped by but able to overcome the incongruous big Victorian west window, with its gaping quatrefoil amid the top tracery. Six gothic niches on the one northern and two western buttresses are a feature found often in cathedrals, seldom in churches. They contain sacred figures. At the base of the main, central tableau, is a belt of quatrefoil and wheel-like panels, rising fom the centre of

*Beaminster. The memorial to George Strode and his wife, Catherine.*

were also removed. The church was gutted and transformed. Every church is accustomed to organic and gradual change, to meet evolving needs and practices. All this, I suspect, was a lesion too many. I believe too the church, like others suffering similar assaults, has never quite recovered. It has good things, the architecture is much the same, but cleared churches move more slowly than cleared garden beds. It perhaps takes longer than the 150 years that have elapsed to give St Mary's back the congruity and consistency which in the best churches allows all sorts of incongruous intrusions, all kinds of rules to be broken, but remains, simply, and in some broad sense, right or good. Which is to say, at too great length: I do not altogether like it.

The church's spacious interior is good in parts, poor in others. The oldest object, the Norman font, worn and chipped and faintly decorated with arches, has the sanctity of age but not beauty. It tells us there was a Norman church here. There was a Saxon one before that, founded in the 7th century and dedicated then to St Bee, or Bea or Begha, an Irish princess who founded a monastery on the Cumbrian coast and gave her name to the town. There is some good but uninspiring Victorian stained glass: the east chancel window, showing the Last Supper derived from Leonardo da Vinci's outside Milan, is

by William Wailes, and the east window of the south aisle by John Hardman. Close to the latter is a squint and the upper steps to the old rood loft. The Jacobean pulpit is also nearby, deprived now of the two lower desks that made it originally a three-decker, finely carved but forlornly outcast. The rood screen was replaced, after an interval of centuries, by the present one, a delicate piece of neo-gothic wood carving – with small birds among the tracery – designed by C.E.Ponting in 1912.

The vault of the Strode family, once owners of the grand mansion at Parnham, a mile or so south of the town, is under the south aisle, with its fourteen coffins in a vault reached by stone stairs. The images of two of the family are floridly above ground. Thomas, serjeant-at-law who died in 1698, is the standing figure, bewigged, robed and high-heel-shod, looking a sort of Dorset Louis XIV, poised for ever to address us in the words contained, perhaps, in the scroll he holds in his right hand. This is said to be the work of Edward Stanton. George, his nephew, dead in 1753, also in Roman robes but wigless, lies languidly beside his wife (died 1746). She seems to be reminding him of some fact or rule in the book she holds.

*Bere Regis, a tower of chequered flint and cut stone.*

The angle of his head suggests resignation, perhaps fatigue. Peter Scheemakers was the sculptor. 'I'm a little impudent fellow,' he said of himself; 'no matter, I can't help it.' He turned out hundreds of such memorials, but almost always there is a wonderful flow and naturalism in his faces, hands, drapery and the rest.

## BERE REGIS
*St John the Baptist*

From the 1300s to the early 1700s the Turberville manor stood over the road to the east of the church. The country round about

was Turberville country. Hardy, in his great novel, changed the name to D'Urberville and brought Tess Durbeyfield, her widowed mother and siblings here from Marnhull, hoping for a family link and chance of inheritance. There was neither. Unable to find lodging they camped under the church's south wall. 'Isn't your family vault your own freehold?' asked the mother vainly.

Despite the fictional gloom, and the all too non-fictional ranks of dull modern redbrick housing that nearly encircle it, and the noisy nuisances of a nearby bypass, the church of St John the Baptist, on foundations cut into rising ground, manages to assert itself very handsomely. Ageing gravestones and a line of clipped cylinder-yews like a procession of top hats grace the churchyard on all sides. The flint and ashlar chequer of the early 16th century west tower, broken by the neat tracery of its bell windows, rises past a course of many gargoyles to battlements and pinnacles large and – on the stair turret – quaintly small. The lead-roofed nave, its two-light clerestory windows peeking over the aisle roofs, links with a steeply sloping stone-roofed chancel, a 15th century reworking (as the Perpendicular windows show) of a 13th century enlargement of an original chancel built on a shorter nave in about 1050. There is a fairly standard north aisle and a much higher and more interesting south aisle, with brick intrusions among the pale ashlar, dark heathstone and flint of its walls. This aisle's east window and another, smaller one on the south side have fine flowing quatrefoil tracery. In the right light you can see from outside suggestions of the stained glass outlines. Entry to the church is by the massive brick, flint and stone-faced south porch. On its walls hang metal flails used, at the end of long poles, to pull burning or threatened thatch off roofs. Bere Regis went up in a blaze in 1788, and not much remained standing. The church did. So, in a town shorn of ancient building, the church alone retains the physical witness of a long and rich history.

Inside, the first impact comes from light, and from the bare and comforting strength of the two arcades flanking the nave – an all but monochrome vista of massive pale shapes, grey shaded stone, white walls, tan of pews and barely coloured glass of the north aisle windows opposite. Walking a few paces towards the nave confounds the pallor with a rich scatter of pigmentation. To the right is the vivid stained glass of the south aisle: the martial array of Turberville armorial shields, and the busy scene within the mullions and shapely tracery of the aisle's east window. This depicts a glum heaven: seated centrally a solemn Saviour; to his left and right a band of all-male cloaked and bearded harpists, none too cheerful; altogether the kind of oppressively pious, monotonously serene heaven that made Shaw's Don Juan (and others) plump for eternity in hell. But the execution is well done, not least the winged angels occupying the window's upper tracery, one per quatrefoil light.

We move under the arcade to the nave. The pier's capitals are enlivened by comical heads: imps, monsters, sufferers from the torments of headache and toothache. To the left, or west, through the panelled tower arch, a fine Norman font carved with a close-knit pattern of circled stars and interlocking arches stands in splendid isolation; to the right, or east, an unremarkable chancel. For the church's priceless and most astonishing feature we need to look up, to the five glorious 15th century beams of the nave roof and their rich mustering of multifarious and brightly painted wood-carvings. There are beams straight and arched, gilt-edged or painted with iterated patterns; heads and flowers and leaves and heraldry in primary colours; but above all there are the twelve apostles, jutting horizontally from the wall, resembling hammer-beams but serving no purpose except ornament, holy indeed but droll enough to lighten the longest sermon or dreariest service, nicely injecting the celestial with a touch of fairground and the cause no doubt of stiff necks by the thousand. Some

TOP *Bere Regis, a headache sufferer carved on the pier of a capital in the nave.*

BOTTOM *Bere Regis, the beams of the nave roof and their painted timber carvings of the Apostles.*

*Bere Regis, painted carvings of the Apostles
Philip and Peter on the roof beams.*

are identified by what they carry: John's
gospel, Peter's keys and church, James's
pilgrim staff, tax-gathering Matthew by his
moneybag. Judas, nearest the chancel on the
north side, carries his purse, painted gold and
filled with silver, and sports a raffishly
oriental-style beard, sign perhaps of
untrustworthiness.

Cardinal Morton, whose face fills the
central boss of the second beam from the east
end, is said to have paid for this florid canopy
as well as for the tower. His chantry chapel
was at the east end of the north aisle. Born a
few miles away at Milborne St Andrew, he
was one of the cleverest and possibly one of
the wickedest men of his time. He helped
engineer the marriage of Henry VII and
Elizabeth of York, daughter of Edward IV, to
strengthen Henry's fragile claim to the
throne. His charge that Richard III killed
Edward IV's two sons in the Tower, true or

false, also helped Henry. Under Henry he
became Archbishop of Canterbury, Lord
Chancellor, Cardinal. Morton's Fork was his
formula to justify the taxing of all clergy: the
rich could afford to pay because they were
rich; the poor because they were frugal in
their habits.

Nothing matches the unique quality of
this lively blending of effigy art and waxwork
art. The chancel has fine painted angels along
the sides of its wooden roof, and a well-
decorated late Tudor tomb-chest with a rich
canopy and brasses showing Margaret and
John Skerne. The 14th century south-side
squint retains its original iron grille. On the
north side the spiral stairway and upper
opening to the long-gone rood-loft remains.
An 1898 wheeled bier stands in the north
aisle. Back in the south aisle we see, close to
the Turberville window, two 16th century
Turberville table-tombs, made of Purbeck
marble and showing serious signs of decay.
Nearby, under a mat, is the stone that covers
the Turberville vault. These memorials, in a
state of decay and ruin, are carefully
described by Hardy when he brings unhappy
Tess in from outside to wander among her
forebears.

## BLANDFORD FORUM
*Saints Peter and Paul*

Summer, 1731. Many houses were timber-
framed; roofs were of thatch; red-hot coals
were carried to kindle a fire, or, in pans, to
warm beds; chimneys built thin; clothes long,
trailing and flammable. Means of putting
fires out were rudimentary – metal-hooked
wooden poles to drag burning thatch from
roofs, besoms and leather beaters, leather
water pails, a slow, horse-drawn or man-
drawn cart to convey the unreliable water
supply. A town burning was no great rarity.
Dorchester burned to the ground in 1613 and
again, though not so thoroughly, in 1725,
Wareham in 1762, Beaminster in 1644, 1684
and once more in 1781. London was
destroyed in 1666. Blandford itself had

sustained disastrous fires in 1579, 1677 and 1713. People were used to fires and to the labours of rebuilding.

It began at a soap-boiler's house in Blandford on the afternoon of 4th June 1731 and quickly reduced most of the town to a smouldering wreck. The medieval parish church, standing alone, was slow to catch, but by two in the morning flames had consumed the tower and were roaring up through the roof, melting lead, turning bells to liquid, splitting stone. Fourteen died in the fire, and many more later – but still as a result of it. There was, as in London, a partial compensation, at least for posterity. Blandford had its provincial Christopher Wren in the form of the Bastard brothers, John and William, well regarded builders and architects, as their father had been, and acquainted with the work of Thomas Archer, architect of nearby Chettle and much in London and elsewhere, and lone English pioneer of Continental baroque. The brothers put Blandford together again and, though the church is their best memorial, most of their work on the town was fine, creating an outstandingly consistent early Georgian townscape. It still survives. Because of the fire, Blandford is essentially a place of brick, roof tiles and slates – thatch was henceforth officially debarred. St Peter and St Paul, one of a handful of stone buildings, opened for services in 1739. The little 1760 pedimented Fire Monument, with its Doric columns, outside the western churchyard wall marks completion of the task, and has an inscription thanking divine mercy for raising Blandford 'like the PHAENIX from it's ashes'.

The church owes a debt to Wren and others, and is usually described as baroque, but the neat disposition of round-arched windows, straight and curved pediments, serried balusters, regular quoins seem far away from baroque's curvaceous arabesques. Archer's influence was mainly in small details like Ionic capitals. The Bastards did not finish the tower or intend the cupola. They planned

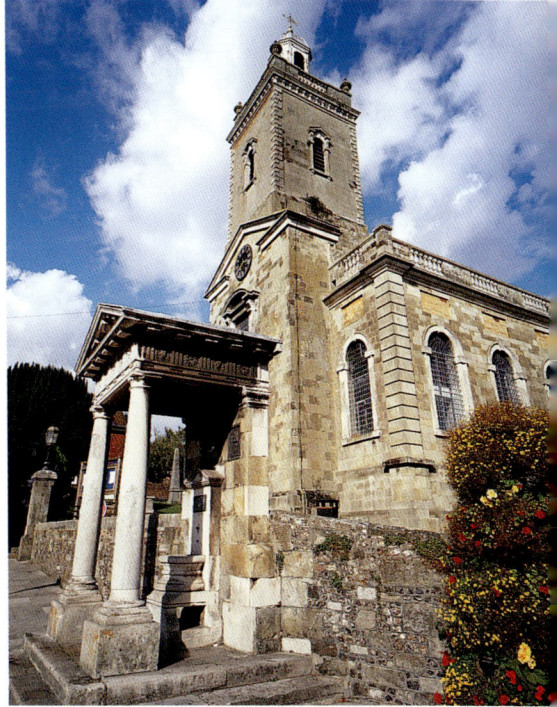

*Blandford, with the Monument to the fire of 1731, in which the town's original church was destroyed, in the foreground.*

a spire but money probably ran out – a good thing, many would argue, since the cupola is probably the best-known and most endearing feature. Their east end has changed too. The brothers provided only the apse by way of chancel, chancels in their day being of very limited function. In 1895, after chancels had come back into use and fashion, the Blandford apse was bodily moved by means of jacks and rollers to new foundations a few yards to the east, and a proper chancel erected in the space thus created. This extraordinary operation was amazingly successful in execution and effect. A year later the organ was moved from the west gallery to the chancel – a bad move in respect of both sound and sight, but one carried out by many 19th century churches. Here it was put right in 1970 when the instrument was returned to its previous home, making a handsome sight at the church's west end and

*Blandford, looking east towards the apse.*

much better sound. Similarly aisle galleries, inserted north and south in 1837 to accommodate a growing population, but spoiling the look of the interior, were removed in 1971.

The church of St Peter and St Paul looks extremely handsome, and utterly Georgian, from any angle. Its greensand ashlar, unfortunately becoming prone to crumble, is nicely set off by neat Portland quoins, architraves, pediments, balusters and so on. The commanding tower, the basic and assured ground-plan rectangle, the sentry spacing of big windows, round-topped and keystone-capped, and the almost continuous line of the balustrade, along with grand protrusions from each wall – pedimented portico on the west, shallow pedimented transepts north and south, even the soft roundness of the eastern apse - all assert the 18th century stateliness of the place. They speak of authority too. Perhaps the cupola, substituting an almost trinket prettiness for

the devout aspirations of a spire, tells something about the 18th century attitude to God.

Within, the nave is all classical space and uplift, broad and tall, light, concert-hallish, with nothing to hide, certainly no mystery. The defining elements are relatively simple: massive, unfluted columns holding not arches but a straight architrave; a fine groined vault with modelled ribs. Windows, but for colourful apostles at the base, are mostly clear and let in plenty of light. Pews, still numbered but cut down to uniform size around 1880, spread either side of the central aisle into the narrow side-aisles. Ahead, a huge chancel arch beckons like open arms. On our way to it we pass, on the right, between the columns beyond the transept, a curious red-plush-covered wooden armchair, facing inwards, under an energetically carved and top-heavy canopy. This was the seat of the bailiff, the 18th century borough's senior official, and dates from 1748. In front of it, facing inward, and almost making a church within a church, run the benches for his council. The bailiff's position would have been more convenient than it looks. Up to the big 1875 rearrangement, the tall pulpit stood imposingly in the middle of the nave, like a ship's prow bringing the message of salvation to the people. Just before the chancel arch, on the right, is the fine oak pulpit which replaced it, designed probably by Wren for a London church, St Antholin's, and brought here when that was demolished in 1874.

The chancel has a slightly warmer embrace than the nave. Use of colour gives a glow to the walls, the windows and their splays, and – forming the reredos – the figure of Christ, below a pediment which encloses cherubs and between Corinthian columns with gilded capitals. This reredos is original and apt, but the Christ, a late Victorian addition, put in place of the Lord's Prayer and Creed, and in the most conspicuous position in the church, jars, giving a very un-18th century smack of high Catholicism.

Our return to the western entrance offers an impressive view of the organ, the gallery it stands on and the attached royal arms, all of 1794. The aisle walls carry a variety of good 18th century memorial tablets; notably on the north wall to the Gannet and Creech families, and to George Vince who accompanied Scott on his 1902 Antarctic expedition and was the only member to die there; and on the south wall, members of the Pulteney, Lewen, Pitt, Bastard and Wake families. The son of William and Amy Wake became Archbishop of Canterbury from 1717-1736. It seems something was in the local air, for five other sons of Blandford became bishops about the same time. At the south aisle's west end is the graceful font of 1739, finely sculpted almost as if it were made of wood. There are records of charities on this same wall, close to the transept door. These, if the name of the town occurred on them, had it deleted at the beginning of the Second World War. Thus, the thinking went, invading German soldiers would remain in ignorance of their whereabouts. Mercifully, the stratagem was not put to the test.

# BOTHENHAMPTON
## Holy Trinity

They demolished most of the old church in the 1880s, on account of its small size and dilapidation. The chancel, all that subsequently remained, was retained as a mortuary chapel. It is still there, half a mile to the east of Holy Trinity. The Churches Conservation Trust maintains it, its table tombs, 13th century font, 18th century pedimented wooden reredos, gold-painted with texts, and graceful altar rail.

By 1890 Holy Trinity was ready for consecration. It doubtless surprised some parishioners, and still surprises visitors today. The dictates of Pugin, the Ecclesiologists, the mid century High Victorian neo-Gothicists, the rule that all the features of a neo-Gothic church must reproduce accurately the forms of the Decorated style of the 13th century and 14th century (with later allowances for Early English and Perpendicular) had by the 1880s considerably evolved. The dogmas of William Morris and the Arts and Crafts movement were of a different order; more to do with spirit, attitudes, honesty, respect for materials, craftsmen and their techniques. The architect chosen for the new church, Edward Prior, former pupil of Norman Shaw and founder member of the Art Workers' Guild, was steeped in this newer approach. He was also his own man, very ready to follow an idiosyncratic line.

Not that Prior was brought into the architectural scene of remote west Dorset for any radical or mould-breaking designs. He was young and promising, and the Norman Shaw stable was well esteemed. Perhaps more important, he had strong local connections. His mother came from a respected Bridport family; his cousin was rector of Burton Bradstock and he himself had married, in 1884, the daughter of the vicar of nearby Symondsbury. He had already designed the Pier Terrace at West Bay, formerly Bridport Harbour. He was the local boy, destined for distinction.

The outside of Prior's church is

*Bothenhampton, with its sweeping arches, consecrated in 1890 and the daring and original work of Edward Prior.*

prominently perched on a grassy knoll, but modest: sizable porch, a long steep coping of stone tiles with a bellcote near the middle, buttressed walls of local stone, pierced by single lancet windows. You approach through a wooden lych gate, its walls dependent on strong timber arches, and already the materials – the tiles, wall-stones and wood – bespeak quality, a sort of sincerity, the real thing.

There are people who gasp at their first impression. If your business is architecture, cooler observers might say, you would surely, before long, possibly while doodling, come up with the idea of arches springing not from the tops of columns or pillars but from floor or knee or thigh level – there is nothing so very remarkable about these. On the other hand, you could not put such ideas into practice much before Prior did because, as we have seen, novelty was frowned on. You followed medieval convention, obeyed the

rules. There were influences and precedents but nobody before had executed a dashing scheme like this: three giant arches, smooth parabolic graduations bending inward as they rise, unbroken, from floor to their lofty apex in the shadowy dark-wood roof.

That, of course, is not all. There are interesting features and furnishings. The pulpit with its panels of linenfold rests on a stone base apparently corbelled out, like an inverted cone, from the wall (not enhanced by a clutter of heating pipe, electric point and electric wires at its base). The chancel floor is tiled in artful triangular patterns (much is concealed by a carpet of hideous deep red). The tall wrought iron chancel screen tends to appear and disappear as the sunlight lights or leaves it. Often shrouded in silken covers, the communion table has on its front a lovely pattern of white roses and foliage done in gesso and painted by W.R. Lethaby, Prior's close friend and collaborator. Most windows are clear, a few are lit by conventional Victorian stained glass. But the three lancets of the east window strikingly and successfully match the impact of Prior's arches. Prior himself invented techniques of glass-making and chose his artist carefully. By the time he died in 1924, Christopher Whall had helped, by example and teaching, change the direction of stained glass design, and his style is clear here. The background to the figures, especially in the two side windows, is of deep, lush colour. Below is a pattern of pale but transmuting greens and near-greens; above of blues and near-blues. There is a striking similarity to Prior's own work at St Osmund's, Parkstone.

The saunter that discloses these items has revealed also a multitude of arches of varying dimensions. There are the arches of porch and uniform arches framing with deep reveals the nave lancet windows. There is the chancel arch, springing – unlike the nave three – from an orthodox height and echoed, along the chancel roof, by arched timbers that resemble whalebone gates. High arcades of small arches on wall corbels support the roof. A big arch leads north off the chancel to the organ. A smaller arcade, rather awkwardly stretched at the ends, encompasses Whall's east window and an arch shelters the piscina on the south wall. The arches' cumulative effect is to tease out, deepen and stress the sweep of those bold nave arches that dominate the scene on entry, to tether Prior's originality to the multiple, mundane requirements of the church, to turn a device into a work of art.

## BOURNEMOUTH
### St Peter

'Hyena in petticoats' was Horace Walpole's opinion of Mary Wollstonecraft, who died in 1797 and is seen today as a brave pioneer of women's rights. Her husband William Godwin (died 1836) ineffectually proposed a world in which, owning nothing, we are given the use of such homes and objects as we can prove we need. Shelley the poet was perhaps the most carefree, inconsiderate and lovable spirit of his age. He married Godwin's and Wollstonecraft's daughter Mary – first seducing her on her mother's grave, grumbled Godwin. Mary (died 1851) wrote *Frankenstein*, a chilling bestseller from that time to this. Shelley was drowned in a storm off the coast of Italy in 1822.

Byron and other friends burned his body in a fine pagan fire on the beach. Everything collapsed to ashes except his heart. This, pressed like a flower in a copy of his *Adonais*, was taken everywhere she went by his widow Mary who, ageing, let it be known that she wanted to be buried with the heart, close to the home of her rich, baronet son, in Bournemouth's first parish church. She asked that her parents' remains should also be brought there, from St Pancras churchyard, which was threatened by railway construction. A massive dark stone tomb, fifty yards uphill from the church, contains this once turbulent quartet of genius, atheism and strife.

The Tregonwell family tomb is a few steps on (there are thirty-nine of these, one for each of the official tenets of the Anglican church). This is a much more Bournemouth affair. In 1812 Lewis Tregonwell, of an old Dorset landowning family, and his wife moved into their new summer house, amid the wilderness of heather and pines. The Bournemouth, or Bourne, they knew was home only to a few fishermen and their families. They bought land and built. Sir George Tapps-Gervis, principal landowner, built much more. In less than fifty years, their and others' enterprise raised the population to about 40,000.

Christchurch-born Benjamin Ferrey designed the first resort, but his plan for a church, quaintly octagonal, gothic and hilltop, was rejected, partly because the steep uphill climb would daunt the faithful infirm. A new plan, begun in 1841, got as far as nave and south aisle, though a small and unpopular tower and spire put in a fleeting appearance. Then, in 1845, the tireless, autocratic, ultra-Victorian Alexander Morden Bennett became vicar. During the next thirty-five years he would oversee the founding of five schools and several other churches, make himself beloved by many and deeply disliked by some for his high-church ways, be burned in effigy as a crypto-papist and finally, in 1879, the year before he died, see the completion of his own greatly enlarged church, St Peter's, to the plans of G.E. Street, architect of the London Law Courts as well as four other churches in Bournemouth. Bennett's grave is a few yards downhill from Shelley's. The remains of Lewis Tregonwell, first buried in 1832, near the main family home at Anderson, were brought to the new family grave here in 1846, on his widow's orders.

Virtue, Bacon said, is best plain set, and perhaps St Peter's benefits from the dullness of the brick blocks that press on two sides of it. The upward streak of its octagonal spire is a striking landmark, and there are fine details on and in the tall tower below – pointed pinnacles, flying buttresses, statues of the four Fathers of the Church (Gregory,

26

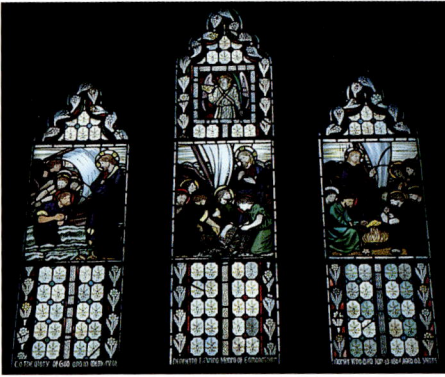

LEFT *Bournemouth, St Peter; the stained glass window by Edward Burne-Jones in the South Chapel.*

OPPOSITE PAGE *The richly decorated interior of St Peter, Bournemouth.*

Augustine, Ambrose and Jerome, all actually made for Bristol Cathedral), large belfry windows. On Ascension Day morning the choir sings from the tower top.

Street had to work as finances allowed. Throughout, he took as the model for his window tracery the mid 13th century Geometrical style – the transition from Early English to Decorated – considered by Ruskin and Pugin as the peak of Gothic, with its point-topped arches and mainly round tracery, before sinuous double curves moved in, as it seemed to them, to corrupt it. The north aisle, with its lean-to roof and tight-packed rank of stained-glass windows separated by deep splays and polished piers, came first, and makes the south aisle, the only remaining pre-Street feature of the church, seem dull. By 1859 the nave had been made fittingly lofty by an added, finely detailed clerestory stage. 1863-4 brought the east end: chancel, transepts and aisle chapels. The tower followed in 1870, and the unusual seven-yard gap left between it and the nave was filled by a kind of western transept (now part-occupied by shop and café) five years later. The spire was completed in 1879.

Under a high hammer-beam roof the nave walls are all colour – but matt and subdued colour. Glimpses of the east-end promise a more luminous, golden presence. Moving to the chancel itself (passing the pulpit designed by Thomas Earp, Street's chosen sculptor) is like entering a jewel box. Matt surfaces, and the restrained polychrome of the nave give

way to glint and glitter – all golds, reds, blues, greens and more golds enhancing rich foundations of marble, wood, alabaster and brass – a dramatic awakening that suggests angels and trumpets. The eye is filled, yet kept restless, by the wealth of ornament. Ninian Comper's colouring of Earp's busy reredos, the great Clayton and Bell east window above with its expanse of flowery tracery, the seven sanctuary lamps glowing red, succulent bunches of fruit and foliage on capitals, the choir's green-shaded lamps, the fat, polished poppy-heads terminating the pews (to the design of the respected G.F. Bodley), and rising above all this splendour Bodley's panelled, crimson ceiling, and the groined gold arches with intermediate angels – the abundance of riches only just stops short of glut. But stop it does. And each component part shows Street's attention to the quality and detail.

There are chapels north and south of the chancel. The north chapel window of 1915, a beautiful study of the Annunciation, is by Ninian Comper, as are several features nearby: the war memorial in the north aisle, the north transept screen, the communion desks and the colouring of the reredos. To the south of the chancel is the exquisite transept, known as the Keble Chapel, now restored for private prayer, its walls made cool after the chancel's colour blaze by a generous use of green. Here is the 1864 window by Burne-Jones, 'the most visited in the church', says the guide; and probably the finest light in a church unusually rich in stained glass. The big *Te Deum Laudamus* window on the south wall of the south transept shows John Keble himself, below the adoring hosts, in the bottom right-hand corner. With Newman and Pusey he had launched the Oxford Movement in the 1830s, favouring a return

to the pre-Reformation rituals and liturgy for which St Stephen's was splendidly designed. In old age, having vainly tried Torquay and Penzance for warm winters, he retired with his ailing wife to Bournemouth, and died there in 1866. Many years later, in 1898, William Gladstone, weeks from death, attended his last communion in a choir-stall on the south side, marked by a plaque.

# BOURNEMOUTH
## St Stephen

In 1974 a suite of churches tumbled into Dorset's sack. To even up the sparse population of this rural county it was given the south-west tip of Hampshire, comprising Bournemouth, Christchurch and a stretch to the north of them. Naturally churches came too. If county boundaries had anything to do with county wealth, power or dominance, rather than the convenience of civil servants, it would have been a massive bounty.

*Bournemouth, St Stephen; 'as convincing an ante-room to heaven as any church in the land.'*

Bournemouth alone brought over twenty churches, amounting to a good record of the high quality of 19th century church architecture. Among them, St Stephen's is as convincing an ante-room to heaven as any church in the land. John Loughborough Pearson designed it between 1881 and 1883 (though it was not complete until 1898) at the behest of Alexander Sykes Bennett. He was the son of Alexander Morden Bennett, first and long-lived vicar of Bournemouth's first church, St Peter's, ten minutes away, to whom the new church was to be a memorial.

G.E. Street was the architect of St Peter's and his chancel there is an effervescence of colour and lustre. Pearson's, on the other hand, is a tall cavern of subtly contrasted shapes and lights, patterns of constructional piety within a tightly unifying fabric. It is, like St Peter's, in 13th century Geometrical style, and striking in its details. Outside, the tower, built in 1908, ends abruptly, having never got the spire of the original plan. A little gothic spire rises above the crossing, and two cone-topped ones to either side of it. The east end is in the form of a polygonal apse, its triple windows alternating with roof-high buttresses. Another apse, smaller and round, projects eastward from the north transept. The site is mostly bound by buildings, woods and roads, one at the east end raised on a roof-high overpass, which affords – at risk to life and limb – the best overall view of the church.

The magic is indoors. The nave has the narrow loftiness of an early French cathedral. Above, the vault is cross-ribbed in Pearson's typical way, and an ornate parapet contains the passage running under the clerestory windows. At ground level, behind the pointed arcades, double aisles offer an intriguing, changeable vista of columns, among which you might imagine you see flittings of medieval priests, monks and nuns. The walls of the eastmost bay of the nave turn slightly inwards, an ingenious step that focuses more attention on the east end. The reverential and Anglo-Catholic character of St Stephen's is reinforced by the Stations of the Cross along the aisle walls, and in the north transept chapel (where most services are now held), by the figure of a gore-stained Christ hanging from the cross, a statue of the Virgin, and a polychrome aumbry for storing consecrated bread after communion. The rose window here, like almost all the church's stained glass, is by Clayton and Bell. From here the sanctuary draws us, with such a warm embrace that it is surprising its style ever went out of fashion.

This is not one of those English country churches in which distracting details of various kinds – tombs, effigies, plaques, royal arms – comprise more than half of the interest. It is more of a unity than that. This is a church to look and wonder in – Pearson wanted it to bring us to our knees – and one whose whole is much greater than the sum of

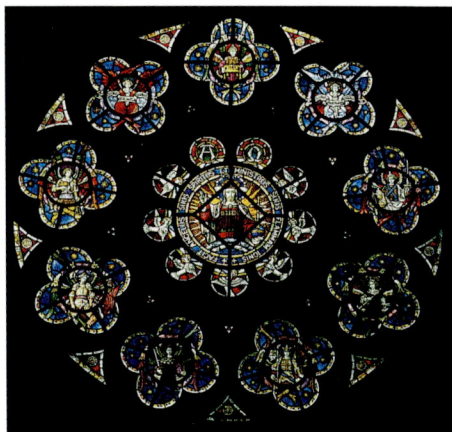

*Bournemouth, St Stephen. The rose window by Clayton and Bell.*

its constituent parts. The tender filigree of the wrought iron screen, the vault ribs braided with gold decoration, the shining figures of the triptych reredos against red or blue backgrounds, the marquetry of flooring marbles, the sundry scriptural images on lights of stained glass, the ambulatory running round the apse behind a screen of wrought iron and under needlepoint arches – they all contribute tellingly to a majestic unity. What puts Pearson high above many others is perhaps that the constituents cohere brilliantly from every direction, so that progress round the church is marked by a constantly and smoothly transforming vista.

## BROWNSEA ISLAND
### St Mary

To get there you catch the ferry from Poole quay and travel about three miles from the town's hubbub, across the world's second largest natural harbour, past woods and bird reserves and residential reserves of the water-loving rich, and arrive on the island's east side, close to the cluttered gothic of Brownsea Castle, now a retreat for employees of John Lewis.

Not far beyond it, in deep rural peace, amid trees and bumpy grassland, tail-flicking red squirrels, strutting peacocks, and

*Brownsea. The Italian well-head marking the grave of George Cavendish-Bentinck.*

sometimes any of three species of deer, is a fairly standard church of late medieval type, with battlemented west tower, nave, south porch, north transept and chancel, a Victorian construction in early Decorated style and all in gleaming Purbeck stone. The most prominent feature of the churchyard is a well-head, or *pozzo*, marking the grave of George Augustus Frederick Cavendish-Bentinck – the forenames ring out respect for the Hanoverian dynasty still ruling at the time of his birth, 1821. The *pozzo* is 16th century Italian, once belonging, as the engraved crest shows, to the Lesa family. It alerts us for what is within.

Cerne Abbey monks built a chapel somewhere on Brownsea in Saxon times, but King Canute's Vikings destroyed it. There was a hermit at some stage but nothing is known of him, which is probably as he wanted it. After the Reformation, Brownsea was fortified against Catholic Spain's recurrent threat of invasion. Later landlords enlarged the castle near the landing stages for residential purposes. Colonel William Waugh bought the place in 1852. On his first walk round he found some white mud that seemed to him, and an expert he hired, to be china clay, much in demand for good pottery. Confident of a fortune, he constructed a factory, made the castle grander, recruited

two hundred workers and built the church. It was consecrated in 1854. But the expert was wrong. The mud was not after all china clay. The business failed and Waugh decamped to Spain, but the church remained. The next owner was Cavendish-Bentinck, grandson of the third Duke of Portland and a hugely rich collector. His acquisitions were distributed round the house but in 1896, five years after his death, and following a catastrophic fire, many items were moved to the church. They were there when a new owner, Charles van Raalte, took over in 1901, introducing an era of Edwardian gaiety and splendour; and again after him, when the unloved and unloving Mary Bonham-Christie, between 1927 and 1961, packed most inhabitants off to the mainland and let nature run riot. Cavendish-Bentinck's residual collection is still in the church, now that the National Trust has taken over and calmed the ruffled course of island history.

We go into St Mary's by the south porch. Pews are plain, though pew-ends have elaborately carved poppy heads, the walls are pale-plastered and the arches of the wooden roof rest, as in a hundred other churches, on the heads of well carved angels. Beyond the high, pointed chancel arch and low wooden traceried screen, the dark-wood walls and ceiling are in contrast to the bright colours in the four main lights of the 19th century east window, with its scenes of Christ's Crucifixion and Ascension to Heaven. What are extraordinary are the detailed decorations, wall ornaments, statues, the 16th century carved wooden panelling of the chancel; the handsome brass candelabra suspended above the nave, each – there being no current laid on – holding sixteen wax candles rather than electric imitations, the chancel's hanging lamps; the two rather blotchily painted 17th century Flemish wooden panels of an angel telling the Virgin Mary of her mystical pregnancy and the three Magi worshipping the infant Christ; the 16th century red-winged golden angel, kneeling; the delicate marble relief of the Virgin with

*Brownsea Island, the church built by Colonel Waugh in 1854.*

the baby Christ and a cherub below, Renaissance work used as a memorial to Cavendish-Bentinck.

But the strangest feature is the room under the tower beyond the western screen, for here, on first look, seems to be set, correct in mood and tone, a London club's lounge or country mansion's drawing-room, with its dark panelled walls, a fireplace you could roast chestnuts on and comforting Turkey-red carpet. It is in fact Dorset's most singular family pew, and it contains the church's richest tally of treasures. Above the fireplace and its grim, painted 17th century Italian Crucifixion of Christ is a beautifully delicate gothic canopy. Either side of it are two fine pre-Reformation Flemish groups of wooden figures, while at floor level are two sensitively done statues: Faith and, it is suggested, February. A charming wood and plaster Annunciation stands atop the centre of the screen. High above is a wonderful wooden ceiling, intricately carved and coffered, with gold bosses at the heart of each compartment.

Then, on the left or south side, the room's character changes. Light streams in from outside, and within a spacious extension to the tower, placed on a sarcophagus of white marble and a Latin inscription, lies the gleaming effigy of Charles van Raalte, proudly moustachioed, dead in 1907 after a tenure of half a dozen years, of no lasting consequence except for permitting the first experimental Boy Scouts' camp to be held on the island in 1907, notable if at all for the splendour of his parties and for this brief, haughty thrust of himself into our attention.

## BURTON BRADSTOCK
*St Mary*

The church stands among handsome stone houses at the southern edge of the village and close to the River Bride, now in its final glide to the sea. Though the sea is unseen, Burton Bradstock has a genteel seaside feel, and long ago, with much flattening and clearing of tombstones, turned its churchyard into a sort of village green with a sprinkle of table tombs. St Mary's is unusual in being an essentially Perpendicular church with a central as opposed to a west end tower. The

*Burton Bradstock. A reminder of the village's closeness to the sea, the lectern carved as a seagull.*

local rough stone or rubble in its building gives its outer surface a pleasing abrasive look, as if a giant could strike an outsize match on it.

A church is recorded here in the Domesday Book of 1086. It was rebuilt on new foundations in the 12th century. But the nave we see dates mostly from the 14th century and later, the porch, tower and transepts from the late 14th century or early 15th century, and the chancel from the early 16th century. The south aisle, which bears close scrutiny, was rebuilt in 1897. The vestry, between chancel and south transept, was added in 1967. The tower clock was made in 1788 for Christ's Hospital, the Bluecoat school, and only acquired when the school moved out of London in 1902. Pinnacles topped the tower till the 19th century, when they were declared unsafe. The stair tower attached to the tower's south-west is neatly square. A few of the gargoyles may be original. Arches visible above the chancel's north wall windows are most likely there to take weight off the lintels below.

We move through the north porch (with its original stoup for holy water), by a door of 1681, into the nave. Above the door, the letters VR for Victoria appear on the royal arms, but the painting was done before her reign and these were added. From the barrel roof, two young females and a toothily grinning male – satyr or Green Man – set among more ordinary bosses, stare down. To the left, the fine pointed arches of the tower, with their inner panelling (a popular West Country feature) and the distant prospect of the chancel and its three-light east window all go to create an evocative medieval vista. But there is also something decidedly unmedieval about our surrounds. The seating is oak, rock solid, clearly hand-carved with care and skill – but modern. The windows over the way in the south aisle, containing pastel-coloured representations of flowers and stems, are strangely opaque. The pretty dado against the walls, clearly hand-painted and with a running text along the top, is certainly not medieval. It is not the conventional eagle but a 1960s seagull whose wings form the book-rest on the lectern.

There are certainly some older interesting contents. The 14th century octagonal font (on a 12th century round stem) has an unusual decorative arrangement of trefoils and cinquefoils. In the nave's north-west corner, a recess with angels and lions' heads on the overhanging cusps is 14th century work and may possibly have served as an Easter Sepulchre, in which the consecrated host was placed and kept under careful watch from Good Friday to Easter Sunday – the days of Christ's descent, after his crucifixion, to hell. High up on the south-west pier of the crossing arch, dark red staining is a tiny remainder of the original paint that probably once covered a good deal of the church's fabric. In the west wall of the south transept is the door to the steps that climbed up to the rood screen. There are good carved heads acting as corbels to the tower roof. In the north transept, the memorial tablets include a mid 18th century one to Elizabeth Best, with familiar visual warnings of mortality: 'Life how short Eternity how long.' The chancel has an ornate altar rail of 1686 and two prayer desks made from late 15th century wooden panels that perhaps first formed part of a chest imported from France.

Pressure of population caused the building

*Burton Bradstock, the nave and south aisle.*

of a cheap south transept in 1833. The columns were of iron and the window frames of wood, but it served its purpose during most of the 19th century. The parish's next expansive mood came in the 1890s. The choice of architect fell on a pupil and apostle of the Arts and Crafts movement, stemming from the ideas of Ruskin and William Morris. Dorset has seldom followed vogues or gone for the man of the moment, and Edward Prior's salient terrace at West Bay – locals called it Noah's Ark – and his new church at Bothenhampton, then and now considered aesthetically electric by the pundits, may perhaps not have played as much of a part in parish deliberations as his strong local family connections. The rector here was Prior's cousin and Prior's father-in-law vicar of nearby Symondsbury. But the choice was good.

A lot happened in the years up to 1897. The west end gallery, and one in the north transept, were removed – a change effected in many churches forty years earlier. The standard box pews went. It was from them that the charming dado was made and decorated by the rector's wife and other parish ladies. Stonework was repaired, windows reglazed. Arts and Crafts principles were observed: local labour, from Burton Bradstock and Shipton Gorge, and local materials used wherever possible, the highest quality aimed at and tasks treated with something approaching reverence. Perhaps this can be glimpsed in Prior's main contribution, the south aisle. Possibly there is an Arts and Crafts gentleness in the south arcade that marries the aisle to the nave, a simplicity in the window shapes and a comforting richness in the wooden roof. The window lights are distinctively Prior's. The thick, almost chunky, pale and opaque glass was his own invention. Their design is simple but agreeably apt. Prior had not finished with Dorset. Yet to come was his dramatic venture into Bournemouth Byzantine, St Osmund's, Parkstone. Here at Burton Bradstock he is quiet, contemplative almost, and strongly effective.

*Canford Magna. The marble tomb near the porch is that of Sir Henry Layard, who excavated what was thought to be Nineveh, and whose collection of ancient Assyrian carvings is now in the British Museum.*

## CANFORD MAGNA
*Dedication unknown*

There is something rather indoors about the outdoor suburb of Canford Magna; comfy, dusted, and suggesting that, should you sit on anything – grass, branch, pavement – it might give a bit, as if internally sprung. Canford School's gothic arched lodge with its cupola, and the turreted tower of the house beyond, appear like paintings. The church is to the right as you approach, and is simply odd: a huge cape of tile clasping a short, flat-headed north tower.

The school is private but the church, though it serves as the school chapel (and the living is at the school governors' disposal), is C of E property and open to the public. It has its own car park, from which you walk towards the broad gable of the west end, then round to the right, or south. A few yards ahead, at the edge of the spreading green tree-hemmed graveyard, is the big marble tomb of Sir Henry Layard. His greater memorial is the collection of massive, exquisitely carved reliefs from ancient Assyria now in the British Museum. For Layard in the 1840s excavated what was supposed to be Assyria's capital, Nineveh, a name that for the Victorians rang with Old Testament, Judaic, even Byronic associations, quite as intense and romantic as

the feelings the Egyptian pyramids had earlier raised, and Tutankhamen's tomb would in time raise in the West. Little remembered now, Layard lies here because he married a daughter of the landlord, Sir John Guest – she is buried beside him. Other Guest graves are set behind them, and inside the church the south aisle blazons the family's social connections and pieties.

In 1846, employing about 10,000 people and sole owner of the Dowlais (Merthyr Tydfil) iron works, the biggest works of any kind in the world, Sir John Guest bought – for his and his family's health and recreation – about 17,000 acres between Wimborne and the sea. Sprung from yeoman stock, he married an earl's daughter. Their son Ivor, Layard's brother-in-law, married well too, earning by the money he lavished on courting his Spencer-Churchill bride the title 'paying Guest'. He had Charles Barry renovate the old house, since 1923 the nucleus of the public school, and between 1876 and 1878 employed David Brandon to restore and add to the church. In partnership with T.H. Wyatt, Brandon had designed the astonishing Italianate church of Wilton near Salisbury, but did not repeat that success here. As happened too often at this time, the air of antiquity in the body of Canford church yielded to a rather soulless gloss, which the place retains. The heavy charmless atmosphere is misleading in what is, in fact, a very long architectural history teasing to historians. Moreover plenty of clues to the church's distant past remain: among them the shapes of windows and arches, positioning of chapels, the angle of the chancel, arrangements of stone, a little broken arch high in the north wall of the south chancel aisle.

About the middle of the 11th century Canford's thick-walled chancel was raised on the site of the original, Anglo-Saxon nave.

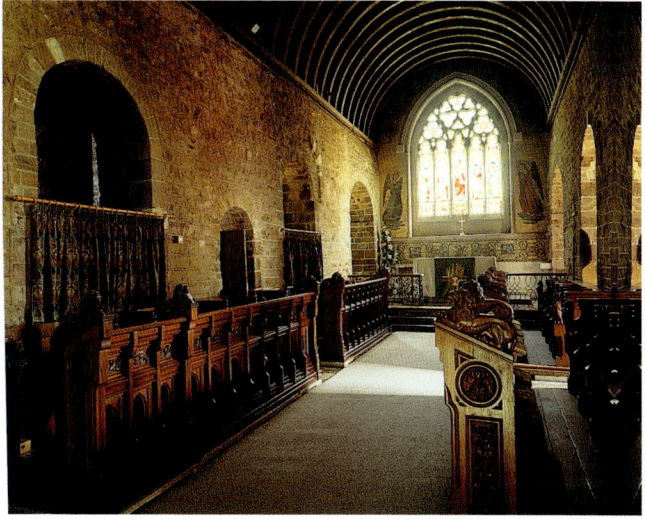

*Canford Magna. Victorian sentiment and piety live on in the memorial of 1918 to Nan Guest.*

*Canford Magna. The 11th century chancel is one of the oldest buildings in Dorset.*

The present nave with its four massive arches was built to the west of the old one in the 12th century, as were the aisles. The pointed arch is due to 15th century rebuilding, making the unusual hybrid of Perpendicular top and Norman bottom. The irregularly spaced arches between sanctuary and aisles date back to the same period, except for those in the north-east and south-east corners which are Anglo-Saxon. The tower, now squatly squeezed between vestry and north nave aisle, is also 12th century. A rear gallery added in 1640 was removed early in the 19th century. So too was the medieval rood screen. The west end with its lancet windows is a Brandon 1870s addition, though it looks older and would be more impressive without the recent bridge carrying the new organ blocking the view. (It is good though for the sound of music). The south-east chapel was an early 16th century addition.

In Saxon times the church is assumed to have had what is loosely called minster status, with a resident, or collegiate, body of priests serving the huge area – stretching to the sea – which later became the parish. The Normans continued this arrangement, placing Canford under the Augustinian priory at Bradenstoke, Wiltshire, which kept it till 1539. The Norman expansion tallies with the erection of several Norman churches in this south-eastern quarter of Dorset. The estate was owned, and the church presumably visited, by William Longespée, earl of Salisbury and king John's lieutenant. His son, also William, was killed on crusade in 1250. Soon after, he was seen by his mother, in a vision, entering the kingdom of heaven in full armour. Beauforts, including Margaret Beaufort, Henry VII's mother and his tenuous but main link to entitlement to the throne, held the land and manor in the 15th century, and both kings doubtless worshipped here. The Guests arrived in 1846.

The 1870s restoration seems to have left little in the way of pre-Guest memorials. There are three workaday relief tablets by the canny John Bacon (who saw that more adventurous sculpting would bring less profit).There was a schoolmaster, Richard Lloyd, who, the Latin inscription tells us, 'placidly breathed out his spirit' in 1752. There was Thomas Macnamara Russell, Admiral of the White, who served his country 'in thirty-six engagements' towards the end of the 18th century and early in the 19th, and was anything but placid. The tablet has him introducing new naval tactics and being offered a knighthood. The *Dictionary of National Biography* makes no mention of either. But mostly it is Guests, packed in during their brief tenure (like the Hambros at Milton Abbey), mastering the Blackmore hounds, being MPs, soldiering world-wide, or simply marrying rather well. One, Montague, had the ill-luck to die while staying with Edward VII at Sandringham – on the King's birthday. Soon after that the family sold up and moved to the Midlands. The house became a school.

Emerging from the church, we see again the grave of that very special son-in-law, Sir Henry Layard. From time to time he brought presents to Canford from his Assyrian finds, and some of these, their interest and value ignored, stayed around when the estate changed hands. In 1992 what had been thought a plaster cast of an original Assyrian relief was discovered to be the relief itself. It was sent for sale to Christie's, who estimated its value at £750,000. In less than four minutes of bidding it went for rather more than ten times that amount. £7,701,500.

## CATTISTOCK
*Saints Peter and Paul*
The Scott tribe has been fashioning and furbishing the buildings of Britain for nearly two hundred years. St Pancras Station, much of Westminster Abbey, the Albert Memorial, Liverpool's Anglican cathedral, Cambridge University Library, the feet-in-the-air power station that now houses Tate Modern are only the peaks of the broad Scott range. Great Scott, they called Sir George Gilbert Scott (1811-78), founder of the dynasty, known sometimes – with wild inaccuracy, even though the number of churches and public buildings he rehashed is astonishing – as the man who rebuilt England. Not everyone applauded. William Morris thought he defaced and distorted the medievalism he professed to protect and replicate, and

founded, in 1877, the Society for the Protection of Ancient Buildings (still energetically and indispensably extant) mainly to stem the Scott flood.

Scott's son, also George Gilbert (1839-97), is more generally approved of: more sensitive, ingenious and practical than his father, the experts say. We hear less of GG junior's work because he converted to Rome and later went mad, youngish. Cattistock shows both father and son at work, for each in his time took on a major share of its 19th century rebuilding.

A church had stood here before, perhaps for a thousand years. There are suggestions of a Saxon and traces of a Norman building. Later medieval centuries brought expansions and a 47 foot tower – less than half the height of the present one. Most of the various east-facing walls are 17th century, though their Perpendicular windows are probably survivals from the 15th century. A massive gallery, half the area of the nave, went up in the 18th century. This and much else was demolished in 1857, when sale of church land to the new railway company brought in the cash to employ GG senior. His remit was the nave, chancel and south aisle: new walls, ceilings, west window and pews and a lowering of the floor level by 18 inches. His external work produces from several angles an attractive huddle of roofs. Inside, the columns of the arcade are comfortingly muscular, and the almost cosy south chapel retains 17th century wood panelling. The elaborately moulded, narrow and pointed chancel arch, of early French-gothic flavour, leads to a chancel with apse-like, three-sided end, sombre light from spaced lancet windows and floor chequer of blue and white Minton tiles. This is all straightforward and impressive.

GG junior's contribution of 1872-76 is what we see first on entering by the main north door. The long north porch, accommodating two different approaches, is his, as is the north aisle, site of the original tower, the stone and iron screen dividing it

*Cattistock. The 100 feet high tower.*

*Cattistock. The font cover in the Baptistery.*

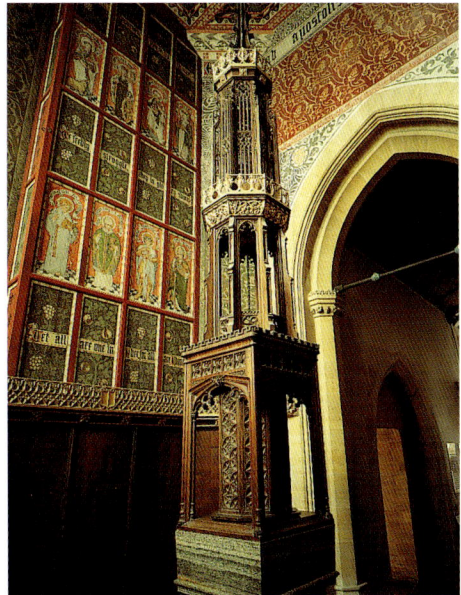

from the north chapel: all admirable in proportions and detail, though the screen's purpose is not apparent. The eye-catcher here is the baptistery to the right, forming the lower chamber of GG junior's new corner tower. Outside, unsurprisingly, the tower is the church's dominant feature, seen, slender and stalwart, from a great distance in several directions. A hundred feet high, it affords room for the belfry stage, clock room and ringing chamber. (The 35-bell Flemish carillon installed in 1891 melted in a ruinous 1940 fire and was too costly to replace; now the peal is of eight bells). The baptistery is one of the county's most colourful and busily decorated rooms, with stencilled patterns, saints and bishops in the stained glass, sun and stars and diapered dividers on the ceiling, a mural of St George sticking the dragon with this tower in the background, all making a Disneyesque wrap for the thin, tapering, twenty-foot, telescopic font cover, of carved and gilded oak, suspended by a chain over the handsome, simple lines of the grey marble font on its five thin columns.

'Original, bold, brilliant . . . thrilling' Pevsner writes of GG junior's additions. This work is 'remarkable for clever planning and self-confident handling' (Gavin Stamp). The tower is 'the finest Perpendicular tower of Dorset' (Pevsner), 'much more grand and eloquent than Charminster's' (Stamp) – to which Betjeman says it owes inspiration. Betjeman also picks out the porch and stone screen as 'excellent', and calls GG junior's work, not his father's, Cattistock's 'claim to fame'. The certainty puzzles a bit. How do they know? True, father's and son's shares differ in style. By GG junior's time Perpendicular was in, Decorated more or less out. GG junior's tower, taken as a whole, is wonderfully graceful. But his father's chancel finely evokes the deep dark sanctity of continental cathedrals. True, father's south side exterior has some clumsy conjunctions. But son's vestry, a low and battlemented addition to the west side, seems incongruous, while the massive frames he created on each of the tower's walls to contain the belfry windows (and two blocked ones below) appear to me to gash the walls to the point of disembowelment, though this effect is eclipsed by distance. But archi-tectural judgment is always tricky. Matters other than architecture have to be considered. What the architect planned may not be what is done. GG junior designed a much busier tower than we see, with niches, statues, friezes, blank arcading and so on. 'All this was omitted,' he wrote sourly, 'through my client's folly and my own weakness.' The truth is that the client rector saw costs rising from an estimate of £2700 to £4000 and called a halt. Even so, upward momentum carried the price to £6046, and still the tower is a long way from the first concept. Then too, the baptistery was not designed by GG junior at all. It and the font cover were actually carried out thirty years later by his former pupil and assistant, the scholarly and enterprising Temple Moore.

For a Dorset church, Cattistock's stained glass is special. The big west-window Tree of Jesse, done probably by Clayton and Bell in 1858, makes a vivid series of portraits – the descendants of Jesse and his son King David. But the finest window by far is by William Morris (*see page 2, the frontispiece*), inserted in 1882 at the west end of the south aisle: six robed, winged angels and archangels against a starry, very starry – perhaps too starry – night sky. Burne-Jones designed St Michael and the Guardian Angels, Morris the rest, using his wavy-tressed pre-Raphaelite models in luxuriant robes. Neither in fact came here; the design is a re-use of one Morris made elsewhere.

## CERNE ABBAS
*St Mary*

The tower of Cerne Abbas church, abutting on a street of fine timbered Tudor, Georgian and high Victorian houses, in a town noted for grace, plenty and rather sleepy complacency, is nevertheless like a very tall model – the mannequin sort: quite out of proportion to its surrounds but, once seen, hard to take one's eyes off. Even the rest of the church exterior, nave and flint-and-stone aisles and chancel, are made flatter by the tower's dominating adjacency.

Yet to understand the church, we must take in the street, Abbey Street, for remains of Cerne's long religious past still attach to it. There are monastic remnants going back to Saxon times, and a spring said to have been set off by a tap from St Augustine's staff, and houses, duck-pond and greenery fit for a cathedral close. Over the hill beyond is a famous feature of different and unchristian character: the undatable, salty, so unCerne Cerne Giant with his mighty erection.

The Augustine story is to be filed with those many others devised to increase the number of pilgrims and revenue of the place concerned. A Benedictine monastery was founded here, probably in 987. With the income from sheep and tenants drawn from massive lands it became Dorset's second richest after the nunnery at Shaftesbury. An early abbot was Aelfric, famous for compiling a Latin grammar for schoolboys, for his compliant attitude towards priestly chastity, and for anticipating the English split from Rome – as perhaps many clergymen did – by denial that communion bread and wine were Christ's actual flesh and blood. In 1015, before becoming king, Canute sacked the place in the standard Danish way. After, he became a benefactor.

For those first few centuries the abbey church would have served in addition as parish church. Villagers and other locals were admitted to the nave for worship and sacraments, but given no seating and screened off from the sanctuary. A similar arrangement at Sherborne caused riots. Here, what is now the chancel of St Mary's was built about 1300 as a separate parish church. There may have been one on the same site before. From then on the church has its own history. In the 14th century came wall paintings of which some have patchily survived. The Dissolution saw the usual vandalism at the abbey – perhaps the survival of the church's statue of Mary was due to the feast of destruction offered just up the lane. Preserved Churchwardens' Accounts for the next three hundred years are a rich source of village information: details of the payments of bills, records of care of the poor, costs of bread and wine, laundering surplices, paying bell-ringers for special work, of payment made in one particular year, 1686, to victims of fire and shipwreck, French persecution of Catholics or to sailors captured by Turkish pirates. Some less virtuous entries, for what seems excessive expenditure on repair of bells, or beer given for odd jobs done, raise suspicions.

The slender Ham-stone tower achieves a marvellous mix. There is the elegant architectural dignity of honey-coloured stone, lank proportions, Perpendicular bell-windows with their tracery of small regular perforations, the eight-light west window, the

*Cerne Abbas, the Virgin Mary and the infant Jesus in a niche on the tower.*

frieze of quatrefoils, the central figure of the heavily overdressed Virgin and her baby, rare survivor of puritan iconoclasts – and all of this punctuated by the salacious vulgarity of leering, squatting, bulging, pouting, face-pulling gargoyles. Light from the broad window accompanies you as you walk through the west door, under the tower, catching glimpses, through pointed arches to left and right, of the closed off aisle-ends and various wall tablets moved there during 20th century clearings of the church's main body. Ahead, a taller arch and within it a charming round-arched wooden gate of 1749 (but looking a hundred years older) open on the nave and its rare brightness. All the church windows but one, including a clerestory of three three-light windows each side, are almost all plain glass. Lightness is enhanced by the pallor of plastic chair-seats – replacements of rush seats and before that, up to 1972, good waist-high Victorian box-pews, condemned for harbouring dry rot. (There is a theory that the pews with richly carved ends at Hilfield, a few miles north, are

ABOVE *Cerne Abbas, with 17th century Biblical texts on the nave walls.*

LEFT *Cerne Abbas, the oak pulpit.*

each arch. A brass chandelier of around 1800, possibly Dutch, run on electricity, before that paraffin and earlier candles, hangs in front of us. The oak pulpit is a fine, dark, slender piece made in 1640. In front of us the screen, pierced by a central doorway and six trefoil-topped Perpendicular lights either side of it, has a stone base. At first, in the 14th century, this was the west-end wall of a church confined within the space of the modern chancel. Until 1870 the wall continued upwards to the roof, blocking sight of the chancel by the congregation, who felt excluded. The arch was made in that year. The east window, inserted in the 17th century, comes from the abbey's ruins, and the heraldic glass fragments in the tracery from an abbey chantry, or private tomb chapel, of 1482. On either side are what remain of the 14th century wall paintings, those on the north and left chancel wall showing episodes from John the Baptist's life, that on the right, obscurely, the Annunciation.

the antique predecessors of these Victorian pews of Cerne). Some displayed old photographs show a busier, more fully furnished church than we see now, but light and abundance of space have not made it a void.

There are biblical texts, mostly done in the 17th century, above us on the walls, and rather drawing-room lamps hanging between

In the south aisle, the church's only fully stained-glass window, done in 1910 by

*Chalbury. The white-washed church sits on a hilltop overlooking the valley of the River Allen.*

Hubert Westlake, shows in rich colour the apostle and evangelist John in exile on the isle of Patmos. To the left, beside the south door, is the site of a medieval fireplace, long covered up. A chimney rises within the wall, and the large mouth of a grotesque face on the wall outside is the smoke's outlet. At the aisle's east end is a good oak altar of 1638. Near it is displayed the copy of Henry Fowke's will of 1502, of interest for what must be the genuine piety of a man many of whose bequests were to holy institutions. A brass of 1702 in the north aisle commemorates Joseph Sommers and an old sentiment with a pert verse:

A little time did blast my prime
And brought me hether
The Fairest Flowar Within an hour
May Fade and Wethar

## CHALBURY

*All Saints'*

They argue about the 18th century. Was God buried under a heap of rationalism, the disbelief of Voltaire or Gibbon, the corruption of prelates, pluralism of pastors, neglect and decay of churches? Was Wesley's Methodism a response to a state church gone to sleep? Did a weary congregation yawn at the hour-long sermon; and watch with dread the hour-glass that hung beside the pulpit lest, as the sand ran out, the preacher should turn it, signifying a second hour would follow? Did parsons deserve to be referred to, as they often were from the late 17th century to early 19th century, as 'ballocks'? Was the poet Charles Churchill exaggerating when, in a nice pentameter, he wrote of the effect of the clergyman's preaching: 'Sleep, at his bidding, crept from pew to pew'; or the wit who, when a bright and lively young curate breathed life into sermons, complained of insomnia in church? The 18th century obviously gets much bad press.

The curious thing is that Chalbury's church, though utterly 18th century in character, seems a thousand miles away from all this. Certainly it displays in its inner arrangement the sharp social distinctions of its time. There is a hint of complacency in the compact neatness of the place. But the message that comes across most strongly is that it is exquisitely functional, the place in which the small local population, mostly involved in farming, were happy to assemble to thank God for his many blessings, not least

*Chalbury, 18th century box pews and three-decker pulpit.*

of which, they possibly thought, was the church itself: neat, small, pretty, idiosyncratic, a little theatrical, a little toylike – a delight. It still is.

Outside, All Saints consists of a modest nave with a south porch attached, and chancel with adjacent north vestry. Rising above the west end and flush with it is a neat bell-turret. Roofs are mostly tiled (with a few strips of stone slate) and the flint and rubble walls rendered white. With its sparsely occupied graveyard and backing of trees it stands on a bosomy hilltop with sweeping views over parts of Cranborne Chase and the New Forest. The building's modesty almost suggests a nonconformist chapel, but it has a longer history than first sight lets on. Some windows give this away, in spite of 18th century updating and the absence of stained glass. There is a 13th century lancet in the north nave wall. Other lancets and the top-pointed trefoils of the east window are of the early 14th century. Drastic rebuilding probably began in the early 15th century. The

original nave was 12th century or even earlier. Most walls are feet thick. A tower, drawn in an old survey, stood at the west end until after 1500. But once we are inside, having entered by the south porch door, all except the 18th century becomes forgettable.

Under a plain plaster roof, and on a part brick and part flagged floor, there are first, to left and right, west and east, the boxes of pews, painted, like all the other woodwork, two faint shades of pale grey-buff. The three largest of these box-pews were occupied by the three local farmers and their families, of whom the one in the front pew might have whiled away duller moments by staring with pride at his own farmhouse beyond the churchyard. The north-side pews, lower walled now but not originally, are more cramped and more easily overlooked by the parson in his three-decker pulpit. The wooden western gallery rests on thin columns. Below it is the 18th century font, of bulbous baluster design. To the east, the chancel is reached through a shallow-arched opening with a clergyman's pew either side, all contained in a dainty wooden framework. The whole structure, with its central curved archway and straight shoulders, is reminiscent of a Venetian window. Beyond, on the left, a village version of an opera box, roomy, with a balustraded front, and containing a long cushioned seat, faces across the aisle to a much lowlier pew. The former must have been reserved for the occasional visits of the patron of the living – for long the Earl of Pembroke, based at Wilton to the north-east, and his family. At least some of the fitments were done not as part of an overall design but as and when need for them arose. The place gains from this, and from its windows and walls, a charming asymmetrical spontaneity which a comprehensive plan would have quite missed.

*Charminster church, which sits in the heart of the village close to the River Cerne.*

# CHARMINSTER
*St Mary*

It rises – long nave and tall, crenellated, pinnacled, feistily gargoyled, honey-stoned west tower – from the valley floor and from its surrounding churchyard, spread with yews and broadleaves and lichened, smartly upright stones. Beyond the boundary hedge runs the east-west road and the north-south, tightly-banked River Cerne, and beyond them a sprinkle of gracious houses, farm fields, a cluster of beeches and, in their boughs in winter and spring, an utterly unmusical choir of rooks. Charminster church, outside and in, is neat but not too neat. Thanks to an urgently needed but sensitive restoration of 1895 to 1897, it hangs on well to its maturity.

The south porch door opens on a fine

*Charminster, the font and bell tower.*

view of the imposing, unusually light nave: almost matching 12th century north and south arcades (the north columns a touch taller and the basal ornament differing from one side to the other), four pointed arches a side, each surmounted by a line (or hood-mould) of tiny pyramid-shaped teeth (called nail's-head) except in one segment where they become round bobbles. To left, and west, is a pointed arch almost the height of the ceiling, its inner side decorated with trefoil-topped panels. It stands between two unexpected buttresses, great stone colossi that together with the arch suggest a desert gateway at Palmyra. Actually buttresses and arch are the eastern part of the tower, Sir Thomas Trenchard's early 16th century addition, whose interior here offers only a plain central font under a girding of looped bell-ropes and, beyond, one of the church's two stained-glass windows, done by Kempe in 1889. Above the nave two rows of clear-glass clerestory windows, on slightly different axes from and possibly older than the arcades below them,

supplement the already generous light of the aisle windows. The four small clerestory lights and a few other features could be of 11th century origin. But, as usual and no doubt as intended, the east of the nave commands most attention. The massive rotundity of the chancel arch, decorated like the arcades, and standing below a large expanse of plain whitewashed plaster, proffers its confident welcome to what proves a let-down. Seventeenth century Puritanism felt chancels set priests and God apart from the people, and the original, much longer, one was pulled down. This is a dull 1830s replacement whose main merit, a preserved 17th century Perpendicular east window (used in the meantime as part of the fill-in of the chancel arch), was inserted the wrong way round.

The north aisle contains the organ, and is broad and Victorian, with Perpendicular windows. The south aisle, headed on the east by the church's second stained glass window, a 1912 memorial by Burlison and Grylls, has a wider east half than west, the wider half containing two handsome canopied Purbeck marble tomb-chests and a striking pillared,

*Charminster, the memorial to Grace Pole.*

pedimented and armorial affair in vivid cavalier colours (restored in 1970) with a kneeling female figure at its centre. This portrays Grace, Sir Thomas Trenchard's unlucky daughter, who married in 1633 William Poule or Pole of Colyton in Devon, bore him two sons, saw both die young and followed them to the grave in 1638. The two tombs are of Trenchards too, as are several others, indicated by floor slabs. Wolfeton House, still standing though much shrunken 600 metres south of the church, was the family home. When in 1506 the Archduke Philip and his wife Joanna, grandparents of Philip II of Spain, were driven into Weymouth by a storm at sea, Sir Thomas entertained them. He possibly brought them to see his magnificent new tower, with its lurid gargoyles and convoluted Trenchard monograms. He also invited John Russell, a distant relative able to speak Spanish. When the royal couple moved on to the king at Windsor they took Russell with them, setting him on the road to becoming first Earl of Bedford and founder of a prosperous ducal dynasty. On the north choir wall is a fragment of an old painted pattern, which once covered a greater area. It is said to represent pomegranates, though some think it is strawberries. Pomegranates have been used as a symbol of Christian fidelity, and a Roman-period mosaic uncovered in 1963 at Hinton St Mary shows Christ's head between two of the fruits. One suggestion is that the work may have been a thank-you gift from a grateful Spanish king, done by a craftsman specially sent by him.

## CHIDEOCK
*Our Lady of Martyrs and St Ignatius (RC)*
Either side of the coast road which cuts Chideock in two, and along which in summer the holiday traffic monotonously heaves, thatched cottages in well-tended gardens remember days when the peace was seldom disturbed. Five minutes away, up the leafy lane towards North Chideock, pastoral

*Chideock, the richly-decoratd altar.*

England still seems to carry on unruffled: tall woods, a grand and rambling (mostly hidden) yellow-stone mansion, rich yields of spring and summer flowers and a church beside a little car-park.

Then, close to it, things become a mite less Olde England. Presiding over the car-park is a tall white figure of Christ on the cross. Above the three matching arches of the church's portico is a colourful roundel with a central statue of the Virgin Mary, surrounded by scenes from her life. A long Latin inscription dedicates the church to her and to St Ignatius, founder of the Jesuits. The truth is, the church in this rural backwater is Roman Catholic. Of course, *all* English churches – all English people – were Roman Catholic before Protestants were ever heard of. But since that time persecution, exile, prejudice, foreign interference, rivalry, resentment, dogma, forms of worship, styles of church and that great alienator, simple difference, have kept them conspicuously apart. The cultural distance is stressed within

*Chideock. The panels above the arches include paintings of well-known Catholic martyrs.*

the portico: on notice boards, images of the Pope, advertisements of pilgrimages to Lourdes and Walsingham; on tables, booklets and posters about appearances of and messages from the Mother of God, delivered at Fatima and Medjugorje, and a large illustrated display about the Chideock Martyrs.

During Queen Elizabeth's reign, in the late 16th century, Catholic priests, trained abroad, covertly infiltrated Protestant England, resolved to restore a religion that had been universally embraced a generation or so before. In doing so, they risked detection by Europe's most efficient secret service, interrogation, torture and sordid execution. Among them, Father John Cornelius, Irish by birth, had trained at Rheims and Rome, moved to London and then to Chideock, where in 1591 he became chaplain to the Arundell family, Catholic owners of the castle there. Three years later he was betrayed by a family servant. At his arrest a relation of the Arundells, Thomas Bosgrave, offered Cornelius his hat. The officer in charge promptly arrested him too, and two servants as well. Cornelius, stretched on the rack, betrayed none of his comrades or

converts. He was offered remission if he renounced popery, and refused. All four men were condemned to death by hanging, drawing and quartering. The other three were hanged before Cornelius. He kissed their feet on his way to the ladder. His suspension was brief enough to allow him, cut down, to watch his own stomach being gutted like that of a pot-fowl, and his innards spilt and burned. The same fate came to another priest, Hugh Green, fifty years later as the Civil War opened. All five men were beatified by Pope Pius XI in 1929, and are commemorated, along with other Dorset victims, by an Elisabeth Frink sculpture in Dorchester.

Chideock castle, with its private chapel, was destroyed by Parliamentary forces in 1645. No part of the building still stands, though an Arundell altar-tomb of about 1545 remains in the parish church. After the Civil War, secret Catholic services were held in a nearby barn. In 1802 the Arundells sold up to their relations the Weld family, an offshoot of the Catholic Welds of Lulworth. The new owners built a chapel on the site of the barn. In 1872 most of the present church, designed for the most part by the then owner Charles Weld, replaced the older building, though the transepts and chancel were added in 1884. The whole interior is intimate, warm and crowded with pleasing shapes, eye-catching detail and a slightly Byzantine flavour. All is contained within a graceful structure: nave, with lean-to aisles behind round-arched columned arcades, painted panels above the arches, clerestory over them, barrel ceiling, a general wealth of colourful decoration. The paintings portray local and national martyrs and other famous Catholics. Charles Weld had an evident restless energy: hardly a capital, step, corbel, spandrel or other wall or ceiling space is left unadorned by his patterns, leaves, flowers, birds, symbols, statues and paintings. Yet everything fits well together. The lavish east end, added to Weld's own design a decade later, effectively changes the style. Its pointed arches and octagon of

*Christchurch Priory. Its Norman provenance is indicated by the blind arcades at the foot of the north transept and the lattice stonework above.*

octagonal columns help to carry the dome and enclose the richly decorated altar. Adding to the baroque effect, a Virgin of gleaming gold ascends on a cloud of golden cherubs into the radiance admitted by a hidden skylight.

Two brasses at the east ends of the aisles commemorate Charles Weld (1812-85), maker of the church and a bachelor, and Frederick (1823-91), the brother who succeeded him and along the way served as prime minister of New Zealand, and governor of Western Australia, Tasmania and the Straits Settlements. An uncle, Thomas of Lulworth, not commemorated here, was made a cardinal in 1830, the first Englishman so appointed for some two hundred years.

There is an interesting local museum in a long room off the north aisle.

## CHRISTCHURCH PRIORY
*Holy Trinity*

There are churches built to a unified plan, visions of one man or a few men, grown without deviancy from conception, each of their separate parts intrinsic to the whole. Then there are evolved churches, bumpily developed, added to or removed from at need or whim. Christchurch Priory, begun in 1094 on the site of a Saxon church of 680, is nothing if not evolved. You see it on the outside, as you approach the north porch, the main entrance. To the right, the west tower – Perpendicular and 15th century (the original was Norman and central, but it collapsed in 1420); 13th century north porch and aisle; north transept scrumptiously Norman, especially the corner turret, with its interlocking round-arched blind arcades and criss-cross stone courses like a lattice tart; and everything eastward of that – the chancel and Lady Chapel – 15th century, their huge windows standing stiffly to attention in

*Christchurch Priory. The memorial to the poet Percy Bysshe Shelley, who drowned off the Italian coast in 1822.*

soldierly, Perpendicular style. Details, of course, both outside and in, add a far greater variety. We have lost most of the voices of the past, and cannot know all the historic causes of and attitudes to diversity. Much that is oldest in our churches may have survived for want of funds to displace it. We have evidence that medieval taste loved the new, inventing fresh styles at home or travelling to France or Italy (as we shall see inside) to find them, and readily sacrificing the old to make room for it. Whatever the intentions of our forbears, Christchurch Priory is a majestic motley of past modes.

Inside, from the first, we are treated to fine vistas. The north porch itself is one, probably the longest in England, with tierceron vaulting and at the end a double doorway, cinquefoil-capped under receding moulded arches supported on thin, dark, Purbeck shafts. Within, we look in at the tower base with its doleful memorial to Shelley the poet and Mary his wife. This was rejected both by St Peter's, Bournemouth (where Mary and Shelley's heart are buried), and by Westminster Abbey. They thought the portrayal of the poet's limp body too closely, and blasphemously, resembled represent-

ations of Christ taken down from the cross. The glass of the enormous west window is of 1861; the font a 20th century copy of the 1220 original. The view to the east from here is splendid, clasped by the might of the Norman arcades, with their patterned arches and spandrels, and the shadowy apertures of the triforia. Above are the illuminating clerestory and the simply ribbed vault – the work of 1819. Beyond the crossing and its screen, diminished by distance, are seen the chancel's lierne vaulting, the tracery of the reredos canopies and a modern painting of the Ascension above them.

All the same, it is in the south aisle, with blind arches that once led into the cloisters and other monastery buildings, that more evocative vistas appear. From mid-point you can look back, westward, along a sequence of gracefully narrow pointed arches, to the classical screen of the War Memorial Chapel; and eastward, under the slightly unruly patterning of the lierne vaulting, towards chantry screens of exquisitely delicate carving. The Cloister Way, off to the right, contains modern stained glass representations of the Priory's history, with charming scenes showing incidents, people and the medieval building techniques used. There is no cloister now – it was destroyed at the time of the Dissolution – so we can return to the nave to look closely at the 14th century Quire (as it is quaintly spelt here) Screen with its delightful carvings of foliage and small animals. Its upper part is much restored and lacks the rood loft it supported till the time of the Reformation. The original piers at the four corners of the crossing were designed to uphold not just the tower but the spire that rose from it, but both collapsed in the freakish storm of 1420 and were not rebuilt.

The early 1500s, just before the arrival of Protestantism blew such things away, were a great time for chantries. Successful people were richer than successful people had been before, and some could afford the costs of an ornate chapel and the perpetual services of a chantry priest. Not only were several constructed in Christchurch but, unlike elsewhere, they were allowed to stand even when their purpose was outlawed. In the south quire aisle we pass the Harys Chantry built for the benefit of the soul of Robert Harys who died in 1525. The picture of a hare and the letters R and YS on a panel within form a rebus - a sort of riddle version of his name. The tomb beyond carries Flaxman's soft and sensitive 1815 statue of Viscountess Fitzharris with her children. One of several wall memorials on the right, commemorating William Cameron of the Cameron Highlanders, recalls yet another of the British empire's probes into the world's hidden parts: he fell 'in an attack on the village of Absari, occupied by the dervishes in front of the Fort of Kosheh on the Upper Nile in the Soudan ... 1885'. At the end of the aisle is the Draper Chantry. John Draper was the last prior of Christchurch before the Dissolution. Where others in his position resisted, failed and in some cases paid with their lives, he negotiated, preserved the church and came away with an annual pension of £133 – enough for a life of considerable comfort. A timber protruding unceremoniously from an aperture in the wall above is known as the Miraculous Beam. Legend has it that, as it was lifted into position, it was found to have been cut too short to span the nave roof for which it was intended. Long delays were expected. Carpenters fretted. But next day it was, magically, the necessary length. It was also in place. One carpenter, a quiet, industrious, impressive young man, was missing, and never reappeared. For some, this was enough to justify the priory's name.

We pass the Lady Chapel at the east end, with light flooding in from vast Perpendicular windows on to the elegant tombs of Sir Thomas West and his mother Lady Alice and the much restored 1450 reredos. In the north quire aisle, above their tomb, lie the worn and chipped alabaster effigies of Sir John Chydioke, killed in battle in 1449, and his wife. The depredations to

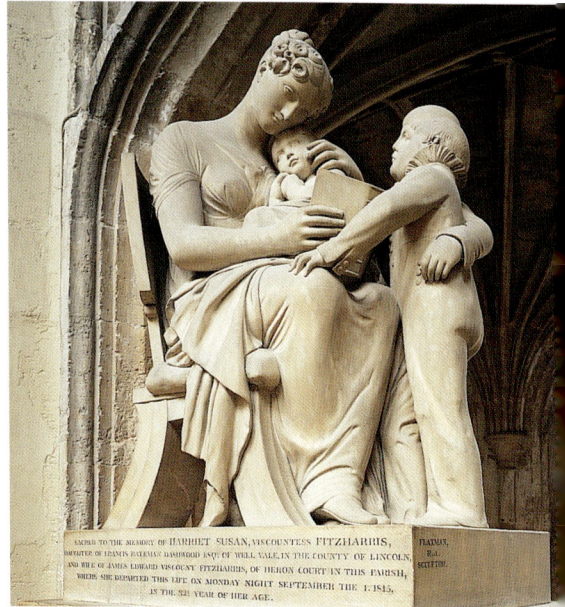

*Christchurch Priory. The memorial to Viscountess Fitzharris and her children.*

the stone are said to be due to an old belief in the benefits conferred by scrapings from such figures, when mixed with pure local water, in the treatment of eye disorders. On the floor a little further on, a small brass within a black slab on the floor marks the grave of Anne, first wife of A.W. Pugin, prime arbiter of the serious, scholarly phase of the 19th century Gothic Revival. She died in childbirth in 1832, aged 18. He fitted another marriage into his short life of forty years, but he always kept a death-mask of Anne, and a cast of one of her hands. Just back from this, we can turn into the quire and sanctuary, in which are situated three of the priory's great glories. There are the carvings: the wooden misericords, bench-ends and arm-rests that remind us of the curious vein of humour that runs through the most august and reverential sanctums. A fox preaches from his pulpit to a gaggle of geese – the cunning to the feeble-minded. A dog bites a clown's foot. Two acrobats swing on ropes. A wild man of the woods prepares to club a malevolent green man. Here is a great richness of whimsy,

*Christchurch Priory, the reredos, showing a pillar rising from King David's father, a sleeping Jesse, at the bottom, and the Nativity above.*

satire and straight portraiture.

There is the reredos, a masterpiece of the mid 14th century, comprising three rows of elaborate gothic canopied niches, most of them bare of the statues they were designed to hold. But the lowest tier and the centre of the middle tier are busily occupied with vivid sculpture. Jesse, father of King David, lies asleep at the bottom, with David (bearing a harp) and Solomon on either side of him. From Jesse's stomach, as prophesied in Isaiah, a pillar rises, spreading out to carry the birth-scene of Jesse's most illustrious

descendant. The Blessed Virgin sits on the left, with the baby Jesus standing on her lap and Joseph behind. The Three Kings have their offerings ready, and there are animals, angels and other important effects. The polish of later artists is lacking. The kings look woefully worried, Mary sits stiffly, Jesus stands precariously, like a little statuette trying to keep its balance. The effect is naive and very moving.

Left, or north, of the reredos, and excelling all, is the Countess of Salisbury's chantry. She was a niece of two Plantagenet kings, Edward IV and Richard III, and a cause of discomfort to Henry VIII, whose Tudor father Henry VII had with dubious legitimacy supplanted their dynasty. Worse, her son Reginald Pole was a Catholic priest and from 1536 a cardinal. Within three years her other two sons were condemned to death; she herself two years later. Aged 68, she was beheaded in the Tower. Fuller records that 'on the scaffold, as she stood, she would not gratify the executioner with a prostrate posture of her body.'

The chantry, built by her in 1529, in white Caen stone, remains an exquisite memorial, though her body was disposed of in London. Strong Italian influence has been traced. It is worth straining every muscle to see as much as possible of the interior, a casket of Perpendicular filigree, fan-vaulting and decorative bosses, canopies, cherubs, roses, honeysuckles and broom – the planta genista from which the Plantagenets took their name. Henry ordered all the heraldic motifs to be destroyed, and they were, but the beauty of the whole thing was hardly affected. Ironically, the Countess's son Cardinal Pole was in royal favour two reigns later, when Henry's Catholic daughter Mary came to the throne. He was made Archbishop of Canterbury and was buried in the cathedral there.

The last section of our circuit takes us past the north transept and the Montacute chantry, where a capital carved in the form of the apostles' heads shows Judas with two

faces. The altar here was done and given by the young Pugin: a carved, curvily ornate five-bay-fronted oak table, mostly hidden from view by modern liturgical drapes.

A small museum is in the loft above the Lady Chapel, for long a grammar school. It is reached by a spiral staircase.

## COMPTON VALENCE
*St Thomas à Becket*

The village is set secretively in a wooded ruck among the bare-topped downs of West Dorset. Most of the 27 houses conceal themselves from the traversing lane, but the church rises beside and above it, conspicuously set against a dark luxuriance of trees. The battlemented west tower, gabled south porch, nave, chancel and east end apse (or more strictly semi-octagon), with their stolid broad buttresses, Perpendicular windows and pithecoid gargoyle on the tower, ranged in long profile within the steeply rising churchyard, look at first glance as if they had been there since medieval builders set the last stone slates in place. But only the tower is that old. Benjamin Ferrey, an architect architects like, fresh from helping to make early Bournemouth, designed the remainder of the church in 1838-9.

*Compton Valence, 19th century nave and medieval tower.*

This is curious. The 19th century had brought into many of its multitudinous new churches a great deal of medieval gothic style, at first careless of period and detail. In his fairly scrupulous adhesion to Decorated modes, in the curvy tracery of the west window (though not the others), pointed tower arch, the apse and its vault, and many other features Ferrey seems to have put a remote rural church into the van of what many historians insist on calling correct gothic revival, and anticipated Pugin, the man most acknowledged as its main apostle. Ferrey, born at Christchurch and designer of many Dorset buildings, was in fact a close friend of Pugin (and wrote a memoir which gives the best existing picture of his personality) and had studied with his father, and no doubt owed much of his professional attitudes to them. In due course he became renowned for his scholarly transpositions of authentic gothic design, anticipating G.E.Street and William Butterfield and other titans of the Revival.

Entering through the south porch you find a tall, slender nave divided from the north (and only) aisle by a four-arch Ham-stone arcade. The arches reach almost to the roof,

*Compton Valence, the nave and chancel.*

level with the clear-cut corbels supporting the wagon roof's dark beams. To the east, a fifth tall arch in the same warm stone leads to the chancel, whose apsidal bulge and binding roof-ribs, along with the pretty patterning of three-light stained-glass windows, give it something of the look of a cave glowing from some inner light. A curious heightening of mystery comes from the 19th century stone pulpit on its spreading stone stem, set in the south-east corner of the nave. Access to it is only from the chancel, and the preacher makes a somewhat jack-in-the-box emergence from behind. This is one token of the ritual change in 19th century churches. Before it, the nave was the thing and the clarity of prayer-book readings within it and the chancel hardly counted. Now the sanctity, mystery and awe of the chancel was reasserted. To deliver his sermon to the people, the priest had to be almost prised through a hole in the chancel wall.

The terminal fleur-de-lys or poppy-heads on the hard but handsome dark pews form lines of simple ornament down the church. The assembly by Ferrey's sure hand of apt and accurately fashioned features, fittings and furniture – the dignified stature of the arches, the plain white stone of walls and west tower arch, the elegant, centrally placed 15th century font, the two glimpsed 18th century north wall memorials (Ann Best's of 1740 has an hour-glass in stone relief to warn of life's brevity), the south wall's two windows and intriguing chancel cavern – all help create an air of powerful restraint and stately simplicity. East of the font a floor brass of 1440, with its inscription on thin ribbon wings, commemorates the rector of the time, Thomas Maldon. He rebuilt the church, at a time when parsons up and down England were doing the same, making the look of the countryside that we have inherited. Maldon's destiny was different. His image survives. Most of his church is gone.

## CRANBORNE
### St Mary and St Bartholomew

A small Benedictine community was founded here in the 10th century and soon owned huge properties. In 1102 it was placed under the wing of Tewkesbury Abbey which had become even grander. Cranborne nevertheless remained rich and influential. The present church consists mainly of a late 13th century rebuilding of the nave; the mighty 15th century tower; and a chancel, vestry and capacious north porch – all three of which date from the 1870s. The north doorway, moved from its first position, is late Norman -early 12th century, and patterned to match. The church is all that survives of the sprawling medieval monastic complex, some of whose stones were used after the Dissolution in the building of Cranborne Manor. In the eighteenth century the town changed character from decayed monastic to time-baked redbrick genteel. Bypassed by nineteenth century railways and turnpike roads, it settled for the quiet ways it had by now become used to. Amid this mature elegance the handsome church – mostly flint, though the tower's base and other bits are of stone and the roofs tiled – stands out surprisingly bright, big, and rather awe-inspiring.

Modern pilgrimages to Cranborne are directed mainly towards the manor house gardens and garden centre. Views of the Tudor house itself, with its chimneys, battlements and quirky corner-towers capped by tiled pyramids, offer themselves here and there, while a wrought iron gate in the churchyard wall gives a pretty glimpse of enclosed orchard and strutting white poultry. References in and out of the church to the Cecils, Marquesses of Salisbury, who have owned the place for over four hundred years, are fewer than we might expect. Hatfield House in Hertfordshire is their main home, and more convenient for running the country, which Cecil prime ministers have made rather a habit of doing since Queen Elizabeth's day. Some Cecil graves, however, lie to the west of the west door, including that of the writer, critic and Oxford don Lord David Cecil and his wife Rachel.

We go in through the 12th century north doorway, under the standard Norman, chevron patterning of the round arch. The interior, predictably, is broad and lofty. The eye is drawn past the outward lurch of the nave arcades, through a rood screen complete

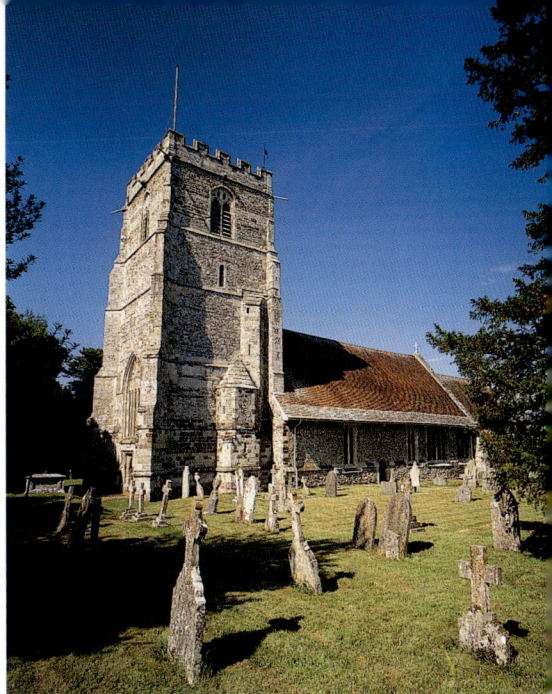

*Cranborne, a happy medley of stone, flint, Purbeck slates and weathered clay tiles.*

with statues of Mary and John the Evangelist standing either side of the crucified Christ, under a Victorian wall-painting of Christ and the Apostles, to an east end rather too light and featureless to hold us long, since the antique tombs and memorials which enriched the chancel before it was rebuilt in 1875 were in that year removed to the far ends of the aisles. The screen itself, along with the reredos at the east end of the south aisle and the tower screen, were done by a vicar at the end of the 19th century. The east window is modern, a Cecil memorial, consisting of diamonds of stained glass set on a pale background and forming a larger diamond that spreads over five lights. The reset recess in the north wall containing a cracked table tomb could be a preserved Easter Sepulchre, in which an image of Christ on the cross would have been covered – or symbolically buried – on Good Friday, to be joyously resurrected on Easter Sunday.

The Early English nave is tall and slim under its plastered wagon roof – probably put up around 1500. The western arches of its two arcades were cut short by the addition of the tower, which is also at a slight angle to

*Cranborne. The pulpit dates to about 1400 and is one of the oldest in England.*

*Cranborne. The Doom, with naked sinners being torn by devils from the tree of evil.*

the main axis. There are traces of medieval murals on the wall above the south arcade: one of them a Doom, showing a smirking, ugly visage lurking within the base of a tree of evil, and naked sinners being torn off the branches by devils. The pulpit is a fine piece, alive with carving and dated to about 1400 by the monogram TP, for Thomas Parker, then abbot. This puts it among the oldest surviving in England. The aisle walls carry most of the memorials, plaques, brasses and in the windows rather richly coloured lights. The doorway in the south aisle was only rediscovered in 1927, probably not used since it opened on to the abbey cloisters in pre-Reformation days. The door itself is a recent copy of a 13th century original. Nearby is the Norman font of Purbeck stone, modestly decorated with shallow panels. Further west in this aisle is a cherub-topped tablet commemorating Susanna Stillingfleet, mother of a future bishop of Worcester, and at the end a magnificent table tomb under an elaborately carved canopy topped by a frieze of arabesques. The pair lying with hands joined in prayer on the tomb, ruffs complete but noses bruised and fingers gone, are

thought to be John and Elizabeth Hooper, parents of Thomas Hooper of nearby Boveridge, chief ranger of Cranborne Chase, whose wordier, splashier, almost flashier monument, also outlawed from its first home in the chancel, stands opposite in the north aisle. Along this aisle the royal arms of Queen Anne hang above the main entrance. Beyond is the sensitive memorial to young John Eliot, a schoolboy who died in 1641, as a result, it is thought, of swallowing a fishbone.

## DORCHESTER
*St Peter*

Most of Dorchester's best buildings – Georgian, Victorian, 17th century – huddle in forced brotherhood around the central junction of High Street and Cornmarket, fearful perhaps that the civic overseers will make as much a bombsite of them as they have of much of the rest of the town's middle. At the heart of these survivals, St Peter's medieval tower raises a spray of spindly pinnacles, while, below, the dialect poet, one-time churchwarden here and later parson of Winterborne Came, William Barnes,

*Dorchester, St Peter's. The statue to the left of the porch is of William Barnes, the Dorset poet.*

replicated in bronze and clad in green verdigris, welcomes trickles of weekday tourists and Sunday worshippers to the church. (Great Hardy, suspicious of God and never liked by the burghers, is made to sit alone, staring at traffic queues at Top o'Town).

St Peter's presents its handsome length, buttressed, Perpendicular and battlemented, to the main road, as do the other two nearby churches theirs. It used to have more room but the railed surround was sacrificed to a road-widening scheme. There was a Norman church here certainly, and probably Saxon and Roman antecedents, but the present building goes back in essence to the 1420s. The south door alone is Norman, with its nice zigzag arch – probably brought from somewhere else and cut in the middle to fit. The porch is big – big enough for an altar and side-seats, and the weddings, churchings of mothers and other services that would have been carried out there before the Reformation. The two little heads at the base of the outer arch's hood-moulding are likenesses of a 1990s rector and verger. The

fine oak doors were done in 1903. The dark, diamond-shaped tablet, placed by Americans in 1902, might, were it more legible, keep alive the memory of the early 17th century rector John White, who is buried below.

The 17th century was for Dorchester – and not least St Peter's – a series of traumas, triumphs, confrontations and cataclysms that leave the rest of its history rather cold. In August 1613 a fire broke out across the road from the church and destroyed 170 houses – half the town. Solemn and self-righteous, hating popery, pomp and ritual, the Puritans who had been making ground throughout Elizabeth's reign saw the tragedy as God's work, retribution for the town's former licence, corruption, drinking, fornication, play performances and dodging of church services. They took over local government and saw to the care of the old and sick and poor and to children's education. For a period Dorchester was rightly called England's leading Puritan town. John White was a driving force behind all this, but his was always the voice of moderation. He also during the 1620s busily promoted the emigration of dissenting colonists to America, planting a colony of the county's men close to what became Boston.

*Dorchester, St Peter's, the stone figure of a 14th century knight probably brought from the former friary at the Reformation.*

But the pendulum swung back. In 1633 the High Church martinet, William Laud, became Archbishop of Canterbury and began to send inspectors up and down the country checking on the obedience of churches to his and the King's decrees: seeing, for instance, whether the altar stood flush with the east wall as he ordered, or – in the way the puritans chose – lengthwise down the chancel, so that communion seemed more family meal than reverential rite. They made sure priests wore the correct surplices and vestments and that the people knelt to pray and bowed at the name of Jesus – both repugnant to puritans. They also made sure readings were given from the *Book of Sports,* the recently revised work of the previous king, James I, which urged Sunday dances and games. This too outraged puritans, yet the parson of St Peter's (or rather plain 'Peter's', as anti-frill puritans were now calling it) was obliged, like all other churches, to declaim specific passages from the pulpit. An answer was found. In mid-afternoon on Friday 11 July 1634 the parish clerk and church-wardens sat in this otherwise empty church listening, perhaps rather nervously, to

a visiting minister read out the required texts. (White would not have been party to the trick, and was not told till it was over). Next day the perpetrators could testify to the visiting inspector that they had done as the archbishop commanded without letting on that the congregation was wholly absent.

Much worse followed. During the Civil War windows were barricaded and a look-out posted on the church roof during services to warn of approaching troops. Nevertheless, armies swept through the town, killing, firing and plundering, and in 1642 White's own house was raided and looted by a particularly lawless royalist force. In 1685 Judge Jeffreys lived opposite the church during the week of his cynical assize, in which bevies of youths were condemned to hang for joining Monmouth's rebellion, trying without success to avert a papist monarchy. No doubt Jeffreys, who remained an Anglican, worshipped at St Peter's, or Holy Trinity just above. In a hundred unhappy years the town tasted Protestant and Catholic monarchy, presbyterian and republican rule, dictatorship, civil war, several revolutions, two catastrophic fires and outbreaks of plague, before settling for the relative sleepiness of the 18th century.

Inside, St Peter's is capacious and stately, tall-ceilinged, tall-aisled, tall-arched, tall-chancelled, tall-towered. Its interior body is symmetrical and open: broad north and south aisles with lean-to ceilings, nave with waggon roof, all roofs white, cut by dark beams and decorated with heraldic, historic or just decorative bosses, re-gilded at the millennium. Almost all windows – three-light and perpendicular in style – have 19th century stained glass, the east ones by John Hardman, others by Albert Moore: decent, pious, forgettable. The chancel, a 19th century addition, is broad, and the chapels either side of it are more or less continuations of the aisles.

Nothing much displeases the eye, but not a great deal delights it either. The church's very loftiness gives it an institutional, somehow impersonal feel, like a school hall in the holidays. Its appeal lies in its detail and history and a few fine things. Among the two hatchments and several wall plaques in the south aisle, where we enter, is a good 16th century tablet commemorating Thomas Hardy of Melcombe Regis and his liberal endowments for the benefit of a preacher, a teacher and the town's grammar school. In the south-west wall is the rough outline of a door that led to the former organ gallery, spanning the church's west end. At the aisle's east end a delicate wooden screen divides off the Hardy Chapel, named after the same Thomas, though a neatly drawn plan of the church by his novelist namesake, done in 1856 when he was sixteen and working on restoration for the Dorchester architect John Hicks, hangs on the left as you go in. There are memorial plaques to young army officers whose careers transferred them from Dorchester to early deaths in India, or in action on the North West Frontier. Memorials of two more warriors, of five hundred years before – magnificent

recumbent stone knights, sensitively sculpted, with lions for foot-rests – are set on window-sills, as if to keep them out of the Hoover's way. They may have been brought from Dorchester's friary, a victim of the Reformation.

The reredos behind the solid 17th-century communion table is a fanciful gothic affair, designed, like much else in Dorset, by C.E. Ponting and framing a marble relief of the Last Supper – given in 1899 in memory of the reforming Earl of Shaftesbury – and coarsely done mosaics either side. More interesting is one of the county's few stone Easter Sepulchres on the north wall, moved here during Hicks's alterations. In this, symbols of Christ would be mournfully placed on Good Friday and joyously resurrected on Easter Sunday. The north chapel is a mess. It is all but filled by the organ (once better sited on a western nave gallery), which thus squeezes into a high, dark, easterly recess the lavish curved canopy, the contained funerary chest,

*Dorchester, St Peter's, the nave and chancel.*

*Dorchester, St Peter's, the memorial to Denzil Holles.*

generous patrons of the town, and they themselves paid for the aisle. Their reward is this containment in outer darkness. In 1814 the clerk and sexton, decorating the church and with senses heightened by communion wine, saw hereabouts the ghost of a dead vicar angrily shaking his head at them before floating up and out of sight.

The way round to the north aisle leads past a fine early 17th century stem-glass carved-wood pulpit, in which no doubt John White preached. The aisle has sober plaques on the wall, among them one to John Gordon, who died here in 1774 but owned an estate in Jamaica where, in 1760, rebellious 'NEGROES whom his BRAVERY had repulsed' finally, 'having confidence in his HUMANITY', gave in. We are left hoping their trust was justified.

Then, against the far aisle wall – removed from its original place in the chancel – but commanding attention by its splendid theatrical pomposity, is the tall, baroque monument of 1699 to Denzil Holles (1599-1680), Baron of Ifield. He lies, skirted like a Roman warrior, bewigged like Charles II, sensitive of finger, looked on by mourning cherubs afloat on a marble cloud, the whole scene set under raised (stone) curtains, with heraldic arms and urns above and a prolix essay, in both Latin and English, engraved below. He was a character of motley mix and his life was stormy; anti-Charles I, anti-Cromwell, in and out of Charles II's favour, brave enough to grip the Commons Speaker to stop him ending a crucial anti-king debate (Holles went to the Tower for that), to challenge opponents to duels, to risk gaol and beheading more than once, to consider his principles before the strength of his enemy, to disappoint his allies by opposing extremes (like killing the king). He could charm but seldom did so. 'Stiff and sullen', Charles II called him, and he was not easy to please, not easy to categorise, and perhaps for that reason less famous than he might be. Independent, tough, quite cussed, very Dorchester.

knightly symbols and to either side the kneeling figures of Sir John and Lady Williams of Herringston – a house just outside Dorchester on the south, and still in the same family. Their successors were to be

# EAST LULWORTH
## St Mary (RC)

After the Reformation Roman Catholicism was on a shaky footing. It carried the scent of incense and conspiracy and the threat of invasion – at first from Spain, later France. English fear and suspicion were periodically fanned to flames: by periodic persecutions, the Armada, the Guy Fawkes plot, the Romeward leanings of Stuart kings, the Jacobite risings of 1715 and 1745. The owner of Lulworth, Edward Weld, was arrested and gaoled in London for a brief while on suspicion of complicity in the 1745 rebellion. Nevertheless attitudes, which had anyway been from time to time relaxed in remoter areas like Dorset, were by now changing radically. The Stuart threat had diminished to almost nothing. Laws that banned Catholics from politics, the army and university, from buying or inheriting land, from holding or attending church services, were often ignored and at last repealed. Some Catholics, concentrating on commerce, which they were allowed, or marrying well, or temporarily handing possession of their estates to trustworthy Protestant friends or relatives, became very rich. Certain of these, if they were not already, became gentlemen or noblemen. They could talk with kings. Thomas Weld (1750-1810), son of the above Edward, whose family had held Lulworth from the early 17th century, quite often did. George III twice stayed with the Welds on the way to bathing in the sea at Weymouth.

This did not involve any compromise of Thomas's religion. He energetically helped refugees from the Continent, provided the Jesuit academy of Liège with the buildings and land of Stonyhurst in Lancashire – earliest of English Catholic public schools – and built and for twenty years after 1795 helped to maintain a monastery at East Lulworth for French Trappists exiled by the French Revolution. At home, though, he had for long had to make do with a room in his castle for family worship, since the building of Catholic chapels remained illegal. In 1785,

East Lulworth, St Mary; finished in 1785 and the first free-standing Catholic church in England to be built after the Reformation.

shortly after Parliament had removed several restrictions on Catholics, and with further reforms in the air, he asked the King to allow him to erect one. George is said to have assented, so long as the building did not *look* like a chapel, but more in the mould of a mausoleum of the kind that adorned many large parks. The structure was complete in 1789 and visited, and so approved, by the King and Queen in the same year. It is in neo-classical style, quite distinct from the Gothic styles then being voguishly revived.

The ground plan shows a central square from which three sides bulge broadly in apse-like curves. The bulge on the fourth side – the one containing the altar – is internal only: enclosed within a rectangular extension which contains the vestry and a staircase to the crypt, in which Welds are buried. The handsome façade of this extension, facing the castle roughly to the east, has niches containing urns either side of – and another urn above – the Tuscan porch. This is the private doorway. The public uses the door at the west end. The whole building is elaborately Georgian, with square-cut clear-glass windows.

The interior is light and large. There is

*East Lulworth, St Mary, showing the broad central dome and carved marble altar.*

none of the shadowy mystery, or repeated upward thrust, of Gothic. The pews, all facing the altar, are painted a pale green. Gold is put about lavishly. The broad central dome was painted in 1988, to celebrate the building's bicentenary, and shows the Blessed Virgin being taken up among clouds and chubby *putti* into Heaven, a Catholic concept not accepted by the Church of England. The carved marble altar with its kneeling angels, ivory and lapis lazuli crucifix and gilt candlesticks were made in Rome. In the south gallery is a permanent exhibition of copes, censers, chalices, crosses, pyxes, thuribles, monstrances, chasubles and other such ecclesiastical trappings, recalling the family's historic devotion to and distinction within the Catholic hierarchy. One of their number became a cardinal in 1830, another a bishop, another Rector of Stonyhurst and several unmarried daughters nuns.

The original architect was John Tasker. It seems he took the general design from James Wyatt's London Pantheon, an entertainment complex based roughly on the emperor Hadrian's original Pantheon in Rome. In the mid 19th century Joseph Hansom, inventor of the two-wheeled hansom cab, gave a Byzantine gloss to the place, altering

windows and impatiently filling bare spaces with artefacts. These were all removed, and austerer dignity restored, by H.S.Goodhart-Rendel in 1953. Hadrian's concept has been carried beyond these shores. John Carroll, first Catholic bishop to hold a see in the United States, was consecrated here at Lulworth in 1790; and, whether or not through this connection, the Catholic cathedral of Baltimore, is clearly inspired by the Lulworth chapel design.

## FLEET
### Holy Trinity

What might be called its foundations are a quarter of a mile away. In 1824 a tidal wave heaved its way over the massive natural wall of the Chesil Bank and drove in its enormity across the Fleet lagoon. Moving 'as fast as a horse could gallop', it rolled much of what

had been the village of Fleet to smithereens. The old Norman church went down with the rest. Its chancel, the only part restored, acts now as a mortuary chapel. The vicar of the day, George Gould, brother of the owner of the surrounding land, took the homeless under his roof. (The road that brings us to Fleet passes through gates which originally marked the boundary of the estate and parish; the raised arm on the present gates forms part of the old Gould family arms).

George paid besides for the building of the church we see now, well away from the storms and thunderings of tide, the men-of-war and merchantmen smashed to matchwood on the shingle; away, too, from the family vault of the Mohuns, in which John Meade Falkner set the chilling early scene of his novel *Moonfleet*, where young John Trenchard hid, cramped, beside an old corpse, while below him smugglers discussed how to rid themselves of the danger he posed. The real Mohuns were the great local landlords throughout the 17th century, and brasses to them still hang in the old chancel.

The new church stands prettily in its Gothic Revival coat by the road in a quiet clearing – the broad, iron-railed churchyard – among tall, lanky woods. It looks somehow as if made from a kit, so neat it is, and nice

*Fleet, the new church sits well inland amidst trees.*

*Fleet. Stained glass casts its glow over the memorial to John Gould.*

and right and rather obvious. There are battlements all round, Perpendicular windows, buttresses, pinnacles like tiny pagodas, the slight blush of the stone; and on the tower a carved winged angel within a quatrefoil frieze and, terminating the tower door's hoodmould, the symbols of king and bishop: crown, sceptre, orb, hat and crook.

You enter through the tower door and on the left a plaque commemorates Sir Morton Peto, Baronet, a benefactor until his construction firm, which, amid much else, built railways around the world and Nelson's Column in Trafalgar Square, crashed in the late 1860s. The nave has a rather novel panelling pattern on the ceiling and there are medieval-style plaster vaults in the sanctuary apse's ceiling. The death of John, the Rev George Gould's brother, in 1818 is mourned in the fine unattributed statue of a young man and two women to the right of the apse. One of the church's treasures links it to the Mohuns and the old church: a silver chalice given in Charles II's reign by Maximilian Mohun and made by the king's silversmith. But there has been more than one theft of church furniture in recent years, and the chalice remains far away, locked in the diocesan vaults. The American flag recalls the occupation of local land and buildings in 1944 by American troops waiting to effect the momentous Normandy landings.

# FOLKE
## St Lawrence

Cattle, sheep and horses are present in plenty on this pastoral, woods-rich, clay-based valley floor, lush the year round. It is prime dairy country, well hedged, with plough and poison less invasive than in the flattened corn prairies to the east. A straight, stone-walled cul-de-sac, flanked by trees, leads to the church which, like the Jacobean manor opposite and other big houses nearby, is of stone and looks lastingly sturdy. The stone is mainly the rough but durable forest marble, quarried locally. Honey-hued Ham-stone is used for church quoins, doorways and window-frames. Here, a couple of miles from Sherborne, the country peace is mostly broken – in spring anyway – by swallow-chatter, dove coo and the occasional small plane's drone. The village itself is easily forgotten. Due to the siting of the new turnpike road in the 19th century, the village was gradually transferred from its first position, close to the church, to Allweston, a mile north.

The churchyard is rucked grass, a smatter of handsome tombstones and two mature walnut trees (the only yew is a struggling millennial novice no more than a yard high) all within a fine drystone wall. Cuffs, Ridouts, Hanns, Days and Osmunds in all their forms (Osman, Osment, Osmond) lie recorded in stone. The medieval church that

*Folke, now separated from the village at the end of a lane.*

*Folke, the nave, showing the carved Jacobean chancel screen and arch leading into the north aisle.*

preceded this one was almost entirely rebuilt in 1628, at the end of James I's reign. Hardly any churches had been built in the previous eighty years, due partly to the uncertainties of the time but more to the capacity of existing churches, after 15th century and early 16th century expansion and rebuilding, to accommodate all worshippers with, at most, some patching and enlargement. Nor would many be built until after the Restoration of 1660. The architectural style for such new churches as there were would not have been decreed by fashion. Gothic had been more or less worked through at the time of the Reformation, but European Renaissance styles were slow to filter into England. The answer at Folke and elsewhere was to prolong Gothic's lifetime in the structure of the church – hence the aisle battlements and the general appearance of the west tower - and apply a new Jacobean exuberance, with faint Renaissance touches, like the patterning of capitals and piers, to the interior design. Curiously, Folke shares features with a handful of nearby churches. Leweston, Minterne and Ryme Intrinseca all have some windows of three or five lights, the central one higher than the rest, in Early English

fashion, with the hoodmould turning up and down to match.

The first glimpse of the nave is almost startling. Ahead, the simple geometry of the prospect above the three-arched oaken chancel screen, is charged with a sprightly, almost cheeky double curlicue – a bit like two benign serpents looking loftily about them. Under the middle arch of the north arcade is another ornate but soberer arch leading to the north aisle. All this woodwork is busy with Jacobean relief patterning. So too is the pulpit, beside which is one of only three hourglass stands remaining in the county – sometimes the object of strained attention as a congregation wondered whether, when a dull sermon reached the end of its first hour, the preacher would conclude, or turn the glass over and start on a second. Pews, under the elegant arcades whose under-surfaces are decorated with roses, are livened by nicely carved bench-ends with semi-circular shell tops. In the chancel beyond, choir stalls, altar rail and the table supporting the marble altar-

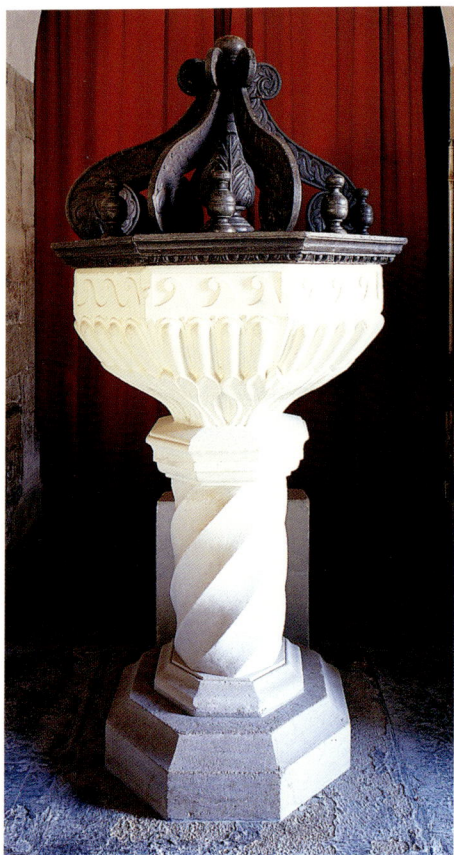

*Folke, the font.*

# FONTMELL MAGNA
*St Andrew*

There is a ripe untidiness, a magnificent, massive, Perpendicular-gothic, asymmetrical bulk about this ascendant castle of Christianity, looming above you as you enter the churchyard gate. It is made largely of blotchy greensand of agreeably differing shades. Its visible component parts – south porch, south aisle, west tower, gabled east end and pinnacled tower – are mostly fringed by buttress angles, spikey pinnacles and a long, wall-top, sometimes horizontal, sometimes canted, perforated stone frieze. St Andrew's looks like a big evolved master-work, set on its mound among the pretty roofs of this picture-book village, well away from the snarling nastiness of the much used through-road. It certainly has a long history: foundation in Saxon times, a parson dying of the Black Death in 1348, another losing his head under Catholic Queen Mary; a passable poet-parson, Thomas Dibden, in the 18th century.

But it was all done or redone in 1862 and 1863 to the design of George Evans of Wimborne, whose work and reputation hardly spread beyond east Dorset. At a cost

*Fontmell Magna, the memorial to Philip Salkeld, who won the VC during the Indian Mutiny.*

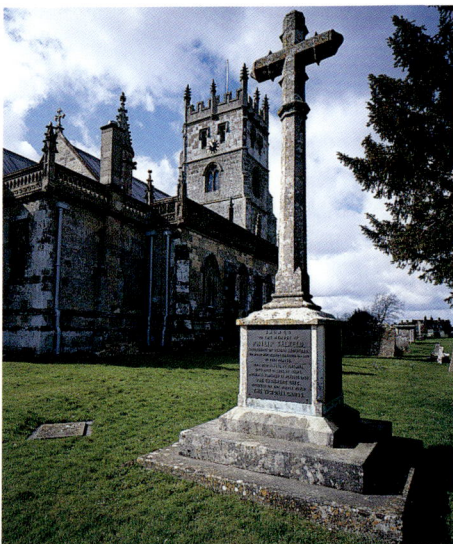

slab are of the same period and as finely made. So is the lectern, unusually a part of the screen. For Folke retains virtually all its 17th century furnishings. Even the graceful font, cup-shaped, with rich wavy ornament on a stem striped like barley sugar, topped by an elaborate oak scroll cover, is contemporary 17th century.

There are some 18th century memorials on the walls of chancel and aisles, and at the end of the south aisle a badly chipped, cracked and crumbling monument to Walter Ridout, who died in 1643, leaving no explanation of his own epitaph on himself, now 'at quiet rest,' but, while he lived, 'by the world oprest'. 'Praised be God', he adds in triumph, 'he hath overcome this evil, and vanquished hath ye world, ye flesh ye devil.'

*Fontmell Magna, framed by the rising downs.*

of £12,000, it was one of the most expensive church restorations in the county, paid for by the Glyn family, banker landlords (like the Hambros at Milton Abbas, ten miles south). The north porch carries an original section of the quaintly carved parapet frieze, brought round from the south and noted by Hutchins to carry the date 1530. It carries various heraldic (and possibly whimsical) devices within solid quatrefoils, and from the corners grimacing long-necked birds protrude.

The sloping churchyard is peopled with large gravestones and mature Irish yews. A cross commemorates Philip Salkeld, lieutenant of the Bengal Engineers, son of the Reverend Robert who was rector for almost half a century, 1819 to 1866, and during whose incumbency the rebuilding took place. When Delhi was overrun by mutineers in early 1857, and the massive arsenal threatened, the British decided to blow it up rather than leave it for the enemy. Philip Salkeld was one who fired the explosives with no hope of surviving – a prototype suicide bomber. Two days short of twenty-seven, he was awarded a posthumous Victoria Cross, within a year of the medal's introduction. The only blemish on the scene is the house set, vexingly, nearest the church: a long low thing of reconstituted stone.

Roomy and airy, the interior is not the shadowy void that naves designed for teeming Victorian congregations have sometimes become. It is light, inviting, well-proportioned, abundantly decorated. But it does not inspire as the outside can. Its appeal is in details. Pier capitals have well-cut leaves and angels. There are three fonts, one Saxon and battered, one Victorian and plain, and the one in current use, near the south door, dating to about 1200, and decorated with a charming relief of leaves and long-necked birds. The chancel has rich tiling from Pugin's studio. On a board in the north aisle are the royal arms – in this case of George III – a legal necessity after Charles II's restoration. The oak screen placed in the archway of the tower, with tracery and a man's and woman's head and the inscription 'Water King and Esbell [Isabel] his Wif' above and linenfold panelling below, is probably a cut-down version of the 16th century rood screen, originally standing across the chancel arch.

A copper plaque to the right of that arch was erected to the memory of Rolf Gardiner, 1902 to 1971, father of the conductor John Eliot Gardiner, nephew of the composer Balfour Gardiner, and in his own right a stormy, cranky, deeply influential patron and promoter of arts, especially among the young. Co-founder of the Soil Association, founder of the Springhead Trust, which still holds residential courses in arts and crafts on the quiet estate a mile upstream, he urged fitness, nature's rhythms, organic nourishment, ritual, dance, nudity, soul, physical work, a 'Celto-Germanic Christendom' – a body of enthusiasm in vogue in the 1920s and 1930s. The German link – his mother was half Austrian – was suspect in this corner of rural England. He was accused, absurdly, of arranging tree plantations in swastika shapes on the downs, and not sufficiently rejecting the Nazi ethos. His place here provokes reflection on the church and its role. He despised the 'degenerated Christianity' which put sermons and catechisms before worship and consecration. He sought to 'recover the sacramental rhythm of the agricultural year'. Facing the congregation as it does, his name may remind some of a version of religion they would sooner forget.

## FORDINGTON
*St George*

In 1902 Thomas Hardy came back to Dorchester from a trip to Bath. What he saw on his approach caused him to resign, angrily, from the Fordington church restoration committee. The handsome 15th century church tower had acquired a prominent pimple – a new top turret to roof its staircase – and the great man disapproved. He also deplored the massive enlargement of the church proposed by the vicar, the Rev. Richard Grosvenor Bartelot. Asked later for a contribution to the costs he said curtly that he was against tampering with the 'old church's excellent proportions'. He was ignored. During the next few years, in an ecstasy of optimism, the Reverend Bartelot oversaw the extension of the nave area and the addition of a huge chancel, doubling the church's area. 'The whole project', says the church brochure, 'is a testimony to Richard Bartelot's vision and tenacity.' A century of

diminishing congregations, services held in side chapels and long days of dank emptiness point rather to his absence of vision and riotous extravagance. St George's belongs to Dorset's herd of prime white elephants.

It makes a good first impression, on its hilltop site, with its fine west-end tower (still sporting the pepper-pot projection), distant vistas of the flatlands to the east, a huge burial ground flung like a voluminous cape over the hilltop's shoulder and, from the churchyard gate, a long profile broken by perpendicular-style windows and pinnacled buttresses. It occupies most of one side of Fordington Green, centre of an elevated area of decent individual buildings, once but no longer administratively distinct from Dorchester itself. Far down below the church on the east side, the mostly dull terraces and blocks of flats towards the River Frome are 20th century replacements of a notorious 19th century concentration of poverty.

There was a Roman cemetery here, as there was along other Roman highways around the town, and, inside and close to the tower arch, stands a possibly 1st century tombstone commemorating (rather successfully, given the nineteen centuries of its survival) a Roman citizen named Carinus. Above the main south doorway is a sculptured stone showing St George lancing a tumbling infidel in the mouth, while kneeling knights pray thanks behind him. This is thought to date from a building of about 1100 and to illustrate the First Crusade, in which, with much slaughter, the united

*Fordington, sculptured stone showing St George lancing an infidel.*

Christians of Europe captured Antioch and Jerusalem from the Arabs. St George's intercession came at Antioch, and turned the day in the Christians' favour. It clinched the saint's popularity in England, and may well have contributed to his eventual adoption as patron saint.

Ahead of us, when we have passed through the doorway, three arches of the south arcade, along with the near stretch of the south aisle wall, represent the 12th century building, of which little else survives. During the Reverend Bartelot's overhaul, the floor was lowered and the pillars here extended downwards, one by inserting the capital of a Roman pillar. South of this, the south transept contains the 15th century font, on which the simple carving of six sides is oddly missing from the other two. A 17th century vessel occupying a niche just to the east of the south doorway is a puzzle, seeming too large for a stoup and too small for a font, but more likely to be the latter.

The tower, behind its massive carved Bavarian doors, is, like most towers, 15th century. We are now drawing to the limit of the medieval church's remains. North and distantly east stretches the 20th century Bartelot enlargement, witness of the vicar's misplaced optimism, but also a none-too-modest memorial to himself and his family. The stone heads looking down from the nave pillars are portraits of himself, his wife and children, variously packed among crowns, wings, musical instruments, scythe, book or quill, and the central roof bosses in the chancel are intended to show his descent from St Edward, the young king murdered at Corfe in 979. Roof apart, the chancel is rather bland. We might have found more interest in the chancel Bartelot replaced, a small 18th century affair described by his architect as like 'an annexe to a shrine of Venus', by which he presumably means a brothel, 'a conglomeration of idiosyncrasies . . . such as would not be tolerated in a butterman's villa.' Still, nave and chancel do contain scattered items of beauty or interest.

*Fordington. The church occupies one side of Fordington Green.*

The pulpit dates from 1592, the only complete 16th century stone one in the country. The relatively few others made at that period were of wood. The helmet attached to the chancel north wall is of a First World War soldier, lost in France. The east window, stained glass figures in plain glass surrounds, is from a design by Burne-Jones. High altar rails, originally at Milton Abbey, are 17th century. The altar in the south chapel, in large part late 14th century, came from Salisbury Cathedral where, starting as the high altar, it had been demoted to a site in the cloister.

The priest's stall by the south wall of the chancel, and a plaque near the main south doorway, (and, over the road, to the right, a blue plaque beside the site of his vicarage) inadequately commemorate the Reverend Henry Moule, vicar for half a century from 1829. At first he was unpopular, a crusading evangelist in an impoverished and slovenly parish, chiding drunken parishioners and getting the town races banned. To get a decent showing, his predecessor had *paid* women to come to communion. Men almost never attended, and one who did, early in Moule's tenure, before sipping from the proffered wine-cup, said festively 'Here's to your good health sir' as if at a party. At a

*Frampton. The unusual rounded buttresses on the corners of the tower are the result of a rebuilding in 1695.*

baptism service Moule asked the clerk for water. 'Water, sir! The last parson never used no water. 'E spit into 'is 'and.' The diseased horror of 1830s and subsequent Fordington – whose population rose threefold in the century's first half – brought out his anger, compassion and energy.

When cholera broke out in 1847, thought to be from imported London prisoners' laundry done by local women, he not only ministered to the sick and dying but studied and urged higher standards of hygiene and devised a system of purifying tainted water by passing it through earth. He was brave enough to criticize Prince Albert for the Duchy of Cornwall's failure to care for its tenantry. His Fordington is mercifully gone. So alas is most of his church.

# FRAMPTON

*St Mary the Virgin*

Around 1840 Richard Brinsley Sheridan, grandson of the playwright and newly owner, through the death of his father-in-law, of Frampton Court and village, had the houses on the south side of the village swept away in order to extend his riverside park to the road. His own house, built of Portland stone, is long gone but the side of the road he cleared is still bare of buildings. The trees and copses which now ornament the park were not mature in Sheridan's time, and his view of the 1695 church tower, with its pin-cushion of thin pinnacles, would have been clear. After the Victorian fashion, he made it grander. In a way, St Mary's is the mausoleum of the Sheridan, Grant and Browne families, recording three centuries of power and prestige and then a final one, the 19th, of premature deaths – infants at home and youths on far-flung battlefields – till this branch of the Sheridans virtually died out in the 1930s and the house was pulled down.

Due to a convenient bend in the road, the most interesting view of the church is seen by anyone approaching from Maiden Newton and the west. Unfortunately, from a distance, the stair turret at the north-east makes the tower look clumsily broader than it is. Close to, you see that instead of the corner buttresses on the towers of other churches, set at ninety or forty-five degrees to the wall surfaces, these are round and plain and envelop each corner. Their style, known as Tuscan, is an ancient Roman one reintroduced by the Renaissance: classical in, here, a firmly gothic context. Such is the conformity to a set style of most churches that this seems distinctly eccentric though rather nice. It was in fact part of a rebuilding in 1695 of the original 15th century tower. The owner, Robert Browne, perhaps designed it. Later, he had the north aisle built. Chancel and south aisle are mostly the work of the 19th century, though the chancel arch, the south arcade and a great many details and fragments go back to the main 15th century erection, and the history a good deal further. Romans were hereabouts in numbers and left a mosaic floor a mile to the west (discovered in 1794, examined and reburied) on which the Chi Rho emblem, the first two letters of Christ's name in Greek, appears. Perhaps they worshipped on the present church's site. There was probably a Saxon church, and Norman Benedictines founded a priory here, which went at the Reformation to the Hatton family, thence in 1566 to the Brownes, in 1833 to the dashing Sir Colquhoun Grant, and a year later to his son-in-law Richard Brinsley Sheridan. The Sheridans owned about 12,000 acres hereabouts: not one of the big Dorset estates, but sizable. Brownes, Grants and Sheridans produced an exceptional number of distinguished individuals, waiting maybe to impress us by their memorials indoors.

St Mary's is hugely spacious, almost as wide as long, with a tiled floor you could

*Frampton, 'hugely spacious . . . big enough to hold a dance on without ever moving the pews'.*

hold a dance on without ever moving the pews, with their delightfully tall corkscrew candle-holders, from aisles and nave. Yet the packing of most available surfaces with detail and colour makes it warm, almost intimate. The pointed arches of the two arcades (the southern being one of the few original features of the church) are the colour of honey, their capitals mostly representing foliage but at each of the extreme ends of the south aisle two rather rustic monks appear to wrestle or dance. Stained glass windows help fill the walls with colour, as do two fresco angels trumpeting high on the chancel arch. Above the nave, the tie-beams of the dark wooden roof end in painted shields, one of which shows the royal arms – English lions couchant, Scottish lions rampant and the harp of Ireland – of Queen Victoria's and modern times. The pulpit is a much reconstructed stone artefact of the 15th century whose panel scenes – some said to be original – are finely worked. Mostly, though, the detail consists of the wall plaques, likenesses of the departed, urns, skulls, hourglasses, mourners, columns and pediments, heraldic devices and tallies of the imperial campaigns in which Brownes,

*Frampton, the memorial to John Browne, Recorder of Dorchester and its MP.*

Grants and Sheridans fought and fell. In the north wall of the chancel are effigies of Rear Admiral Sir John Browne, who died in 1627, and his wife – he a veteran of the Armada campaign of 1588. Opposite, Robert Coker commemorates 'Mrs Joane his deare wife . . . fifth daughter of John Browne of,' as it says quaintly, 'this PISH ESQ'. She died in 1653. Dates are given in unusual style: 8BR for October, 9BR for November. Other Browne monuments crowd the north aisle. The window in the centre of its north wall, framed by Corinthian columns and a round arch topped with a heraldic cartouche, recalls Robert, builder of tower and house, vicarage, school and much else. On the east wall the satisfied smile, smooth and baggy chins and periwig curls of his son John, Recorder of Dorchester and four times MP, are convincingly sculpted above a eulogy that might leave some less than convinced: 'Elected . . . by the united voice of all his Constituents . . . The Good and the Virtuous were always sure of his Friendship &

Protection, The Bad, he had no Connections with but by his endeavours to make them better.'

General Sir Colquhoun Grant links the two main Frampton families. His sister married a Browne and his daughter a Sheridan, creating, for want of direct male heirs, a direction for ownership of the estate to go in. On the south wall of the choir, his colourful record appears: Mysore, Seringapatam, Cape of Good Hope, Vittoria – twenty years of winning his country an empire and depriving Napoleon of his, with the climax fought at Waterloo where, commanding a brigade, 'he had no less than five horses killed under him'.

In the tower, where the family pew was, a plaque lists the Sheridans buried here or beside the local stream, the Frome. They make a more literary dynasty. There are fourteen of them, the last interred in 2003, all descended from, or married to spouses descended from, the mainly 18th century Irish playwright and polymath Richard Brinsley Sheridan and his wife, Elizabeth Linley, renowned for her beauty. Their daughter-in-law Caroline was beautiful too (and wrote novels, read in her day if not later). Her daughters, Linley's grand-daughters, the three sisters of the playwright's namesake grandson, were the most famous beauties of their time. One mothered a viceroy of India, one was a well-known poet and song-writer, and the other, the scandalous Mrs Norton, best-seller poet and novelist, was accused with likelihood but without certainty, of having an adulterous affaire with the prime minister Lord Melbourne. It was their brother who moved half the village and rebuilt much of the church. Of later Sheridans, one married the daughter of John Lothrop Motley, assiduous historian of *The Rise of the Dutch Republic,* who spent many of his latter years here. All these, if not buried here, spent part of their lives at the house and on Sundays occupied the Sheridan pew.

Above the south door, a simple plaque

supplies a refreshing finale. The Revd William Butler died in his eighties in 1843. Second, no doubt, to God, his love and enthusiasm went to hunting. When weekday services were unavoidable he would wear his scarlet coat under his ecclesiastical robes and hurry the service to be in time for the meet. As he knelt at the altar, his hunting boots were visible to the knowing congregation. Dorset produced a breed of these hunting parsons. They did their rounds on horseback, intoned services to the sick from outside their windows, interjecting incongruous sounds designed to calm their mounts. Hardy tells of one who left a pregnant bride and unwilling bridegroom locked in church all night, having forgotten his promise to the girl to return early from the chase to marry them.

## GUSSAGE ST ANDREW
*St Andrew*

Farmhouse and church are what, with two or three more distant houses, Gussage St Andrew consists of. Sometimes the church is called after Minchington, the next hamlet westward. You could easily pass along the quiet lane, in the midst of orderly, undulate Cranborne Chase farmland, without noticing the church was there at all, unless you read the small wayside sign. What does stand out distinctly is the handsome, 17th century Chapel Farmhouse, with its banded brick and flint walls and well-tended gardens. The house is on the site of a Saxon nunnery founded by King Alfred's daughter Elgiva.

The church, whose predecessor would have served the nuns as chapel, lurks rather shyly behind the house, and you get to it through a gateway, past a line of chestnuts, up steps, along a path. Its east and south walls are squeezed by a small but steep earthen bank and the wire of a paddock fence. In fact the church owns nothing beyond the walls that define it. They, made partly of exposed flint, partly plaster rendering, form a plain, rather dull rectangle, with diagonal buttresses and flat brick ones on the far, south side – all

under a tiled roof, tiny bellcote, and weathervane on which a fish turns in the wind. Some of the few windows hint at antiquity. So does the arm-length thickness of the walls. In fact the nave goes back to the 12th century, the chancel to the 13th century – though much was restored in the 19th century. Until the latter half of the 15th century it was one of the many properties owned by the wealthy nuns of Shaftesbury Abbey.

Once we have reached the round Norman arch on the inside of the doorway, the view towards the altar is entrancing. All the familiar furniture and elements of a chancel are there, but in particularly quiet and unassuming form: small 17th century altar table, dark wooden reredos with linenfold panelling, fashioned from old box pews, two lancet windows in the east wall, and twin lancets in the south, the twisted balusters of the altar rail, the plain panelling of the 17th century pulpit, the simple tie-beams of the roof – all this modesty of form reinforced by the subdued tones of wood, stone quoins, whitewashed walls; and made punctiliously perfect by two or three glinting highlights, the 18th century brass chandelier, brass candlesticks, the coloured heraldic symbols set in the plain glass of the east windows.

There is an oddity under the altar. The tomb slab of William Williams of Woodcutts, who died in 1725, occupies the choicest position in the church, yet runs north-south. Burial rules have generally been strict, though seldom consistent. The good were buried (and usually still are) with their heads to the west and feet to the east. Thus, when Resurrection is trumpeted, they will fittingly sit up facing the Holy Land. The bad, by and large, had they sat up at all, would have faced the wrong way. Executed criminals were likely to be buried front down (though the head might have been retained for public display). So were unbaptised children and suicides: the latter outside consecrated ground, often at crossroads. William Williams was clearly none of these, and his

*Gussage St Andrew. Rare survivals, the medieval wall paintings on the north wall of the nave.*

prime placing is a puzzle. It may be that only the slab is oddly placed, while the bodily remains lie conventionally east-west below.

More remarkable is the state of the medieval paintings that decorate the nave's north wall, as well preserved – at any rate restored – as any in Dorset. Before the Reformation, you stood or paced or possibly sat on one of the few available benches throughout the service, while the voice of an unseen priest – cut off by the rood-screen, chancel arch and tympanum (filling the semi-circle between) – intoned the appropriate Latin liturgy. Till well after the Reformation, pews and pulpit were rare. There may have been whispers, even winks, but the main legitimate occupation was to look at the instructive, improving cartoon-strip paintings that covered the nave walls. They are mostly done in the depressingly limited range of pigments available at the time: red and yellow ochre, with black. Other colours were rare and expensive. Though often skilfully painted by travelling craftsmen, they were not great art-works. But those we have are so few as to be precious. 1540s reformers ordered their destruction, but some were simply plastered over and have been

discovered in the last hundred years. The ones here came to light in 1951 and were restored in the 1960s. Different experts attribute them variously to every century from the 12th to the 15th.

They show scenes, not always easy to identify, from Jesus' Passion, the last events of his mortal life. There are two rows, and the human figures are between two and three feet tall. The first scene is in doubt. In the next, Judas betrays by a kiss Jesus' presence to the Jewish priests, and two men seize him. Judas, in an agony of remorse, hangs himself – we see only the tree, the drooping hands, legs and lifeless feet. (This subject is not, as the guide-board says it is, unique among medieval murals, but occurs again at Breamore in Hampshire and Slapton in Northamptonshire). Jesus, his hands bound, is mocked by the soldiers. In the lower band we see Jesus carrying the cross; the Crucifixion, with one soldier spearing his side, another offering a sponge of vinegar. Jesus is removed by Mary and John, the almost invariable spectators of his death. Next, Jesus is received into heaven, and later appears to the disciples.

In the church's west end interest lessens. The Norman font is round and unadorned. Texts, probably 18th century and moved from the chancel, hang close to the door.

Above the walled-up doorway on the south side hang the royal arms of George III, very badly done. Endearingly, the guide makes a nice judgment: 'possibly,' it says, 'possibly the worst example of its kind anywhere.' No matter. St Andrew's is a box of quiet delights, all the better for its imperfections and the modesty of its hiding-place.

## HILTON
*All Saints*

From down in the grassy tree-rich graveyard to the east, cushioned in the rural greenery of this upper branch of the Piddle valley, All Saints presents a delectable geometry formed by the embattled tower and attached but slightly taller stair-tower turret, the overlapping gables of nave and chancel walls, the trim south aisle with its majestic five-light east window and gabled porch, and the oddly obtrusive north aisle – and all these mellow stone surfaces interrupted and adorned by the neat tracery of their large Perpendicular windows. The north aisle invites special attention. Its east window, seen from this eastern viewpoint, is more seasoned than others, and because of its size the sloping top of its alternating flint and stone wall awkwardly overshoots the chancel roof. But round the corner the aisle's main wall displays a grandeur not quite appropriate to the church as a whole. It boasts four large Perpendicular four-light windows identical to the eastern one, divided by buttresses stiff and spruce as guardsmen, overlooked by vivid gargoyles – two lions' heads, two devils' heads and a man playing bagppipes (*see page 7*), a curious sight met also at Piddletrenthide and Stinsford. A blind bay closes the wall at each end, and rather over-prominently in front stands the 1778 table tomb of the Reverend Boucher Syndercombe. The windows at least are intruders, brought the mile or so from Milton Abbey cloister after the 1530s dissolution of the monasteries.

Here at Hilton nothing is quite so good, assured or stylish as this north wall. All the

*Hilton, the trefoil-topped niche and fan-vaulting in the porch.*

same, moving round to the south, and after noting the 1690 sundial and some high-up 17th century stones with masons' initials marked on them, we come to the very handsome Ham-stone porch with a niche above the entrance and, inside, a trefoil-topped niche and a marvellous fan-vaulted ceiling. Pre-Reformation porches had acquired a number of functions, including serving as site of certain services, but they are seldom as decorative as this. The favoured explanation is that it started life as a chantry chapel in Milton Abbey and, like the north aisle, was brought here at the Dissolution. We shall come on even more Milton cast-offs.

The distance from the church's north wall to south is actually longer than that from the west to the east. The interior is consequently broad, spacious and, by virtue of those mighty traceried windows, unusually light.

*Hilton, a detail from the wood panelling brought from Milton Abbey showing ten of the apostles.*

The nave roof is held on wooden arches resting on hammer beams, that of the chancel barrel shaped and plastered. The timbered aisle roofs, with their wooden bosses, have more character. The pulpit's leafy design is typically early 17th century – Jacobean. Pews are modern, flooring wood parquet. The columns of the north arcade and chancel arch are older than those to the south, but all are likely to be 15th century. The openings that gape behind the south pier of the chancel arch show where the usual cramped staircase once rose to a spacious rood-loft. Opposite, in the north aisle, high on the north side of the eastern respond, or half-pier, is a little stone carved face, possibly a mason's mark. Almost the only stained glass lights in the church form the pious, lifeless but colourful scene behind the altar, placed there in memory of two generations of Woodhouses, a family who produced soldiers and brewers. John Hutchins noted that in 1730 'idle persons' smashed many of the church's stained glass windows. Not all breakages go back to the Reformation or Cromwell. In fact the list of Hilton's vicars seems to show there was little trouble here during the first of these

changes. Elsewhere some fled and some burned, but William Stily retained the cure of souls in this rural backwater through the arch-Protestant reign of Edward VI, the Catholic reversion under Mary and the first decade of Anglican Elizabeth.

There are two more Milton Abbey relics. On the north wall, a rather anomalous 15th century stone panel carries the arms of Cerne Abbey, St Anthony, and Richard, 13th century Earl of Cornwall and (a hollow honour) king of the Germans. They are almost certainly acknowledgements of benefactions. A more treasured import, brought when the old abbey stone was being transformed into Milton's present grand mansion, is the wooden panelling, set on the inner walls of the tower, showing ten of the apostles, (Bartholomew, being perhaps already on the rood loft, and treacherous Judas are missing) plus Saints Paul and Matthias. These were restored in 1961 and 1962. Below stands the square, Purbeck marble, lead-lined font, with round-arched relief arcades cut into its sides: Norman work. This and a few other traces – the two-light window west of the porch, some masonry blocks, some tower-building materials – suggest the present building was preceded by a Norman, and that by a Saxon church. As so often in Dorset it is the Perpendicular style that lasted.

## KINGSTON
*St James*
The Isle of Purbeck is noted for Norman churches: Studland, Corfe Castle, Worth Matravers, St Aldhelm's Head, Wareham St Martin. Yet in among these, with their worn remnants of elemental Norman muscularity, rises this lofty, ornate, narcissistic pile, like a tropical orchid among buttercups and daisies. You could take the pink of St James's Purbeck stone for a blush of embarrassment, at being so nakedly exposed to the gaze of Corfe, town and castle, Poole Harbour, a good half of Purbeck and, perhaps more

*Kingston, the 'cathedral' of the Purbecks.*

shamingly, of the petitely pinnacled central tower of its predecessor, the older – though not much older – Kingston church. Not that St James's lacks vigour. The tall tower is masculine, assertive, crop-headed, with no fancy battlements, pinnacles or finials. The big three-light clusters on each tower wall, the high apse bulging from the east end, the steep gables and ridges on nave, transepts, and chancel, repeated patterns of thin lancet windows, narrow cone-topped stair-turret and the great rose window at the western end, speak of energy, power and ingenuity. And, when all is said, the blush is bogus. It comes, not from within, but from a red lichen that thrives on Purbeck stone.

There was little obvious point in building it. The first Earl of Eldon, stalwart enemy of religious freedom and longest-serving Lord Chancellor in our history, bought the vast surrounding estate of Encombe in 1807. He rebuilt the existing, then dilapidated medieval church, whose tower we have noticed, in

1833. Forty years later the Chancellor's great-grandson, the 3rd Earl, commissioned George Edmund Street to build another, infinitely grander and more expensive, in honour of his distinguished great-grandfather. (A family story, remembered from childhood by a living family member, has the earl's wife returning home one day to discover her husband in bed with the vicar's wife, naked but for one of the countess's hats. Barred from the existing church, the earl found himself obliged to build a new one). The older church became successively storehouse, village hall and, recently, privately owned house; the new one a vast and costly encumbrance – but something more too. St James's, and particularly the interior – is one of England's greatest Victorian churches.

The testimony is abundant. 'The most perfect Victorian church,' Alec Clifton-Taylor

*Kingston, a Victorian masterpiece.*

calls it; 'a cathedral in miniature'. For Betjeman it is 'superb . . . so stately on a hill slope.' Pevsner is, for him, almost abandoned: 'one of Street's masterpieces, wholly Early English . . . of a calm perfection inside, economic in its effects, yet sumptuous throughout.' Street was beyond doubt one of the outstanding Victorian architects. His London Law Courts, built over the same period as Kingston church and only finished after he died – of overwork, they said – is his best known work and perhaps the last great public Gothic building erected in England. He was working at a time when the obsession with Early English style was giving way to an interest in earlier, robuster prime-Gothic French models. Kingston has more space than would have been allowed before – much of the nave has chairs, easily cleared away. It dispenses with fuss and frippery, relying much on the orderly repetition of effective features. Most of all the aisle arcades,

clerestory windows and particularly the tall arches of the crossing give it the thrusting upward surge that in French cathedrals can seem so expressive of spirituality.

From the narthex, the elongated porch at the west end which for obscure reasons shares its name with the Latin one of the giant fennel plant, we enter the church and at once – most particularly if the sun is not shining – all colour is bled from the scene. The lichen-pink drains away. Almost everything bar the stained glass windows is of a monochrome shade: the pale and grey of the local Purbeck wall stone, the dark dark shiny grey of the round and moulded columns (also Purbeck, but polished with linseed oil to make what is known as Purbeck marble), the wrought-iron tracery of screen and pulpit, the darkness of the nave's oak roof. The mood of the world is kept out and a sombre but still vigorous sanctity put in its place.

The workmanship is everywhere superb. Quality is palpable. 'Let your deeds be done as well in the dark as they are in the light,' Street's foreman said to his workers. God can see, even if the congregation cannot. The wrought iron is to Street's own design, as is the great west rose window, with its interplay of squares and quatrefoils. He himself made the clay models from which a former pupil carved the stone capitals. In everything – the eagle lectern, candle standards, the pews and tiles, the fine piscina or wash basin and sedilia or stone seats in the chancel's south wall – Street's diligent scrutiny is in evidence. Where he relied on others, he employed tried and tested craftsmen. The sensitive relief in the chancel, under a long inscription to the first earl, was done by Chantrey. The stained glass in the lancet windows, pleasing if not inspiring, was all done by Clayton and Bell. It is not surprising that Street's influence on the new Arts and Crafts generation – Norman Shaw, Philip Webb, Morris himself – was considerable. For Shaw, who worked under Street in his office, the blessings were not unmixed. In his experience, Street left no design undone. 'During the whole time I was with him,' Shaw complained, ' I never designed one single moulding.'

The central arches and rising couplets and triplet of steps lead one on to the chancel and sanctuary. As often with Street, the altar does not monopolise attention. Altar, altar rail, candlesticks, cross and the emphasised pointed lines of the window arches seem like stage properties. It is the inward curve of the ribbed ceiling that draws aspiration upward and perhaps achieves holiness. Still, something is missing. It has been absent ever since we came in and felt the bleeding away of colour. Colour is warmth, and a shadowy coldness pervades the church which all Street's virtues and skills do not dispel. Bright sunlight penetrating the stained glass gives the interior a dawn-like glimmer of glory, and perhaps that is what Street intended.

# KNOWLTON
*Dedication unknown*

The ruined medieval church stands alone in the middle of a rather irregular circle of grass, about a hundred yards across and hooped by an ancient ditch and a bank. The enclosure is mown but bumpy, in a way that suggests the vestiges of ancient walls and buildings. Ditch and bank are neolithic, from somewhere not far off 2500 BC. In spring, the long grass growing on them is spattered with cowslips, buttercups and Queen Anne's lace. There are three gaps in the bank. The one on the south-west is now the main entrance to the circle, close to the gate from the quiet lane, but the one on the east is likely to be the only original one. In most directions there are flat or gently sloping fields and hedges, and woods on rising land in the distance. A rounded clump of trees and shrubs in a neighbouring field to the east marks a prehistoric barrow. There is an 18th century farmhouse roughly south-east, on the Cranborne-Wimborne road. No other buildings are close, though a few farms are distantly visible. From the air it is possible to see the outlines of other vanished prehistoric henges and barrows.

So people wearing skins and daubed with paint have no doubt worshipped here, and buried their distinguished dead – great hunters, perhaps, or warriors, breeders, forest clearers, hereditary grandees, story-tellers, priests – under these barrows, and died themselves or gone away. There were Romans all over these parts, and not long after most of them had left, Christians. It may be that these followed the advice of Pope Gregory the Great around the year 600. Don't destroy, was his message; adopt and adapt sacred pagan sites. Gradually bring local heathens round to the new faith. All we know for sure is that in late Norman times – the twelfth century – and at the heart of what must have been recognised as a place of ancient sanctity, a church was built, whose round-arched remains now form the nucleus – nave and chancel – of the ruin. It served a village a few hundred yards north-west,

beside the River Allen. A century and a half later, as a result of exhaustion of the poor chalky soil, bad summers and around 1348 the appalling climax of the Black Death, which entered the country through Dorset and killed more than a third of the population, villages themselves were dying. Yet Knowlton survived, and was thriving enough in the late 14th century or early 15th century to add a Perpendicular tower, south porch and north-east chapel to the existing church. Prosperity was short-lived. Enclosures, the pendulum swings of state religion, emigration to the new world and civil war reduced the population again, perhaps wiped it out. By 1659 permission was sought to demolish the church. It was refused, but time and neglect did what the diocese would not. Curiously, the church was used briefly in the 18th century – enough to warrant the building of a north aisle. But later in the century the roof fell in. There has been no formal worship here since.

All the same, it was a long run of worship: well over four thousand years, possibly continuous. Scraps of history have been garnered. Excavations of the earthworks have disclosed burials, paths, dwellings, utensils, tools, weapons. We know enough of the styles used in the church – round arches, trefoil lights, the alternation of bands of flint and stone in the tower – to deduce the details of its past. The essence eludes us. The Knowlton scene is evocative, awesome in some lights, poetic; but it gives little away.

## LEWESTON
### Holy Trinity

This little chapel was built in 1616. Shakespeare died the same year. Donne, Herrick, Bacon, Hobbes were writing. The Authorized Version of the Bible had been published five years before. It was a time when the English language, without yet having dressed itself in the stately finery of the 18th century, reached a peak of idiosyncratic verve and subtlety. That seems to hold true of some other forms of workmanship, not least woodwork. The sublime finesse of Grinling Gibbons' heads and fruit-swathes were still half a century away. But there is something in the conception, energy and fallible quirkiness of much Jacobean carving and construction that can be even more agreeable, particularly perhaps to an age as suspicious of refinement as ours. Few places in Dorset bear this out so well as Leweston.

It is set in bosky parkland, beside a handsome, pedimented 1774 manor house, which became in 1938 the nucleus of a Roman Catholic girls' school, St Anthony's, whose clutter of more recent buildings, including the starkly cut outline of a 1970 chapel, do no favours to the westward view from the older chapel. The latter's exterior is compact but handsome: rectangular, gable ended, stone roofed, plaster rendered, with three three-light windows, one on the north side and two on the south, the central light of each being taller than its neighbours (like those at Folke, a few miles away and built twelve years later, and other nearby churches). A porch projects from the west end, and above its shallow-arched, Ham-stone south doorway appears the framed image of a dolphin, heraldic symbol of Sir John Fitzjames who, a Latin inscription proclaims, built the chapel in 1616 to replace an earlier, tumbledown one, of which the circular font we shall shortly see is the only visible survival. The Fitzjameses later got the nearby Longburton estate. There is a gold-numeral clock on the main west wall above the porch. Above it sits a Ham-stone bell-cote, open-ended like a gabled boathouse, topped with a cross and engraved with ornamental strapwork.

Inside the porch, a narrow wooden staircase leads away up to the clock's workings. Its weights hang down beside us, as does a pendulum, whose tick-tock will be loudly with us during our visit. A studded oak door leads to the nave – indeed to the church's body, for there is no chancel – and there, through the doorway, is, for those with

*Leweston, the little Jacobean chapel of 1616.*

a taste for such things, one of the more entrancing sights that Dorset's churches offer. What we see is almost purely the Jacobean of the original: a light but intimate interior, handsomely barrel-roofed, walls palely plastered, four mostly plain-glass windows, a floor of honey-hued stone, and between walls and floor tall panels of limed wood. There are the pews, seven a side, and each with room for three or four worshippers. All the round-topped, five-foot high bench-ends are incised with different patterns and diagrams. The wooden panelling, from which simple

*Leweston, carved bench-ends and two-decker pulpit.*

wooden coat-pegs project at intervals, covers the walls to the same height. Ahead and one step up, the wooden altar-table is part of a 20th century restoration, though made of old panelling. The small tabernacle (for holding the sacrament) and crucifix standing above the altar-table and under the east window *are* modern, supposedly made and given in the 1940s by Italian prisoners of war who worked on local farms and used the chapel for worship. But practically everything else is of 1616 or close to it.

The Jacobean gem is the rare two-decker pulpit (combining exalted preaching-place with the parson's or clerk's lowlier reading-desk) in the south-east corner, with deeply cut decoration on the outside. Its height and placing, and the resounding six-sided tester or canopy above his head, ensured attention to the sermoniser. Built in wood that matches the pews and panels, it rounds off a wonderful organic unity.

In a grave to the left of the altar lie the remains of Sir George Strode and his wife Grace, born Fitzjames and great grand-daughter of the chapel's builder. (For reasons not explained she was first buried at Longburton church, a mile away, and later transferred here). Their daughter, also Grace, inherited the estate and married a Thynne of Longleat. To Longleat at their invitation came the old and battle-worn Thomas Ken, one-time bishop of Bath and Wells, whose pluck in opposing three successive kings on points of principle had earned him the increased respect of each of them. He refused a courtesy to Charles II's mistress Nell Gwynn, obstructed James II's regeneration of papism and refused allegiance to William III. In 1710, frail and sick, Ken came here for his last winter, looked after by Mrs Thynne. He preached and worshipped here. He may have joined the congregation in singing the hymns he wrote, of which two, *Glory to Thee my God this night* and *Awake my soul*, are still popular.

Permission to visit the chapel is to be sought from the school office.

# MAIDEN NEWTON
*St Mary*

Seeming to be almost as much a work of nature as the stream which, ten sheer yards below, flows along the eastern edge of the Frome valley, the pale, patchy, massive walls of the church of St Mary seem less to have been built than to have grown like a living organism to their untidy cross-shape, set among static yews and swaying beeches. Buildings hem much of the churchyard in. The ranked dormer windows of the handsome old Victorian rectory peek over the boundary hedge, and recently a smart housing estate has occupied the higher ground across the road. The church is not disturbed. It is heavy, bulky, old, unkempt, forgetful, and seems startled – and not in the least gratified – to be reminded, by the visitor pausing here and there, of features of interest and value surviving in its fabric.

Given the relics of ancient occupation in this Dorset downland, there may have been a place of worship here for two thousand years or more. The Saxons built a church – probably destroyed by Danish raiders. What we see of the structure is mostly 15th century work, but much of the nave's north wall and the lower parts of the tower are Norman. On the north side is a rare Norman door hanging on rare Norman hinges. From the outside it is protected, but not improved, by a dirty glass panel, which greatly detracts also from the zigzag Norman arch above it. This Norman wall leans outward, but seems to have finished its leaning before the 15th century walls on either side were built. The outside of the church sports numerous amusing gargoyles and corbels. On the south wall, the generously broad span of the pointed-arch porch has the inviting effect of spread hands. Intriguing carved fragments – one of them including a curiously beaked face – and three empty niches are set in its interior walls.

A roomy 15th century south aisle, attached to a south transept which houses the charming 1855 organ, and three broad arches, lead to a nave of barn dimensions.

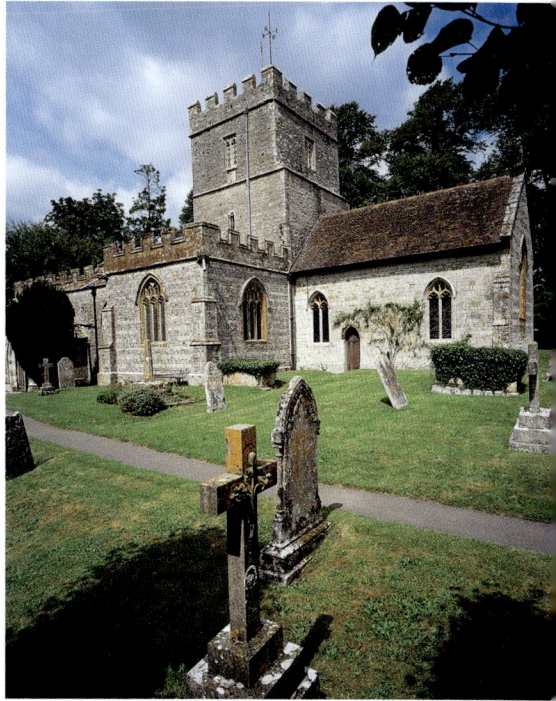

ABOVE *Maiden Newton, the Norman door and zig-zag Norman arch.*

RIGHT *Maiden Newton, with the 15th century chancel on the right.*

The roof, which is its own mix of purlins, rafters, tie-beams, struts and posts, has been repaired from time to time. The corbels on which the main rafters rest have comical-rustic subjects including a dog with a bone. Behind the pulpit two blocked doorways mark the former staircase to the rood loft, a feature probably removed, as so many were, on the orders of the Privy Council in 1548. Royal arms – those of George I – still hang above the tower arch. Close by, a door leads to the ringers' floor. The area under the tower has recently been covered with a wooden dais supporting a small altar, allowing for a more intimate service. The 15th century chancel, much restored by the Victorians but made remote by the new development, contains a good monument to a rector of the reigns of James I and Charles I.

Amid these commodious whitewashed spaces lots of little details are easily overlooked: wall-memorials, inscribed floor-slabs, medieval and Victorian corbels, carved keystones, piscinas, squint, chests, scalloped capitals and unexplained fragments of carving inset arbitrarily in walls, probably saved from some early refurbishment. They are almost eclipsed by the scale of the whole.

During the Civil War, in October 1644, when Charles I's still formidable army took, lost and took again most of Dorset from the Parliamentarians, the king's men, exhausted by a march from Exeter to Chard and by illness, stumbled through Evershot to Kingcombe, intent on recapturing Dorchester. The king himself stayed with the vicar of Maiden Newton, Matthew Osborne, at the rectory, and perhaps came to the church for a prayer. He decided to turn back to Sherborne, where he was surer of welcome than in the county town. A year later Osborne, says the burial register, was dismissed from the living by 'the Rumpish Triers' (a nicely sonorous 17th century phrase) until at the Restoration his Puritan replacement, Andrew Bromall, was himself 'turned out by almighty God as a base and unworthy successor.' Maiden Newton has

had few brushes with history, but the church guide proudly records that in July 1952 Queen Elizabeth slept, not at the vicarage, but in the royal train, drawn up in a siding a few hundred metres away. The Parish Council delivered an Address of Welcome.

## MELBURY BUBB
*St Mary*

A few yards to the church's west, Bubb Down rises steeply, like the high back to a padded chair of which Melbury Bubb is the seat. Next door to, and seeming all of a piece with the church is the handsome gabled 17th century manor house. There are a couple more houses, farm buildings, and further off a slew of oak-mantled Dorset downs, and the green flatlands of the Blackmore Vale stretching far away to the north-east. Hardly anything else stands out in the view, though three centuries ago a pond was reported close by, whose water would dye anything red in the morning and green in the afternoon. This is about the most agreeably remote and secluded settlement in the county. Another main attraction is the upside-down font, to which we come in a moment.

The body of the church is an 1854 rebuild

*Melbury Bubb, the church and hamlet from Bubb Down.*

of a 15th century reconstruction of a Saxon or Norman original; all except for the tower, which was built new against the south nave in the 15th century, in Perpendicular style. It supplies a porch to the main entrance and has some quirky features. Pathetically thin central pinnacles rise from the battlements on each of the four sides. Below are bell-chamber windows with stone louvres, then a frieze of quatrefoils among whose engraved decorations are the initials WB, standing for Walter Bokeler, the rector who in the 1470s – prime period for Perpendicular – probably paid for the tower. Below that each wall carries a central shaft of triangular cross-section resting on an angel's head. 'Walt. B' occurs again on the right pier of the tower doorway. Nearby, on the grass, a number of 17th century table tombs, at slant angles, include one of 1622 to Alexander Buckler, an evolved spelling of Bokeler.

Inside, the church is simple, short of items of specific interest but enchantingly rich in its air of modest rural piety, savoured by the comedy of the font, to the left of the door. Various carved beasts – dog, stag, horse, maybe lion, and sinister-miscellaneous, inter-twined with long twiddly tails – decorate its round side, but they are all upside-down. If you up-ended the font the animals would be the right way up but the lead-lined bowl would disappear, which is presumably why it stays as it is. The design could be Celtic or Saxon. The standard theory is that this is the plinth of a 10th or 11th century column, no longer wanted as the base of a churchyard cross, and turned over to provide a font bowl with minimum effort. But this is only a guess. The enigmas of the font tell of our ignorance of large areas of Anglo-Saxon life.

The stone reredos with its carving of the Nativity is very Victorian. Likewise the oak pews and choir stalls and screen with its simple tracery. Some of the stained glass is 15th century and beautiful, most of this being contained within the tracery of the upper window. Puritan iconoclasts were perhaps too heedless or drunk to hit anything but the big glass lights below. Arms of the Warre and Maltravers families, and symbols of the gospel-authors, appear in the east end window. In north wall windows of the nave, the Archangel Gabriel announces to the Virgin that she will mother God, the wise and foolish virgins appear, Christ displays his hand wounds, and a bishop ordains kneeling youths (*see page 9*). Faces are crudely drawn but everyone has character. Originally, the whole figure of Christ would have appeared in a main light. Church windows often displayed all seven sacraments instituted by Christ, one of which is ordination, and that is likely to have been the case here. God, some apostles and other figures and scenes occupy the west window tracery.

From its brush with the 20th century almost all the church seems to have gained is a stove, placed to the east of the entrance, and two homely scuttles standing close by. The parishioners have not even admitted electricity, admirably preferring ten or so oil lamps bracketed to walls. For the rest, little is notable except for the rare peace.

*Melbury Bubb, intertwined upside-down animals circle the Anglo-Saxon font.*

## MELBURY SAMPFORD
*Dedication unknown*

Here it basks, you might say, this conventional English church, amid the very ideal of the picturesque English landscape, cared for, tucked into the hillside, pampered even, and as permanent as human works can be. A neat border containing hydrangeas, escallonia, climbing roses, magnolia and varieties of holly runs along its outside walls. Statues of the gospel writers, biblical patriarchs and heraldic lions and foxes in greater number and better condition than the external ornaments on most churches stand atop the corners of nave, chancel, transepts and central tower. The classical façade of the big house smiles on it, and in all directions lies rich rolling parkland stippled with rare trees of the highest pedigree, groves and avenues of oak, beech, lime and chestnut, Capability Brown's lake, post and rail enclosures, horses, bison and free-wandering deer. Much of the house and grounds have been roughly as they are for nearly five hundred years. The present owner's ancestors have been hereabouts for perhaps eight. Everything suggests more than half a

*Melbury Sampford, snowdrops line the path leading down to the beautifully maintained church.*

millennium of peace and plenty and continuity of care.

Then you learn, for instance, that when the church was built it was the parish church, surrounded by a village. Not a visible trace of that village remains. You discover that a 16th-century owner went to prison for debt. A 17th century successor was twice captured in the Civil War and paid a fortune for his liberty and – but willingly this time – more than that to enable Charles II to escape England after the disastrous battle of Worcester in 1651. Since then there have been unsettling scrapes and blips in the succession and a half-century ago two heirs, brothers, lost their lives tragically young, one through an accident, one on active service. Numerous Dorset estates have gone under and been split up and redeveloped in the same period. All the same, for the time being, the feel of Melbury is like that of Arcadia, safe since the beginning of time, and with any luck for much of the rest of it.

The church, the shape of a cross, warm Ham-stone, 15th century perpendicular style with window tops of lacy tracery, central tower with a south-west stair turret, transepts north and south, all walls battlemented and surmounted by the statues mentioned, was heavily restored in Victorian times, between 1874 and 1878, when the nave was extended a few feet westward. You enter from the west. The interior is dark, solemn but full of lively particulars. The nave is narrow – narrower than the chancel – with a dark wood hammer-beam roof, supported on stone angel-head corbels. There is a mildly medieval look to it. If all the Melbury staff were God-fearing and church-going there would be a space problem – as there is, it seems, at family weddings and funerals. The pews were carved by a Victorian estate carpenter with reliefs of plants, birds, a spider, a butterfly. There are brass plaques on the west wall and marble ones north and south. The prospect, here at the west door, closes with a fine east window full of heraldry, and a carved-stone, fancy-cake reredos of the Last Supper that is quintessentially and in this case depressingly High Victorian. But on the way up we shall see a number of historic family monuments and memorials, which are, religion apart, the main point of coming here.

For a few years in the 13th century Melbury was owned by Sampfords, whose name continues to distinguish the place from other, nearby Melburys. But marriages and

*Melbury Sampford, the chancel and narrow nave.*

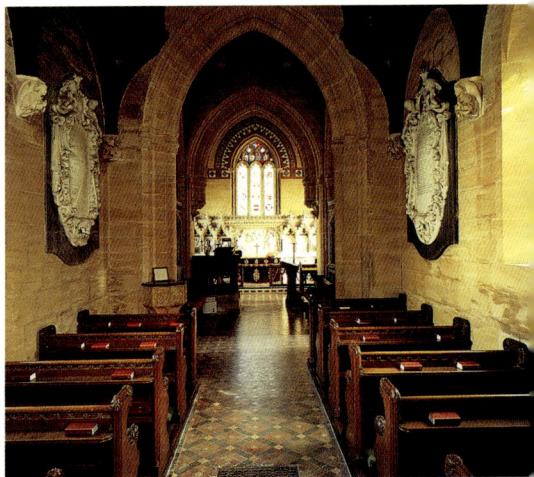

female inheritance brought name changes. Brunings or Brownings were here in the 15th century, and the magnificent Purbeck marble canopied table tomb of William Bruning who died in 1467 is to the left or north of the crossing. His alabaster effigy has him in armour, helmet under his head, a somewhat light-headed lion at his feet. He sold the estate to Henry Strangways, related to him by marriage, in 1500 – the only time it has ever been sold. Henry's son Sir Giles, one of Henry VIII's commissioners for closing down monasteries, rebuilt the Bruning house and vastly increased the family's properties, acquiring among much else the manor and lands of Abbotsbury. But he is not buried here. His grandson, though, another Sir Giles, lies under the south transept table tomb, but a question hangs in the air above him. The effigy, identical in almost all respects of face and armour to the effigy in the north transept, almost certainly initially commemorated a 15th century Bruning. Sir Giles, soldier, wildly extravagant, often in debt, and occasionally locked away for it,

seems simply to have collared the tomb for himself. There is a brass to him on the nearby wall, originally on the floor. Back in the north transept, against the east wall, is an ornate tablet to Sir Giles's grandson Sir John, loyal royalist imprisoned for two and a half years in the Civil War and punitively mulcted by the Commonwealth parliament in return for release. His grandson Thomas's marble memorial of 1713, with attendant cherubs, skull, scroll and arms – very 18th century – hangs on the south wall of the nave. Other nave tablets record various of his children.

One of these, Susanna, married Thomas Horner of Mells in Somerset. In 1735 their daughter Elizabeth married Stephen Fox, who brought his cousins, the dazzling Lennox sisters, subjects of the recent book and television film *Aristocrats*, into the family circle. He was made Earl of Ilchester in 1756 and another nave tablet records his

*Melbury Sampford, the memorial to Caroline, Countess of Ilchester, who died aged 31 having produced 4 children in 7 years.*

death in 1776. He combined the two family names into Fox-Strangways. His daughter Susan shocked her family by eloping with an Irish actor – we meet her and her husband again in Stinsford church. In the chancel here is the kneeling figure of the third earl's wife who died young in 1819 having produced four children in seven years of marriage. The life-size marble figure of her, loosely draped, bare-shouldered, doleful, is by Francis Chantrey, good at soft flesh though this is not the best example of his work. One other memorial we passed at the entrance, against the southern face of the west wall, of discoloured brass and not easily read, celebrates Brigadier-General Thomas Fox-Strangways, put in command of the Royal Artillery in the Crimean War at the age of 64, almost forty years after being wounded at Waterloo. Noted for leading from the front he was killed at Inkerman late in 1854. He combined, says the inscription, 'the courage of the soldier with the faith and virtues of the Christian.' Last of the grand commem-

orations is of Denzil Vesey Fox-Strangways, who died in 1901 aged 22. A full-size effigy seems excessive for one so callow, but there it is. At his feet stands a short-legged hairy terrier, clearly a likeness of his pet.

The church thus exhibits several centuries of tomb and memorial style. A parallel, fuller companion to family history is seen in the windows, in the form of heraldic coats of arms. Originally hung in the house, and of great interest to students of heraldry, they blazon the lofty lineage of its long-lived family, the kinship with Staffords, Blounts, Herberts, Horseys, Paulets, Trenchards, national leaders, Dorset and neighbouring grandees (many of whose names recur in these pages), bishops and generals and statesmen – a prime genetic pick possibly daunting to those sprung therefrom.

## MELPLASH
### Christ Church

With the Napoleonic wars over, those English with money and leisure began to scramble for the medieval past. Georgian houses grew battlements, people called Burke or Morris became de Burgos and de Montmorencys. The romantic recreation of the castles, costumes, heraldry of five hundred and more years earlier culminated in the Eglinton Tournament of 1839, where amid extravaganzas of spectacles and feasting Victorian knights and barons biffed each other out of saddles with wickedly authentic lances. In church architecture, the backward look was towards medieval gothic: early Decorated to start with, later the glorious Perpendicular of the 15th century. But Classicism was not dead, and other styles had their moments. In particular, the 1840s saw a small flurry of Norman or Romanesque and related round-arch styles. The sheer ungarnished strength of Norman structures made them good protective packaging for Christianity exported to far-flung colonies. Besides, Norman survivals such as Studland and Worth Matravers were inspiring models.

Even architects dedicated to Gothic were prepared to chance a Norman church or two before returning to the mainstream. Benjamin Ferrey, zealous gothicist and close friend of Pugin, high priest of the Gothic revival, was one of these. Melplash church was built to his plans in 1846.

James Bandinel, who served as translator for the Foreign Office for fifty years, was a friend of William Wilberforce and wrote a history of the slave trade, funded the church in memory of his father, seventeen years vicar of Netherbury. Three inscriptions on slate insist that all the pews and seats 'without one single exception' should be free, 'open always entirely equally to the poor as to the rich, by desire of the founder.' Some churches were less liberal. Gladstone's father, for instance, not long before, aimed to get a 5% return on the £14,000 he spent building two churches in Liverpool, from pew-rents. Liberal as he was, however, James Bandinel would have raised a brow at modern developments. To pay their way, insufficiently endowed churches nowadays become conference halls, classrooms, nurseries, deconsecrated museums and private houses (one of these, Chedington in Dorset, has an Aga where the altar was). Melplash chose a different way. The nave is cut off from the rest of the church

*Melplash, built in 1846 and paid for by James Bandinel in memory of his father, vicar of Netherbury.*

by a moveable glass partition. A net hangs from a line stretched across its middle, and the wooden floor is marked by a pattern of white-painted lines. Melplash's nave, under its dark, unNorman hammerbeam roof is a wholly unNorman badminton court, available for rent at £5 a session.

The rest of the church, which is cross-shaped with transepts, has been reorientated. The altar-table is in the north transept, the pews, facing it, in the south – which has in other words become the new nave. The eastern apse, where the altar used to be, holds little but the font. You enter by the south transept door and, facing the altar, see the fine square of arches – broad, tall and of course round, resting on twin half-columns, topped by trumpet capitals – which define the central area below. Ahead is the altar. The apse, darker, is to the right. The vestry door and five slim windows, framed by slim shafts at the sides and chevron and dogtooth bands above, break its curved surface. The roof's dark rafters splay out like a curved fan from the apse top. Opposite, the glass partition, filling the crossing arch, is an eyesore, as most glass screens are in old churches. Eyesore too is the pink carpet, chosen – but could it be? – as a feminine counterpoint to the male brawn of Norman masonry. And all about is that keynote of Norman, the round-headed arch: ahead, above, behind, single, matched or in rising tiers (in the transepts) reminiscent of the walls of a Roman amphitheatre, these smooth semi-circles, plain, moulded or ornamented, over doorways and windows; a form first used in Europe by Etruscans, adopted by Romans – the word derives from the Latin *arcus* – unknown (but is that possible?) to the Greeks.

Outside, these rounded caps turn the bland wall-surfaces of flat-topped tower, nave, transepts, porch, the soft curve of the east-end apse (and its little calf, forming the vestry on the north side) into a busy patterning of chamfered, moulded, plain, dogtoothed, chevroned, twisty-roped arches and arcades overhanging apertures of many sizes. It must have looked stately when first completed, close to thatched cottages on a dawdling lane – the next-door schoolhouse came a few years later – with views in most directions to the strange green bony contours of west Dorset. It is sadly different now: a nice old neighbouring pub, yes, and good views too; but some ugly houses and an unpleasantly busy road with no provision for walkers. Badminton players doubtless come by car.

## MILTON ABBEY

*St Mary, St Michael, St Samson and St Branwalader*

Beside the paler, rather skittish fancy-gothic of Lord Milton's 1770s house, the massive bulk of the hacked-off abbey church, with its dark, cold flint, warm Ham-stone dressings and big foursquare tower, looks solid, masculine and indifferently handsome. The hacking is no more than apparent. There never was a complete nave extending from the tall, blocked up arches you see now in the west wall under the tower. The abbey King

Athelstan founded here in the 930s had a wooden church. The Normans put a stone one in its place but in 1309 that was reduced to rubble by lightning and fire. The present building was begun soon after but in two hundred years proceeded no further than chancel, tower, transepts, cloisters and some monastic buildings. Sir John Tregonwell (usually pronounced Tregunnell), selling off monasteries confiscated by his master Henry VIII in 1539, kept Milton for himself. The monastic buildings were converted for domestic use and the abbey church switched to parish church, serving the occupants of a busy market town, called Middleton or Milton, comprising more than a hundred houses and spreading down the hill immediately to the south. After a period in the possession of the Bancks family, the estate was sold in 1752 to the startlingly upward-bound Joseph Damer of Winterborne Came, south of Dorchester. He, a baron and on his way to an earldom, married to a Sackville bride, master of the mansion he got Chambers and Wyatt to build him here, felt bothered by the populace on the neigh-bouring slopes.

Heir, in Swift's words, of the 'old miser and usurer Damer of Dublin', Joseph Damer was, wrote Horace Walpole, 'the most arrogant and proud of men, with no foundation but great wealth and a match with the Duke of Dorset's daughter. His birth and parts were equally mean and contemptible.' His doings at Milton dwarf those of most modern exploiting developers. In the course of twenty years he evicted all Milton's occupants the moment their leases fell in, persuading stubborn citizens by such means as the release of village pond-water to flood their homes. He removed all head-stones and bones from the graveyard and dumped them out of his way, then called in Capability Brown to turn the wasteland into a picturesque park. The result was exquisite. To be fair, the new model village he made for the evicted is fine too.

The abbey church now became an

*Milton Abbey, with the mansion (now Milton Abbey School) built by Joseph Damer on the left.*

inordinately large family chapel, and remained so when the estate was sold in 1852 to banker Charles Hambro from Denmark. In 1865, during their time, George Gilbert Scott restored the church. Having occupied much space with their wall plaques and grander memorials, the Hambros sold up in 1932. Owned by Salisbury diocese and open to all, it now serves as chapel to the boarding school installed in the house in 1954.

Some of the building's history, along with some unexplained puzzles, is proclaimed by the exterior. Projections from the west front, either side of the porch Scott built, suggest that a pre-Reformation start was made on the north and south aisle, as well as the nave. Either side of them come the west windows of the transepts. Rounding the south-west corner, we see the flowing tracery of the huge south window and the leaden outlines of the stained glass design. Flying buttresses, seen forming airy tunnels from raised ground to the east, rise from double pinnacles placed along the aisle parapet. There are intriguing terminal labels – faces wild and placid, torsoes, sly heads – to the arch moulds that hood the windows.

Scars of arches on the east wall show where aisle chapels, ambulatory and central Lady Chapel were in the mainly 14th century rebuilding. (Directly to the east, surmounting out-of-bounds grass steps and reached from the boundary road, is St Catherine's Chapel, a simple Norman structure looking timeless and sequestered among the woods. Pilgrims visiting it, according to an inscription, were formerly granted 120 days indulgence). The abbey church's north side has an aisle like the south and blocked archways in the transept, originally providing passage between church and cloisters.

Through the west porch we enter what would have been the crossing had there been a nave to cross. This space, canopied by fan vaulting, and the transepts, roofed by coarser lierne vaulting, form together a vast and lofty hall, ending in a massive window at either end. The vault bosses – bishops, kings, horse-riders, trees, angels – are fascinating. Some photographs are on display, as well as some

*Milton Abbas. The Norman St Catherine's Chapel sits snugly in the woods above the abbey.*

old prints and fragments of masonry from razed walls. The 14th century Decorated tracery of the southern transept window we have seen from the outside, but now its plan and rich colours show it as an arrangement of human figures, mostly kings but with the Virgin and Child top middle. Designed by Pugin and executed by John Hardman, one of the great glass artists of his time, in 1847, it is intended to show the line of descent from King David (placed below the Virgin) and his father Jesse (below David) to Jesus. Some such windows show, often very beautifully, the family tree, allowing a movement and dynamic that this window perhaps lacks.

The north window, perpendicular in style and perhaps a century later than the south, contains, where not rather dustily plain glass, some good 18th century panels of Damer and Sackville heraldry. Underneath is the church's most memorable memorial, the marble tomb, based on Robert Adam's design, of Joseph Damer's Sackville wife, who predeceased him in 1775, with a sensitive sculpture, by Agostino Carlini. Damer is shown pensively posing beside his wife's dead body, both of them dressed in the height of opulent fashion, her chest copiously bejewelled. Walpole gave her higher points than her husband: 'very sensible, has even humour, if the excessive reserve and silence that she draws from both father and mother would let her . . . ever show it.'

Nearby stands an unusual font: two marble angels flanking a marble rock with what any sensible dog would take for a dog bowl on the floor. A Dane, Adolf Jerichau, did the work for Baron Hambro in about 1860.

In the south transept some twenty wall and floor tablets commemorate members of the Hambro family who during their eighty-year tenure impressed their name firmly about the church without greatly adding to the place's glory or legends. In the south-east corner of this transept is a fragment of Ham-stone wall – part of an unfinished chantry. An ogee-arched piscina or wash-bowl occupies two of its cusped panels.

The south aisle leads to the Lady Chapel and an altar by Wyatt. On the way we pass, high on the north wall, a rebus of William Middleton, last abbot but one before the Reformation. Possibly aristocratic, certainly rich, he paid for – besides much else – the building of the north transept and the vaulting of both transepts and crossing. He also founded a free school in the town. The rebus, clues to the syllables of his name, shows a house that is clearly a mill, and a barrel or tun. Middleton and Milton were by his time used interchangeably. Further on is a stone statue of the apostle St James the Great, whose supposed burial at Compostela made that place one of the chief objects of medieval pilgrimage. Above the altar a plaque records the material gratitude of a John Tregonwell who as a small boy fell from the abbey roof in 1605 and was saved by the skirt he wore opening like a parachute. The St James statue rests on the 14th century sedilia – priest's seats, seen clearly as we move into the central presbytery.

Opposite us is the 1877 tomb of Baron Hambro under a florid canopy Scott designed. It might be a shoot from his Albert Memorial. The 15th century reredos is bare of the bright colours with which it was originally painted, and the thirteen statues it carried before iconoclasts smashed them. Fine work, but the empty niches still beg for them back. The oak tabernacle with Perpendicular adornment that hangs against the north wall was once suspended by ropes attached to pulleys over the altar. Its function

*Milton Abbey, the memorial to Caroline Damer (1775), with her mourning husband, Lord Milton, lying beside her.*

was to cover the pyx containing the Host – the bread that was converted into Christ's body. It is the only one in England to have survived the Reformation. The two paintings against the stone screen dividing choir from crossing, are 15th century and represent King Athelstan and his mother. They are quite bad in a charmless way. The screen itself supports the Gray and Davison 1868 organ and under the arch is a glassed treasury containing a remarkable ivory triptych and other valuable objects.

Before leaving by the north aisle, we find two tombs. On the aisle's south wall, opposite the exit, is a charming marble altar tomb, with delicately carved canopy on twisted shafts. On the wall at the back are brasses recording the death of the wealthy first private owner of the place, Sir John Tregonwell, buried here in 1565. Beyond, at the aisle's east end, and seemingly intended to dwarf the older tomb, is the grandiose and uncomfortable Bancks memorial, all moulded columns, Corinthian capitals, rounded top, cherubs, urns, coats of arms and a prone damsel with shapely prominent breasts holding skull and book.

During Easter and summer school holidays, the fine Abbot's Hall, built under Abbot Middleton in 1498 and now contained within the school buildings, is open, just across the way.

# MINTERNE MAGNA
## St Andrew

*Minterne Magna, winter sun and a dusting of snow.*

The setting is magical: period village, richly wooded valley, the fields and tall trees of its eastern slope making an almost theatrical backdrop to the church itself, with its tousled graveyard, pinnacled tower, nave, north transept, chancel, all in flint, and a gold-number clock on the tower's south face, above the engraved inscription *Le temps passe l'amitiée reste*. There are traces of a Saxon church under the chancel, and the list of rectors starts with Walter Hudd in 1350. However, nave and chancel are early 15th century, as the Perpendicular windows suggest. The transept or north chapel was added between 1610 and 1620. This was unusual. For 70 or more years, since the Reformation, almost no churches in the county had been built or expanded. For one thing there were sufficient already: 234 Dorset churches in 1535. For another, the hazardous switchback of 16th century state religion – RC to C of E to RC to C of E – discouraged expensive commitment. Now, between 1610 and 1630, radical rebuilding or extension took place at Minterne and three churches nearby – Ryme Intrinseca, Leweston and Folke. Their manorial patrons were often related to each other. More

obviously, each carries an easily identified signature, not common elsewhere: some windows of three or five lights with the middle light rising above the others. The north window of the chapel here is one such. After these churches little was built till the end of the century, when William III's Glorious Revolution brought in Protestant permanence. The tower was rebuilt in 1800 and heightened in 1894. There was a wholesale restoration in 1869. Along with much else the nave roof was raised a foot and a half to accommodate a monument inside.

We go in, straight off the road, by the west door of the tower. Ahead, the nave looks quite long, thin, simple, and circumspect. Eastward progress discloses unremarkable Victorian stained-glass windows, wall brasses and other items commemorating members of the Digby family. The personal flag of the 11th Baron Digby – his Garter banner, 'azure a fleur-de-lis argent' – hangs from the gallery, as such noblemen's flags, doubtless battle-tattered if possible, did in medieval times. Sensibly moved from the chancel in 1963, the organ is in the gallery. A 15th century octagonal font stands on a modern plinth.

Gallery and pew-ends have pleasing carvings, and Benjamin Grassby's corbel angels are heavier than his best but good all the same. More conspicuous than any of these is the nave's north-wall memorial – the one that raised the roof in 1869 – with its wordy tribute, sobbing putti and almost audible bunchings of the arms and implements of war, to Charles Churchill, who died loaded with honours in 1714 'Esteem'd one of the best commanders of foot in Europe'. Of course. He left no heir, and illegitimate children get no mention here, still less a family capacity for inventing pedigree and political and romantic intrigue. These are most clearly seen at work in Charles's brother John, the famous first Duke of Marlborough and victor of the Battle of Blenheim in 1704, their sister Arabella, mistress of James II, and her son by him, the Duke of Berwick, who commanded the French and Spanish armies which opposed her brothers at the same battle. Doubtless all of them worshipped here in childhood.

Charles's grandfather John died in 1659. His remains lie under a stone further along the nave. He had achieved a hike up the social ladder by marrying, as his first wife, Sarah, a Gloucestershire Winston, who brought him a limited fortune, distant kinship to the Cecils, a name that would last with lustre into our own time and a grand but largely invented pedigree – 'a nightmare of bogus genealogy', A.L.Rowse calls it, that traced the family back to Welsh princes and Strongbow, conqueror of Ireland. Another of Charles's sisters, Ellen, would get no mention among this galaxy were she not buried here, beside her grandfather, under a floor tablet of heraldic interest. The bow above her coat-of-arms indicates that she was unmarried. The diamond (as opposed to shield) that encloses the arms announce her gender. The cross of St George appearing within a square (or canton) over the lion signify the augmentation, or honour, granted by Charles II *after* her father the first Sir Winston Churchill's death, in recognition of his unerring loyalty to Charles I

his father.

Two other families in particular, Napier and Digby (still inhabiting the big house next door) share the honours of Minterne, and turning into the north chapel we find an eruption of Napier grandiosity, of which the main outcome is the vast, ceiling-high, marble monument, complete with trumpeting putti, heraldry, garlands of flowers, Corinthian columns holding a broken pediment, skulls, crossbones and mourning maids on the east wall. Covering the entrance to the Napier vault, it lists several 17th century Napiers, the last-named of whom, Lady Blanche, in 1695 'received ye fatall stroke from ye cold hand of death.'

## MORETON
### St Nicholas
At around 9 pm on the night of 8 October 1940, with Hitler intensifying his blitz on London, a lone and unaccountable German bomb exploded close to the north aisle wall of St Nicholas' church on the rural periphery of Moreton village. Much of the church's exterior and most of the content was destroyed. All the prized 19th century stained-glass was blown to bits. And when, after ten years of rebuilding and restoration, the Bishop of Salisbury rededicated the church and worship resumed within, the windows were plain, and calling out for content. Boldly, the architectural historian Howard Colvin suggested an approach to the glass engraver Laurence Whistler. The German bomb had made possible a new direction in church art.

There had been a church on the site since 1298. We know the first rector's name: Ysemberd. Within a century the Frampton family arrived on the scene. They have owned the land, the successive manor houses, and the living of the church ever since – probably no other family in Dorset has longer records of possession. Hutchins describes a church here in the early 18th century – 'a small but very ancient fabric' – in which, he says,

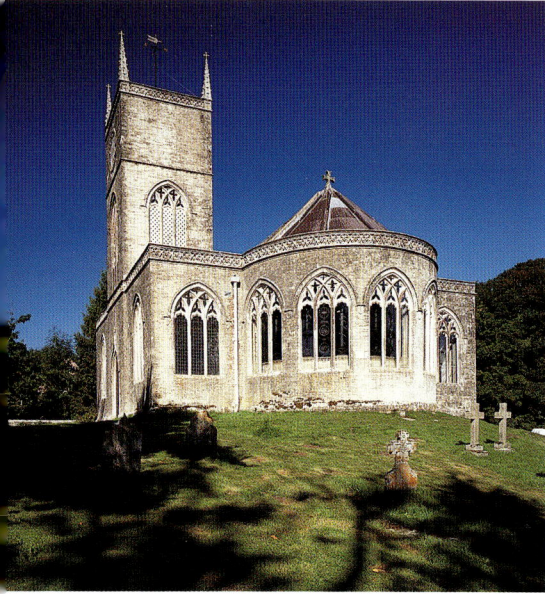

*Moreton, an 18th century church whose 20th century engraved glass windows by Laurence Whistler have made it amongst the most visited of all Dorset churches.*

Framptons had been buried at least since the Reformation two hundred years before – probably longer. An 18th century head of the family, James Frampton (1711-1784), married as his second wife the heiress to a West Indian colonist, which often meant a fortune based directly or otherwise on sugar and slaves. In 1776 he had the church built anew in the bright, light, Georgian gothick style. It had a nave which swelled at its eastern end into a graceful apse containing five equal pointed windows, and on the south two side-chapels with decorative parapets flanking a tall and pretty pinnacled tower with a clock on its southern face and a main doorway below it. The western chapel served as vestry, the eastern as the chapel of the Trinity. This, divided from the nave by a pew, was to be reserved for the family, its walls loaded with family memorials including a brass, saved from the old church, showing a kneeling James Frampton who died in 1523. A beautiful tablet, also preserved from the previous church, hangs on the east wall,

within a surround of wreathed flowers, commending the wifely virtues of Mary Frampton who died aged 35 in 1762. All this was in essence the church that stands there today, set on a sharp rise of land and making a handsome landmark in the flattish valley of the dairies east of Dorchester. The chief external differences are that the main entrance has gone round to the west; the south and far the best front, partly obscured by churchyard trees, is less conspicuous than it was; and that a north aisle, which presents visitors with a rather enigmatic first view, has been added.

This northward expansion was put in hand in the 1840s by the Reverend William Charlton Frampton, younger son of the owner, and one of those long-lived, dynamic parsons who seem to crop up more often in the Victorian era than others. He was rector for fifty-seven years. His alterations were rather well done, modifying but not ruining the church's essential Georgian character. There was new stained glass in all the windows supplied, as was much work for Queen Victoria, by Thomas Willement; new wooden pulpit, lectern, pews, font stand, painting and decoration, encaustic floor-tiles over nave and aisle, reredos of ogee-shaped niches and candelabra for the ninety-one candles needed to light winter services until electricity was introduced. It took on a 19th century cosiness but the broad light span of the apse windows and the rib-vaulting above, as well as the exterior, kept alive the spirit of the original.

The churchyard has global associations. It contains – now unmarked – the remains of Prince Clarence, son of the King of the Mosquito Coast in what is now Nicaragua in Central America. Sent here for schooling, probably with a view to continued alliance between Britain and his homeland – which contained part of a possible canal route across central America before Panama was selected – he was dead at fourteen in 1849. Far better known, and visited by many, is the grave of T.E. Lawrence, in the graveyard over

the road given by the Framptons in 1930. He was killed when the motor-cycle he was riding collided with a car in 1935, near his small and sparsely furnished home, Clouds Hill, two miles from here. Not everyone is convinced it was an accident. Among those who came to his funeral were Winston Churchill, Siegfried Sassoon, Augustus John and Bernard Shaw. A stone engraved by Eric Kennington marks Lawrence's grave. It identifies him only as a Fellow of All Souls College, Oxford. There is no mention of Arabia.

Then in 1940 came the bomb and in 1950 the church's reopening. By 1955, Laurence Whistler's five east windows, paid for by war

*Moreton. The Trinity Chapel window is a memorial to a pilot shot down over France in 1940.*

compensation funds, were in place. The theme was light in all its manifestations. Some find the candles and the scrolls of text around them too stiff, and some of the ornaments too whimsical, even sugary, for their taste. In the 1970s, after a gap of years, Whistler began to fill the other windows, in the north aisle, the south chapels, the porch. His style had evolved to freer concepts and lines, though the execution of the minutest detail – flower, church, house, flame, jewel glitter, smoke, face, bird, rain – was always done with an almost magical pin-point sharpness and sensitivity. In some cases both sides of the glass are engraved, giving an impression of depth and, to a moving eye, of motion. In 1984 he did the climactic west window: the whirl of an astral galaxy, white hot and in furious motion. Filling all the windows with engraved glass, and that by one artist, was not at first envisaged. The plan grew and finally was done. The more oppressive elements of Victorian taste were swept away, and in particular the ribbed ceiling was painted plain again. Such a complete series of windows is thought not to exist elsewhere. It has become as famous a feature as any in a Dorset church.

No, not quite all the windows. The east wall of the Trinity Chapel conceals from the eyes of those within a three-light window, matching those in the apse and perfectly visible outside. Its plain glass is divided by lead lights. Whistler's later windows were paid for by private patrons, usually as memorials. But Whistler offered a new window, as a free gift, for this south-eastern vacancy. The subject was Judas, the apostle who betrayed Christ for thirty pieces of silver, and it shows him hanging from a tree and the coins spilling to the ground. It is perhaps the most powerful of all Whistler's work for the church, but it has never been installed. Instead it languishes, seldom seen, in an awkward and badly lit position in the exhibition room of Dorchester's County Museum. Its subject offended the feelings of those whose family dead lie close to the window it would have occupied, and it was, alas, outlawed.

## PARKSTONE
### St Osmund

The Orthodox Christian Church of Poole – for that is what St Osmund's became in the year 2005 – gets high marks from all the commentators. Quality of design and workmanship is of the highest. But, to my mind, and thinking mainly of the outside, it

fails, albeit magnificently. It might work on a bare Thracian plain or treeless Turkish tableland, but here it is too hemmed, hunched and heavy, too squashed, too pinioned. A tall gothic spire of stone might fit the scene better, yearning upward towards heavenly release. All the same this is a church that fascinates, as does its principal architect. Edward Schroder Prior (1852-1932) was determined to break the High Victorian mould. Pupil of Norman Shaw, and child of the Arts and Crafts Movement, he helped found and became Master of the Art Workers' Guild. A guiding ideal was that a building's designs should grow from the innate potential of local materials and the skills of the local craftsmen employed to work them. The architect should sensitively guide and oversee this natural and organic process. There was, too, a puckish, radical strain in him, that put his work in its own category, not always a snug one. St Osmund's, Prior's last great work, done between 1914 and 1916, is not an altogether comfortable construction.

It is made mostly of local bricks, formed from carefully selected and moulded clays, fired in a variety of old, well-tried kilns, to produce a broad spectrum of texture and colours – brownish, purplish, yellowish. At this point the local links dry up. St Osmund outside is of basically Byzantine cast (and roughly contemporary with another essay in brick and Byzantinism, Westminster Cathedral). It has a central dome, terminal apse and transept roofs like high shoulders under a squat neck.

Eclectic detail is everywhere: a tier of round clerestory windows above the broad brick aisle, aisle windows separated by rather edible-looking brick shafts, a couple of massive brick buttresses like giants drunkenly flopped against the south wall, and a sizzling west front with a turret-hemmed pediment on top, arcaded gallery below, central rose window under that, and a broad, shallow arch above the entrance, the omnipresent brick an animated motley of colour. When a bright sun in a blue sky picks out the glinting pigments of glass and brick, you can forget the suburban terraces all about it, the conifers, adjacent crossroads, traffic lights, fumes, weed-tangled railings, pebbled car-park. But on a dank and drizzly day it blends more with the surround, settling for an earthbound lumpiness.

It had some early structural troubles, making necessary the rebuilding of the dome in 1922 and of the south aisle in 1950 – when the buttresses went up. By 2000 other grave faults were said to have emerged. The church was closed, declared dangerous and barred to the public. Estimates for making everything safe flitted between £300,000 and over a million. Anyway the diocese, with dwindling congregations and several sizeable churches only minutes away, had no need of St Osmund's. The church was declared redundant and offered for sale. Copts, the Bournemouth Symphony Orchestra, the next-door dancing school (whose lissome girls in tutus are said to have shocked the Copts away) and film studios are said to have shown fleeting interest. During the years the church stood locked, gathering dust and deteriorating, rumours were rampant about the price asked and whether it was about to fall down. The ultimate outcome was unlikely.

A rich and munificent Texan bought the church for the Romanian Orthodox Church, and the structure seems quite safe, in need of no more than occasional repairs and maintenance. There is nothing particularly Romanian about Parkstone or Poole. Indeed the church comes under the Orthodox deanery of Antioch. Nevertheless the Orthodox Church had in recent years gained numbers through the defection of disenchanted Anglican priests – followed in some cases by their congregations – from what they saw as the post-modern liberalism, desertion of old forms, ordination of women and pervasive political correctness of the Church of England. The part-time priest here (otherwise a teacher), Father

*Parkstone, St Osmund. Now the Orthodox Christian Church of Poole, for which its Byzantine cast admirably suits it.*

Chrysostom, is English, Bristol-born, a former Anglican minister, and superbly content and fulfilled by the teachings and forms of service of Orthodoxy, and by the Byzantine flavour of the church itself. Its acoustics are superb. Resonating off the high dome, the chants and harmonies, much in minor key with a hint of the Levant, fill the church. Yet often the only voices are those of the priest, his male assistant and the 'Cantor', actually the priest's wife, with a fine, pure, boyish voice.

The church's interior seems huge, and almost as wide as long. The nave is taller than it seems outside, and on each side of it three massive, round-headed arches, from which hang clusters of lights, rest on lanky square piers and give on to broad, well-lit aisles. The ceilings of these, as of the dome, are of dark, curiously dull, reinforced concrete. (There is nothing dull about the

*Parkstone, the pulpit. In the background, piers with winged-angel capitals beneath the dome.*

antler-like wings of the angels placed at the tops of the piers below the dome). Eastwards, steps rise from the lower parquet floor to a marble sanctuary, with balustraded projecting wings either side, and marble seats at the back of them. Ahead lies something of a stylistic jumble – the work not of Prior but his predecessor G.A.B. Livesay – under the apse's sky-blue ceiling. An open passage or ambulatory leads round the back of the apse, and a semi-circular arcade of fluted Ionic columns in dark terracotta, linked by iron railings, separates this from the high altar. Above the altar and behind a set of 18th century wooden rails brought from the London church of St Mary-le-Bow, rises a striking altar canopy, or baldacchino, copied from one in the Roman church of San Clemente. Seven lamps hang on chains in front of the altar.

The war memorial statue of Christ in the church's far south-west corner is by MacDonald Gill, as is the grille dividing the two south-eastern chapels. The inscriptions are by his more famous brother Eric. The window glass is very Prior. Chunky, opaque, hand-made glass squares of various colours are arranged in abstract patterns among paler squares. All these were his own design. Blues and greens predominate in the big south aisle windows, pink, yellow and watery green in the north. (Prior windows are also to be seen at Burton Bradstock church). The south transept window is starkly, darkly blue – an exception. The great window is a masterpiece of subdued but glowing tints arranged in neat symmetry.

# PIDDLETRENTHIDE

*All Saints*

The Bridge family, formerly of Piddletrenthide Manor, and substantial landowners, were introduced to King George III when he was inventing summer holidays at Weymouth around the end of the 18th century. They talked of their cousin John Bridge, born at Piddletrenthide but by then partner in a firm of London goldsmiths. Back in the capital the king scrutinised John and his work, and soon appointed his firm Rundell and Bridge royal jewellers and goldsmiths. (Among their employees, a little later, was Augustus W.N. Pugin). Much plate, including a silver-plate dinner service for state banquets, still existing and of superb quality, was done for the king's sons, the Prince of Wales and the Duke of York. Over the years the latter's unceasing orders landed him in such huge debts that when, in 1826, by his father's wish, the incalculable mineral rights of Nova Scotia came his way, he transferred this unlikely asset to the firm in settlement. The Bridge family fortune soon reached its apex. Although it was dispersed later in the 19th century, this was not before so many pious tributes to various Bridges had been erected in the church that it can easily be seen as a family museum and testament to their virtues.

The impressive tall and slender tower of 1487 stands high and pinnacle-rich above the stringy line of the village, which is tucked deep in the north-south Piddle valley. The church body is big and broad: broad nave, broad north and south aisles, broad chancel; and the honey-coloured interior arches separating all these are broad and tall too, so the whole interior has an all-disclosing, nothing-to-hide look. The zigzag pattern on the south doorway and the scallop capitals on the south side of the chancel arch announce the church's Norman ancestry. The chancel dates entirely to an 1852 restoration, but almost all the rest is late 15th century. The exterior is enlivened by the stone's character, rich in the pigments of lichen,

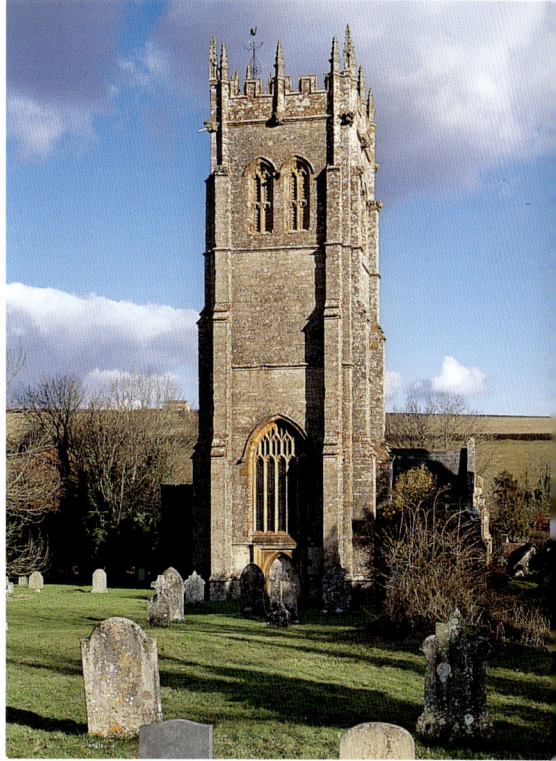

*Piddletrenthide. The high medieval tower is one of the landmarks of the Piddle Valley.*

*Piddletrenthide. Looking east towards the chancel.*

*Poole. The church lies at the heart of the tiny fragment of Georgian Poole that still survives.*

mould and age; also by gargoyles and other sculptures. One of these shows a puff-cheeked face playing a form of bagpipes. There is a sundial above the south porch.

Inside, on the aisle walls, marble urns are mournfully draped, angels comfort and veiled women loll piteously over graves or wipe away tears shed on account of 18th century Colliers and Coxes and 19th century Bridges. Captain Robert Bridge is portrayed, under a spray of flags, wings and weaponry, having withstood the hazards of battle, siege and disease in mid 19th century India, but dying on his way home in 1858, after a brief illness in Ceylon. More of the family are commemorated in the stained glass which decorates but darkens the three windows of the chancel and four of the south aisle. In the westernmost of these, Christ hangs on the cross, which is grasped by a rather

photographic representation of a seated, dapper, moustachioed figure in First World War officer's uniform, dead at 25 in 1915: perhaps the final hope of the depleted Bridge family. John Bridge, from whose skills and royal connections came the family's ephemeral glory and several benefactions to the village (including the gates of the former school, said to have once guarded the tomb in Westminster Abbey of Margaret Beaufort, Henry VII's mother) died in 1834. He is commemorated, on the chancel's north wall, by a remarkable but too polished (in every sense) monument comprising a profile in relief hung between statuettes placed under finely done gothic canopies; fitting more perhaps for royalty than one who made cups and plates for them.

## POOLE
### St James

St James's is set in an opulent enclave not far from quay and shops. It rises, clean, white and sensible among Georgian brick-built terraces, domestic double-fronts, porticoes, pediments, railings, balustrades, burglar alarms, warnings of car clamps and prodigious fines, an unfenced churchyard with trees and warnings to dogs not to foul the grass or the few remaining flat tombstones, a palpable aspiration to material security and a notice on the wall to the effect that the church may be visited when the church office is open, Wednesday to Friday 9.30 to 1.00.

It is just fine, it is OK, St James – and more than that when the Purbeck stone ashlar gleams in sunlight. Walls are topped by rather pinched battlements. Windows – two tiers of them along the north and south aisles – are routinely two or three lancets bracketed together. There is a blue clock with gold numerals on the west tower, through whose doorway we enter. The vestibule, flanked by vestry and office, is gothically decorated, with walls, arches, ribbing and so on painted in dark and light blue, pink, beige and gold

Poole. *The fishing nets, flags and Newfoundland pine piers are a reminder of the town's past as a port trading in cod, fur and timber.*

paint. Its east wall has copious records, gold on black, of charitable gifts and endowments: '1739 . . . paid for a Workhouse for the poor . . . silver communion cup . . . brass double chandelier . . . 1897: Lord Wimborne . . . gave the Cornelia Hospital'. (With the mighty south Wales ironworks under his belt he could afford to). On the wall to the right is a saddening framed watercolour of the old church, with fine box pews and a magnificently commanding pulpit placed square in the middle of the nave.

The fact is, old St James – the worse for 18th century wear and tear – was knocked to the ground in 1819 and reopened, new in style, content and materials, in 1820. They used some of the old stone and retained a few wall memorials, and, mercifully, the big 1736 wooden reredos. Poole's population was swelling rapidly, while her lucrative share of the Newfoundland cod fisheries and skin and fur trade was giving way to other fleets of other nations. Based on the pressing need for more pews, St James was almost the last throw – and a dubiously successful one – of the old prosperity.

So, as we move into the nave, we see hugeness and munificence and thrusting confidence: the high plaster ribbed vault covering the mighty sweep of the continuous south, west and north galleries, the sea of pews. There *is* something nautical about the scene: the deck-like look of the galleries, the wooden piers (Newfoundland pine) that support the ceiling like sturdy ship-masts, the flags (Union, US, and others) hanging from them. A distinct change of mood comes in the chancel. First, a pleasant wooden screen consisting of a dado with a row of metre-high round arches above it narrows the stage by cutting off the end of the north aisle; another, that of the south, the aisle here being occupied by the organ. Within the screens choir-stalls face each other. Things are a touch warmer, a little less commodious and impersonal than in the nave. The sanctuary is one step up. Carved wooden thrones backing on to the wall north and south of the altar look, it is true, massively uncomfortable. And, above the altar, the stained glass window inserted to mark Queen Victoria's diamond jubilee in 1897, is deadly dull. But between altar and window the 1736 dark wooden reredos dominates the scene, probably the church's best thing, its pediment sheltering a grey-painted round relief of the

Holy Ghost as dove, amid waxy grey clouds, while the three panels below, divided by Corinthian pilasters, display the Lord's Prayer, Ten Commandments and Creed, with short biblical texts at the base.

Eye-catching details are scattered. Above the clock on the west gallery the royal arms show within the main heraldic shield another, smaller shield. The white horse of Hanover gallops in its lower third and the crown of Charlemagne occupies the centre. If we were not anyway supplied with dates from other sources, the crown which surmounts this inner shield would narrow the possibilities. From being a mere electorate (with a vote to cast in the election of Holy Roman Emperors) Hanover became a kingdom, sharing Britain's king, in 1815, after Waterloo. Hence the surmounting crown. But Salic law barred female monarchs, so when Victoria became Britain's queen in 1837, Hanover passed to a male relation. The crown appeared in the royal arms only during those few years. This example was in fact a parishioner's gift of 1821.

The 18th century mahogany font, now in the south aisle, is pretty. There was a large stone Norman one in the original baptistery at the north aisle's west end. Deemed too heavy to move at the 1964 rearrangement, it was lowered below the new floor level and left unseen. Among the few coloured windows, the latest, dedicated in 1999, at the west end of the south aisle, looks as a yellow sheet might if a pot of blue paint had been spilt over it and little wiry fish outlines scattered over the surface. It is intended to show God's love penetrating the ocean depths, and commemorates a family of Poole marine pilots, fishermen and dock workers. 18th and early 19th century memorials salvaged from the old church and hung around the walls upstairs and down include a 1718 cartouche to George Lewen, thrice mayor of the town, several draped female mourners and a curious carved panel of 1824, at the end of the north gallery, to Thomas Parr, put up by fellow freemasons and showing a cherub among clouds with dagger, skull, sun, moon and stars and other masonic flummery.

Two memorials, both eloquent, are striking for the contrast in tone of their inscriptions. The Reverend Peter William Jolliffe, (memorial in the chancel) who died aged 94 in 1861, was a man, we are informed,

of childlike simplicity,
of unaffected courtesy,
of unblemished reputation,
of unbounded benevolence,
of singular disinterestedness.

His near namesake, Peter Jolliff, who died at 71 in 1730, wore a coat of different cut. 'In the late wars' which would have been Marlborough's, he 'Signaliz'd himself against the French with uncommon Courage And frequently reveng'd their Insolences towards the English By Captivity and Death.'

## PORTLAND

*St George, Reforne*

From either side, St George's looks like three attached buildings: a perfectly handsome city-centre Georgian courthouse in the middle, squeezed between an east-end apse and, on the west, a belfry tower removed from the front of St Paul's Cathedral. This sprightly tower relieves the ugly heaviness of a massive lead roof covering the other two component structures. The whole unlikely hybrid is dramatically ambitious and grand. It is also most strangely sited, amid a flat, almost treeless, acre-and-a-half churchyard of waywardly tilting headstones, within the white windswept wasteland of the old Portland plateau – with its giant cut blocks like the liths of Stonehenge felled and swept into heaps, and huge scooped weed-splotched quarries, fidgety with nibbling or scampering rabbits. It is hard to see where the church's congregation or even its rector could have come from. Indeed there are 19th century reports of the sexton, once the Sunday flock was in place, climbing to a high window and peering through a telescope to bring advance warning of the parson's approach from his distant home.

In fact, in the middle years of the 18th century, there would have been several wealthy quarriers, their numerous employees, and all their families in hamlets scattered round about. Medieval St Andrew's, up to then the island's sole church, perilously situated above Church Ope Cove a couple of miles to the east, could be patched and propped no more. Today's densely populated townships had yet to be built. The site chosen for St George's was at the time perfectly sensible.

St George's was built between 1754 and 1766. Thomas Gilbert, 'GENT. ARCHITECT and Master Builder of this CHURCH', as the wall-plaque describes him, was a Portland native, and grandson of the quarry-owner who supplied the Portland stone for St Paul's, an event commemorated perhaps in the rough resemblance of the church's tower to the cathedral's. No other building design is attributed to Gilbert.

The churchyard contains styles of gravestone very much its own, with deeply sculpted and often beautiful carved relief figures or designs surmounting the incised texts – texts which show that 18th century Portland was a harsh outpost. Quarry workers, choked by daily inhalations of dust, were lucky to last to their forties or fifties. Their wives and children might go before, as did, in 1775, 'Grace, wife of Edward Combe who died in childbed with two daughters who also died, on the 29th of November . . .' There is too a grim profusion of graves of shipwrecked sailors.

Inside, the church has shallow transepts, north and south, and a shallow dome above the crossing. Each transept, and the west end too, contains a large gallery divided by pews and supported on thin columns. The western gallery also holds the organ. Central aisle and apse apart, the ground floor is covered with numbered box pews. The place is practically awash with seating. The apse, with its engraved Ten Commandments and Lord's

*Portland, St George, Reforne. Quarrymen and shipwrecked sailors are remembered by the gravestones in the churchyard.*

Prayer, is curiously small, and the stained glass Crucifixion in its east window is perhaps the church's least attractive feature. The interior's most conspicuous items are the central twin pulpits resting on narrow stems and set either side of the aisle. One – serving as reading desk – would have been used by the parson conducting the service, the other – the pulpit proper – for preaching sermons. What might seem odd here is that the pews to the east of the pulpits are facing, not the altar but the pulpits themselves. This is a rare but not a unique arrangement. There are cases of *all* the seats turning their backs on the altar to face a west-end pulpit. The Sacred Word, in the form of lessons, sermons and liturgy, was still, in Georgian times, taking precedence over the Sacraments, symbolised by the altar. Communion may well have been celebrated only four times a year – certainly no more

*Portland, St George Reforne. The twin central pulpits on their narrow stems.*

than monthly. Not till the 1840s and the coming of the Tractarians, Ritualists and Ecclesiologists, with their insistence on a return to medieval Gothic forms and practices, was the altar generally restored to its ancient prominence.

And yet the pews and much of the rest of St George's furniture, it became clear not long ago, date back, not to the time the church was built, but to a refurbishment carried out during the years 1849-1852, when the Gothic revival in churches was well under way. It clearly had no influence here. A Cornish parson said at about this time that every hundred miles' distance from London took you back a hundred years. St George's on its island, still lacking a road to link it to the mainland, was simply behind the times.

All the same, this is in essence an 18th century church. Both George II and George III contributed to the funding. The exterior could only be Georgian, and, inside, the apse, dome, rounded plaster vault, round-topped windows, and round arches of the crossing are characteristic of 18th century classicism, as is the curvy grace of the 1766 font, signed

by Thomas Gilbert's brother William.

There are some sparse references to people and events. East end plaques commemorate members of important families: Gilbert himself, Penn, Addison. A plaque on the north wall under the west gallery recalls the memory of what is hyperbolically called the Easton Massacre of 1803, in which three Portland youths were killed while resisting the efforts of a naval press-gang to carry them off to the French war. A woman, Mary Way, was also killed in the scuffle. Her grave and that of one of the men are marked to the south of the church. The round and domed bell-room under the ornate west tower (the single bell was cast in 1777) has a panel on one wall showing various ringing routines. 'When a person dies,' it instructs, 'a knell to be rung, and afterwards strike six times for a man and three for a woman . . .'

By the first decade of the 20th century, Portland's population was burgeoning elsewhere, needing – and getting – several new and convenient churches. St George's, unwanted, was demoted to mortuary chapel, then abandoned, bombed during the 1939-45 war, allowed to rot, pillaged, vandalised ('and worse' says the guide) till in the late 1960s a group of locals raised funds and toiled to save it. Due to them, and the Redundant Churches Fund (since 1994 the Churches Conservation Trust), into whose care it was one of the first four churches to be entrusted, no obvious effect of the neglect survives and the church's future seems assured.

## PUDDLETOWN
*St Mary*

Puddletown has been lucky. A few years ago the dissecting route of a main road was budged to a bypass, leaving as its mark only the slight, steady soughing of deflected traffic. The village centre is tranquil, richly green, lushly gardened, with glimpses of manor and other grand and humble houses in square formation around the churchyard. Within it, among a rich crop of yews, stand scattered an unusually good, legible, handsome collection of 18th century and later tombstones, commemorating old Puddletown families: Hand, Kingman, Daw, Cousins, Dunman and so on. Jane Lovelass and John Lovelass Junior lie under adjacent stones, she dead at 21 in 1770, he at 19 in 1771, leaving a stoical message to posterity: 'Short was my time the longer was my rest: God called me hence because he thought it best . . . ' Nearby lies a man remarkable, as far as we are told, for nothing but his name: Zabulon Gape. One of the Antells, John Antell, Hardy's uncle and possible model for Jude, lies here, as does his aunt Maria Sparks, mother of Tryphena, of whom young Hardy thought tenderly. All of them are in a green ground perfectly proportionate and appropriate to the venerable stone church that stands handsome and mostly perpendicular in the middle.

Or, rather, were, for the green ground is no longer so proportionate and appropriate. In 2002 the parish council decided to cut down several churchyard yew trees, and cover in the graves of Hardy's and several other people's relatives to erect a new building of modern design and containing lavatories,

space for meetings and so on. In spite of passionate opposition, the building went ahead. The churchyard will never be so lovely again.

The pity is the greater since St Mary's had emerged magnificently, though not wholly unscarred, from more than eight centuries of existence. There is some evidence of a Saxon foundation, but the oldest parts of the fabric go back to a 12th century building. The tower was built, lower than at present, along with north and south transepts, in the 13th century. But most of what we see is late 15th century work, after which, in 1505, the church was rededicated. In the 17th century most of the furniture was made and installed. That is part of the place's glory. In 1910 the chancel was radically enlarged. That was a pity.

We enter through the north porch by a fine, ancient, broad, battered, curve-topped, iron-nailed, iron-hinged wooden door, and find ourselves in a big well lit interior that simply breathes character. It is a church of stone bones and wooden sinews, for the stone walls and windows, floor flags, chancel arch, and pointed arches of the north aisle are all, in a way, bound or bracketed by wood: the panelled oak roof's laden beams and rafters, the balustraded west end gallery, the clumps of panelled box-pews. The roof (of around 1500) apart, all of these and much more are of precisely the year 1635. The rector of the previous twenty years, a graduate of Cambridge's most puritan college, Emmanuel, had very likely been happy with the plain minimalism of church furniture puritans loved. But now Archbishop Laud's examining envoys compelled attention to ritual and formality. The three-decker pulpit, the screen across the south chapel arch, the communion table, communion rail and other items all date from the same year.

You can see immediately that the 1910 chancel is wrongly proportioned, awkwardly big, a bland annexe to the church's engrossing body in spite of Huntingdon and other memorials and the handsome three-

sided (as opposed to straight-across) altar rail required by Laud. There is also a small 1517 brass to Roger Cheverell, moved to the south wall from the nave floor. But it is the structural grandeur and all the little features and curiosities of nave and south chapel, known as the Athelhampton Chantry, which

*Puddletown, the effigy of the builder of Athelhampton, Sir William Martyn – the family emblem of a chained ape rests at his feet.*

*Puddletown, the fine wooden roof and musicians' gallery.*

are more likely to hold us. There is the gallery, with its wooden shields. One – possibly taken from a ship – is heraldic. The other has a Latin text which translates 'You come here not to be seen but to hear and pray' – a very puritan injunction. Under the gallery four canvas fire buckets hang. They date from 1805, property of the Sun Insurance Company of Bath, and were there to serve the village. (Some churches contained an archetypal fire engine). On a bench near the gallery steps the name 'Henery' is cut. This was Hardy's grandfather, who in early life was one of the players of church music here. Till 1845 music was provided from clarionets, piccolo, bassoon and two bass viols. In that year some kind of barrel organ was introduced and the village

*Puddletown, one of the four canvas fire buckets of 1805.*

*Puddletown, the effigy of one of the Martyns.*

ensemble became resentfully redundant. Hardy's *Under the Greenwood Tree* describes the consequent rancour. Unlike other villages, though, Puddletown retained its gallery and sensibly kept it for music, as the placing of the modern organ shows. Behind it, the royal arms of George II, dated 1753, are painted on the wall.

The beautifully carved Norman font with its conical Jacobean cap stands in the aisle a few yards east of the gallery. Sketchy remains of Queen Elizabeth's royal arms, of which few examples survive, are above the south door. To their east, painted hands hold a painted book with a text from the end of the book of Revelation. It was done in the early 17th century – by the end, since most households had bibles and the ability to read was spread wider, wall texts became rarer, until the Victorian revival.

Between painting and pulpit is the arch leading to the chapel of St Mary Magdalene: the Athelhampton Chantry. It is an astonishing cache of medieval tombs, shrines, brasses, effigies, statues and statuettes. A prone and pious knight (of about 1300) joins his hands in prayer, a robed and wimpled wife turns her eyes devoutly upward, a feistier knight clasps the handle of his sword, as if bent, even in death, on slaying more Saracens. There are friezes and niches of angels and apostles. Not all the figures are identifiable but those that are are Martyns and their forebears and successors. The canopied Purbeck stone altar-tomb lying partially under the arch is thought to be that of Sir William Martyn, Knight, who in 1485 built the magnificent nearby mansion, Athelhampton. He died in 1503, but his alabaster effigy seems to have been made twenty or so years before. Within, to the left, is a mounted brass showing his son Sir Christopher, kneeling, sword in sheath, and praying to God, who is seated. On the south wall is a brass to Sir Nicholas, with his wife, three sons and four daughters. He died in 1595 and brought the male line to an end, all his sons having died before him. The broad, Perpendicular window above shows the arms of the Martyns and many of their kin.

## SHERBORNE ABBEY
*St Mary the Virgin*
In the panoramic view from New Road, which runs along the hill south of the town, the central tower of Sherborne Abbey suggests a huge architectural bird with outspread wings mantling a clutch of lesser buildings widely strewn around her. The warm look of the Ham-stone, of which both the abbey and its surrounds consist, reinforces this impression of maternal care. No other church in Dorset so possessively oversees its setting.

Sherborne was made a bishopric in the year 705. The bishop was the saintly, bustling Aldhelm, famous in his day for hanging his cloak on a sunbeam and converting Saxons to the perplexing Roman method of working

out the date of Easter – cause of one of the bitterest schisms in English history. He started work on a cathedral for the new diocese, and the 13th century of its foundation was commemorated in 2005 by the installation of a sensitive and moving bronze statue of Aldhelm by Marzia Colonna in a niche high on the south porch, the present church's main entrance. The building lost its cathedral status in 1075 when the see was moved to Old Sarum. The northern doorway in the west front of the present church (hidden on the outside by a drab modern porch), as well as some of the central stonework of that front, are remnants of the pre-Conquest, Saxon church. The giveaway to the dating in the case of the door is in the 'long and short work' – alternating horizontal and vertical stones up and down the door jamb.

Meanwhile, in 998, a Benedictine monastery had been founded, whose buildings in due course occupied the land which now contains Sherborne boys' school,

*Sherborne Abbey. Sherborne was made a diocese in 705, and a few fragments of the pre-Conquest Saxon church still survive.*

adjacent to the north side of the abbey. The present abbey church was begun in the early 12th century, in late Norman style.

For a couple of centuries the monks – reluctantly it seems – let the public use the nave as their parish church, reserving the chancel for their own exclusive use. Towards the end of the 14th century, in order to repossess the nave, they built a church, All Hallows, especially for the townspeople. Its east end came right up to the abbey church's west end. Indeed there was a doorway between the two buildings, leading into the abbey's south aisle, and baptisms were still conducted at the font in the abbey's nave. This earned fees for the monks, but did not suit the people, who made a quite illegal font in their own church. Moreover they rang their bells at times when the monks were trying, between periods of prayer, to snatch sleep. For their part, to make life awkward for the citizens, the monks reduced the size of the linking doorway. This remains in place, though completely blocked up now, in the abbey's west wall.

About 1425, following the national trend, the monks started to pull down portions of the nave and choir in order to rebuild them in the new Perpendicular style. The eastern part was temporarily protected by a thatched roof. The spring and summer of 1437 saw popular demonstrations against the monks, who seem to have paid a powerful butcher to smash the citizens' illicit font. Provocation continued and tension mounted until, in October, the All Hallows priest, in support of his parishioners, shot a burning arrow into the abbey choir's thatch. Most of the building took fire, bells melted, timbers and scaffolding fell to the ground. Stone, where it remained standing, was deeply scorched, and some of it bears the marks to this day – particularly in the piers of the crossing and adjacent choir, and conspicuously in the base of one of the choir fans.

The feud rumbled on for years, but so too did the programme of rebuilding. Norman work remained in the nave and transept walls and tower piers, and Early English in the Lady Chapel at the east end and Bishop Roger's Chapel (a vestry now, and not open to the public). But for the most part the outside of the abbey is a solid statement of 15th century Perpendicular.

Hardly had the monastery reached its peak of wealth and size, than the 16th century brought its dissolution. The monks were expelled in 1540 and the buildings bought by Sir John Horsey, one of the great Dorset landowners of the day. He sold the church on to the townspeople, and what had started as a cathedral and continued for four centuries as an abbey church became, as it has since remained, and in spite of the retention of the word 'abbey', a parish church. There is a Bishop of Sherborne but he is a suffragan, serving as assistant to the Bishop of Salisbury and without a see of his own.

The abbey's greatest treasure is the broad span of fan vaulting extending, with changes of pattern, from the nave's west window to the chancel's east. But we can take a brief clockwise walk around the church before settling to examine the ceiling. The huge nave piers, rising smoothly and without the interruption of capitals to their pointed late Norman arches, are elegantly panelled, and hidden within the panels of the western four (which are closer together than the rest) are the original pre-Conquest columns. We pass under the great west window – best seen from the chancel – to the north aisle, covered, like the south, by lierne vaults, a form which preceded fan-vaulting and in which the straight, narrow ribs defining the groined ceiling criss-cross to form additional patterns.

In the north transept we see the fine 1856 organ, its patterned pipes contained in

*Sherborne Abbey, the fan-vaulting in the nave.*

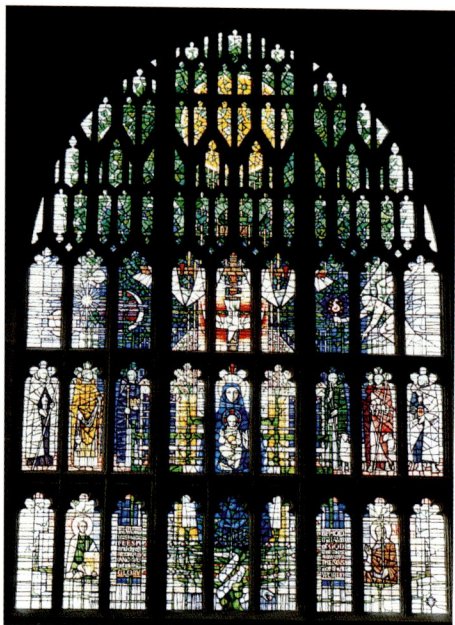

*Sherborne Abbey. John Hayward's west window, commissioned to mark the abbey's Benedictine millennium in 1998.*

curvily carved wooden gothic casing, under a lovely fan-vault, enriched with painted bosses. This vault is a very advanced example of the species; much more elaborate, and probably later – early 16th century – than others in the abbey. In the 1970s its survival was found to be threatened by outward movement of the walls, and a hidden network of steel was constructed to support it from above. Another, very beautiful fan-vault covers the cramped Wykeham Chapel east of the transept. Already it is evident that the form allowed variety. Patterning in the central portion of this ceiling within the fans shows it. So does the curve of the rib containing the fan's top. Corresponding ribs in the abbey's other vaults are not curved but made of a series of straight lines.

The bright white tomb against the north wall, with its two finely carved male effigies, rows of heraldic shields and strong pedimented canopy bearing punningly heraldic horse-heads, marks the grave of Sir John Horsey of Clifton Maybank, he who

bought and sold the church after the Reformation and died in 1546, and his son John, whose death followed eighteen years later. In the north aisle are the sparse remains (mainly the sturdy, bearded face) of a tomb effigy of 1165, thought to be one of the two earliest examples in England and portraying the abbot of the time. Close by, a panel marks the grave of the poet Sir Thomas Wyatt, who died in 1542, the objects of whose love, expressed in subtle, haunting rhymes, are said to have included Anne Boleyn, Henry VIII's doomed second wife. The vaulting of the aisles to either side of the chancel and in the ambulatory – the area behind or to the east of the reredos – are made heavy by a wealth of bosses covering up rib joints. In later vaults their number is much reduced.

This east end – a Lady Chapel with a closed-off vestry to the north and the Chapel of St Mary-le-Bow to the south – is more satisfying to the archaeologist than to the worshipper. First built as a three-bay chapel in the 13th century, when chivalry and the holy passion of the troubadour poets gave strength to the growing cult of the Virgin Mary, it was partly remodelled as the school's headmaster's house after the 16th century Reformation. Its present incarnation, a redesign by the ageing W.D. Caroe in the 1930s, presents something of a mish-mash. Caroe's stately trio of pointed arches leading from ambulatory to Lady Chapel hardly counters the jumbled nature of the areas they enclose and abut. A stern, rectangular barred window presses rather brutally on Caroe's arches. In a small space we try and quite likely fail to assimilate dark Purbeck shafts that seem raised awkwardly aloft, ill-assorted surfaces, odd unions, dusty regimental banners, a gruesome skull (bakelite?) occupying a First World War helmet – all amounting to an uneasy incongruity.

There is much to approve of or admire: a graceful 1657 brass chandelier, probably brought from Holland, perhaps the oldest of its kind in England, the fine 1930s Christopher Webb window showing the

Annunciation and Nativity, the Lady Chapel's ribbed vault (one stage before lierne), the mostly modern screen leading to the Chapel of St Mary-le-Bow, and the 16th century fireplace within. Attracting most attention, forming a not always lit reredos under the east window and not pleasing all tastes, is Laurence Whistler's engraved glass panel of 1967 to 1968, with its strong flavour of adept doodle – all flowers, hearts, horns, and riddle-me-ree allegory in demure symmetry.

Along the south aisle, on the left, the Sepulchre Chapel (reserved for private prayer) reminds us of the antecedents of fan-vaulting, in this case a simple quartered pattern with a ring of linking lierne ribs at its centre. In the neighbouring south transept, with its 19th century copy of a medieval wooden ceiling, the big south window was designed by Pugin and made by John Hardman in 1850. It is one of only a handful of contributions made by Pugin to the county. Inadequate firing has led, as so often elsewhere, to the fading of faces. The design is a serried sequence of ninety-six biblical figures, fitted in uniform groups into the regular main lights, with a further thirty-one angels, cherubs and seraphs in the tracery lights. Pugin liked this kind of ranked arrangement, and it is often admired. He did it in the great south window at Milton Abbey and he or a colleague did it in the old and now replaced west window of the nave here. There is something encyclopaedic about such a tally of scriptural figures – yet you know that all the portraits are invented, so that it is really more ornament than encyclopaedia.

Over to the right, embowered in a sumptuous backdrop of stone armour, swathes of tasselled cloth, putti, scrolls and fluted columns, the figures of John Digby, 3rd Earl of Bristol (he died in 1697, the last of that creation) and his two wives, sumptuously sculpted by John Nost, command attention. His legs placed in that favoured officer-like pose – one foot at right angles to and pointing away from the other – the Earl

*Sherborne Abbey, the altar-tomb of John and Joan Leweston in St Katherine's Chapel.*

displays all the magnificent, pharisaical, posturing vanity his Saviour was at pains to warn us all against. 'He was naturally enclined to avoid the Hurry of a public Life,' runs the inscription, 'Yet careful to keep up the port of his Quality', which seems to mean he liked his honour without effort, or both having and eating his cake.

Next door, in St Katherine's Chapel, under a fan vault with a *square* of liernes in the middle, stands the impressive 1584 altar-tomb of John and Joan Leweston, whose effigies lie in praying pose under a fan-vaulted canopy. He, of ancient Dorset lineage, is in armour, with neatly curled beard and a swirl of a moustache; she wears a ruff, an embroidered gown and many rings. Most of the church's 15th century stained glass that survived the Dissolution is in the two windows of this chapel, scanty but exquisite reminders of 16th century vandalism.

So to the centre, the crossing, choir and sanctuary, with great sweeps of fan vaulting stretching away over the nave to the west window: a controversial millennial replacement of the old Pugin window, strikingly bright, over-detailed perhaps in parts, in others scrappy, with its pale edging giving an impression of premature fading. Under the rear rows of choir stalls is a collection of those fine wooden carvings – misericords,

*Sherborne Abbey, the choir and chancel.*

seats of pity or compassion – designed to buttress the backsides of clerks forced to stand each day through hours of worship, and a chance for the carver to forget solemnity in fashioning, for instance, a man in a tussle with a lion, Christ at the Last Judgment, saints, vegetation, a schoolmaster birching a boy's bared bottom, a chained monkey or a woman knocking a man about. There are other superb carvings on stalls and bench-ends.

Eyes are soon drawn up to the fan vault, an exquisitely delicate form of ornament, spraying out from corner piers or corbels. The style developed, as part of the Perpendicular style, in England alone while the Continent hurried forward to Flamboyant and Baroque. The earliest example is in the cloisters of Gloucester Cathedral, but it was here at Sherborne that the brave step of vaulting a really wide roof-space was taken. The vault above the choir was begun before the great 1437 fire, devastated by it and resumed after. The vault above the crossing is of the same pattern, that of the nave differing in detail. Both were done later in the 15th century. Sherborne's fan-vault is not as wide nor as fancy with rings and pendants as those of Bath, Peterborough, King's College, Cambridge, or Westminster Abbey – but these were done after 1500. (The latest major example is made ingeniously of concrete panels, inserted in Eton College Chapel in 1959, and replacing a rotted

timber roof). Spacing and clarity of design make Sherborne's one of the most satisfying. For some, the warm colours (added by Victorians) of the contained panels at the east end make this the most beautiful part of the building, others prefer the barer elegance of the nave. Detailed scrutiny, preferably with the help of binoculars, brings out the charming designs – heads, animals, heraldry, scenes – on the bosses, placed where main ribs intersect.

## SILTON
*St Nicholas*

It is not easy to find, but worth the journey, worth the detour, worth the wrong turnings and poor signing in this northern flap of Dorset flung across the green and fertile Somerset borderlands. Around the antique asymmetry of the church a broad, bumpy but uncluttered graveyard stretches to a stone boundary wall. Some 17th century table tombs survive. Across the wall, to the east, you see a field falling away, an oak tree of massive girth – some thirty-five foot – lake, woods, fields and distant hills and the towers

*Silton, showing the lovely 1869-70 stencilling by Clayton and Bell.*

of at least three more churches.

Silton has a thousand years or so of past – the first church was certainly Saxon – but almost no history. Few such sequestered hamlets do have, there being seldom anyone about who could or cared to write it. The accretion of pitch roofed aisles and chapels and the features they enclose tell us the outlines. The Saxon and Norman churches would have been simple. The late Norman south aisle, divided from the central aisle by a pointed-arched arcade, would have been added around 1300. But in essence the church is 15th century and Perpendicular. Off the chancel to the north is what was a chantry chapel, also 15th century, provided for the recital by a paid priest, daily and in permanence, of prayers pleading for the soul of some local grandee buried below. The Reformation would have done for that. Priest, sepulchre, even the subject's name are gone and forgotten now. But a fine fan-vault remains, sadly forbidden to the public since the room is now a vestry.

*Silton. The memorial to Sir Hugh Wyndham, flanked by the weeping figures of two of his three wives.*

The south porch dates from the early 16th century. But much of Silton's present character comes from two features of later date, and the porch interior prepares us for one. Its colourfully painted wagon roof is decorated with gold-painted bosses and stencil work. Within the church, light is at a premium but the place is dense with decoration, crammed with colour: more gold bosses, stencilling in spandrels and interstices of roofs, on walls, even the organ. Some south aisle bosses are decorated with swastikas – the name comes from the Sanskrit for well-being – a symbol of rebirth and revival used in the East as well as Europe and the Middle East in prehistoric times. Early Christians made it a symbol of Christ's resurrection or of the Second Coming, and its sinister link with Nazis is entirely of our time.

All this is the work of Victorians – Clayton and Bell, famous for stained glass, did the stencilling in 1869-70 when a major restoration took place. The east window has a stained glass Crucifixion, with the usual bleak piety on the faces of spectators. But ahead of us, against the north wall

(reinforced for the purpose, as can be seen from outside) somewhat eerie if the light is poor, looms the pale but grandiose stone figure of Sir Hugh Wyndham, dressed as a judge, smiling serenely, proffering a scroll with his right hand, his death (in 1684) mourned by two cloaked females at his feet. These are the first two of his three wives, one holding a shell, the other an hour-glass. Barley-sugar columns hold up a round arch topped with heraldic shields and drapes of vegetation. John Nost was the sculptor. He did the equally posturing, even more splendid Digby monument in Sherborne Abbey. Here, his sensitive fashioning, seen in the serene smile, the natural fall of clothes, the slight swell of the belly under Wyndham's belt, seem absent from the other figures, possibly wrought by assistants. This baroque memorial stood originally against the chancel's south wall, and Wyndham's remains lie in a vault under the chancel floor. In life, Wyndham, who bought the manor house, was said to have liked sitting under the massive oak tree we have noticed already in the field below the graveyard.

Wyndhams came in the 16th century from Norfolk to the West Country, through marriage to a Sydenham heiress. Their main estate became Orchard in Somerset, but they proliferated in central and north Dorset, intermarrying with many local gentry families. Other Wyndham memorials are described at Minterne and Trent.

Over the south door hang the royal arms of the present queen, Elizabeth II.

## ST ALDHELM'S CHAPEL

Strong, solid, 25-foot square, thickly buttressed and, over the years, much rebolstered against wind, the stone chapel stands a few yards from the cliffs of this swollen headland – south tip of the Isle of Purbeck. The chapel goes back to the Normans, but why they built it is not clear. There is the story of a man watching helpless from here as his newly married daughter and

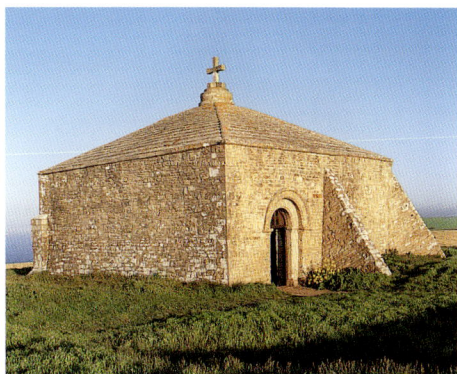

ABOVE *St Aldhelm's Chapel, overlooking the sea on the cliffs at St Aldhelm's Head.*

RIGHT *St Aldhelm's Chapel, the stone and vaulted interior.*

her bridegroom were wrecked and drowned 350 feet below by a sudden squall, and building a chapel in their memory with an ever-burning lamp to warn sailors of the rocks below. Perhaps it was a chantry chapel for the drowned. Or the simple urge to plant God's flag among the inimical winds and cold of territory that seemed naturally the Devil's (on occasion in recent centuries it has been known as the Devil's Chapel). It seems certain to have been built in the early 12th century, four hundred years after St Aldhelm, first bishop of Sherborne, toured Wessex, and presumably came here as a missionary.

There is little around but a coastguard lookout, a row of whitewashed coastguard cottages, pasture and ploughland, the coastpath, a rambler or two and, a few yards south-east, a bronze sculpture, like the skeleton of a hemisphere, commemorating the vanished RAF station, with a camp stretching to Worth Matravers a mile away, in which important experiments were done with radar during World War Two. Ancient graves have been found within a quarter of a mile. On cliffs a hundred yards to the south, clean-cut shelves and ledges on the cliffs are the imprinted relic of stone quarries. The Isle of Portland, the long wedge-shaped silhouette to the west, ends a magnificent view (on a clear day) of loping green downs

and chalk-white headlands.

St Aldhelm's does not look like a chapel, though there is a record from the mid 13th century of a chaplain paid fifty shillings a year. At about ten yards distance an irregular earthwork, three feet high at its highest, surrounds it. Within the east face of that are remains of a crude, tiny building claimed by some to have housed a Saxon hermit. The chapel's corners point to the compass points, so there is not the usual (though by no means invariable) east-west orientation. It is built symmetrically round a central thick pier, which at a packed service would block important views of most of the congregation. The modern altar, as presumably the original one, stands a little awkwardly in the east corner.

For all that it is a deeply impressive chamber. The entrance is by a brawny round-arched door in the north-west wall. As the interior darkness sufficiently lightens, the massive central pier emerges, heavily engraved with initials, supporting a spray of ribs; four of them dividing the chapel's space into four quarters, while four alternating ribs rise to support, along with cross-ribs, one of the four resulting vaults. Sometimes architecture creates material features – of stone or wood or brick – to admire in themselves. Sometimes – and this is a case – it is more the *spaces* thus created which impress and intrigue the eye. St Aldhelm's possesses a certain spatial enchantment.

It keeps its history mostly to itself. It overlooked the passage of the Spanish Armada in 1588 and saw the Battle of Portland and, next day, an attack by Drake close by. Innumerable shipwrecks have occurred in sight of it, with bodies and debris washed up on the rocks below. In the 17th century and 18th century it was neglected. Part of the roof fell in, though some old initials on the central pier, and pins later retrieved from an aperture within it, point to a habit of depositing these in superstitious hope of marriage. From time immemorial a procession of locals was held on Whit Thursday, with music and dancing. In 1874, after a full restoration at the expense of Lord Eldon of the surrounding estate of Encombe – he who caused the building of the second church at Kingston – St Aldhelm's resumed its religious functions, albeit irregularly. Nowadays there tend to be evening Sunday services in late July and August. Some gatherings have been organized by the ecumenical Taizé community

## STINSFORD
### St Michael

The church, with the old redbrick vicarage on one side and pale stone manor-house, recently revamped, cut into flats and hemmed by a score of new houses, on the other, has become a place of pilgrimage. The veneration is of course directed at Thomas Hardy. He was born a mile to the north-east, at Bockhampton, and lived most of his adult years at Max Gate, which he designed, a mile to the west. His father, uncle and grandfather had played fiddles and cello in the gallery during services, until in 1843 a new vicar (like many others about this time) imported a new organ, and did away with the need of them. The Hardys loathed this disdainful vicar, Arthur Shirley, who once preached a sermon, probably aimed at them, denouncing

*Stinsford. After Thomas Hardy's death in 1928 his heart was buried amongst the Hardy family graves in the churchyard.*

ambition in the humbly born. Baptised here, Hardy was led by experience and the observation of his maturity to forgo faith in God. Fate, with an ironic smile, was the great power, toying with the lives of paltry humans. Still, from coming to church regularly as a boy, Hardy knew the Sunday services by heart, taught at Sunday school and never entirely gave up attendance at the church. One Christmas in his old age, he saw the ghost of his grandfather emerge from his grave and greet him. The ashes of most of him are buried, against the instructions of his written will, in Westminster Abbey. The heart, cut out by a surgeon and placed in a small box, was buried beside his first wife (the second arrived later) in the line of Hardy family graves on the left of the path after you enter the churchyard. Not everyone took the arrangement seriously. 'Almighty', 'e'll say, "Ere be 'eart, but where be rest of 'e?' was repeated locally, while it was rumoured that the vital organ was consumed by a cat the night before interment.

With its gently sloping walled churchyard and woods beyond, St Michael's makes a handsome picture, though with the exception of the battlemented south aisle its defining outlines are plain. Since the raising of the nave roof in 1870, the west tower is relatively short. The chancel and nave arcades, with, as we shall see, pointed arches and compound piers, are 13th century: Early English. The tower is early 14th century, and the upper half has no buttresses. The south aisle is 15th century Perpendicular. The north aisle, west tower window and chancel's barrel roof date from the 17th century. Inside, the initial impression is of a rather cosy, almost crimped nave giving on to a generous chancel and north and south aisles. The feeling of constriction is increased by the outward lean of the Early English chancel arch's sides (with the unusual lines of its unbroken mouldings), as if bulging from a basal corset.

A sensible soullessness seems to preside. Parquet flooring has long ago replaced the old flagstones, and individual chairs the box pews Hardy knew: a victory of bottom over eye. Much of the enamelled Victorian glass has lost detail and been replaced by clear glass. Eight foot high wooden panelling round the whole interior (some of it the recycled box-pews), though it helps pull the place together, seems a little incongruous. Otherwise the appeal lies in detail and links – and not only with Hardy.

The font on the west of the nave has survived eight centuries, having been at some stage broken into seven pieces before a full restoration in 1920. In the south aisle, past the south arcade's west respond – the shapely half-column, surmounted by its capital's rich, deep-cut leaves, and engaging with the outer wall – a honeystone Saxon relief of the wide-winged archangel Michael is set high on the western wall, transferred in 1996 from the tower's outer wall to free it from weather's further wear and tear. Eastwards along the south wall comes a striking window of 1930 by Douglas Strachan, illustrating an episode in the Book of Kings. The prophet Elijah, discouraged by failure, watches from a cave on Mount Sinai the effects of a freakish succession of storm, earthquake and fire but only recognises the presence of God – who needs no pomp or show – when he hears a still small voice speak out. The passage was a favourite of Hardy's, and he has the moralistic Henry Knight read it in *A Pair of Blue Eyes*. Not a believer, but convinced that

ABOVE *Stinsford, showing the battlemented south aisle.*

BELOW *Stinsford. Douglas Strachan's 1930 Thomas Hardy Memorial Window illustrates a favourite passage of Hardy's from the Book of Kings.*

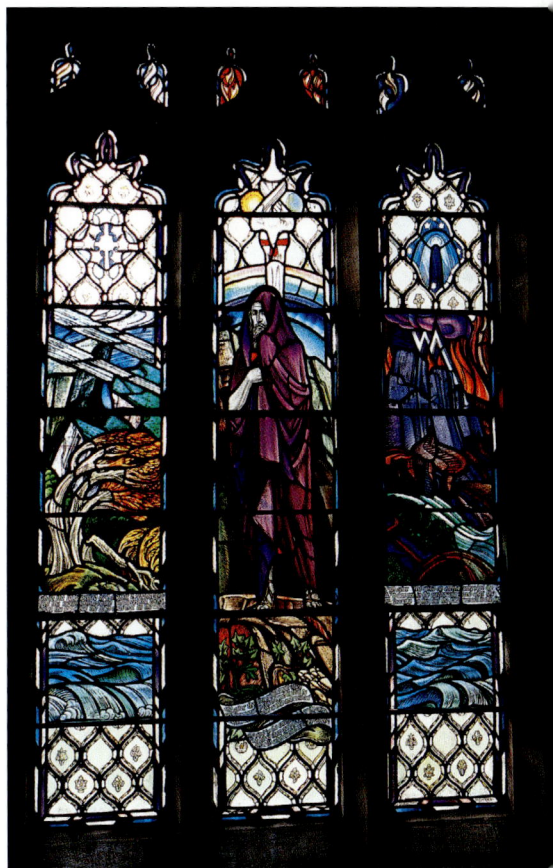

*Studland. The oldest and purest Norman church in Dorset, and one of only a handful in the country.*

church-going was 'a moral drill', Hardy always attended when this lesson was read, and the window is a memorial to him. Left of it, above the piscina or washing bowl, is an elaborate 15th century niche.

The chancel is dull but commemorates an old romance. Lady Susan Fox-Strangways, daughter of the Earl of Ilchester, resident at Melbury some twelve miles north-west, horrified her noble family by eloping in 1764 with William O'Brien, a glamorous Catholic Irish actor. Each attribute must have seemed worse in their eyes than the last. Horace Walpole was unwilling to believe she could 'stoop so low'. They choked his acting career, though he was brilliant, and got him lucrative, dull sinecures in America. On his and Susan's final return they were given Stinsford manor house. They were still in love, childless, and lived on, he to 1815, she to 1827. Giving orders for their vault, she said they must be together and alone. So they lie nearby, in a tomb just big enough for the two of them, with twin plaques to mark their

presence.

What seems to be the organ opposite is no more than the facade of the instrument given by Hardy's youngest sister Kate in 1931, and recently replaced by the modern model on the new west gallery. Round the corner is the north aisle, with impressive wall memorials, to the Grey family, 17th century owners of nearby Kingston Maurward, and the Pitt family who succeeded them through marriage. John Pitt's second son George, we read, died in 1769 aged fourteen, 'speedily . . . taken away, Lest Wickedess should enter his Understanding or deceit beguile his Soule'. The earliest Grey's Christian name was Angell, doubtless the source of Tess of the Durbervilles' vacillating lover. In these parts Hardy is never far away.

## STUDLAND
*St Nicholas*

Set on rising ground, three hundred metres from the broad sweep of Studland's beach, the church of St Nicholas crouches resigned – under its short, saddle-back tower, strapped in by buttresses – to the worst that foreign men-of-war, privateers, wind or storm could or can throw against it. Its gruff facades are in contrast to the neatness of a crowded graveyard, adjacent farm and terrace of houses, all once part of the 25,000 acre Bankes estate, now owned and groomed by the National Trust. A parallel contrast obtains inside. As you enter the church, your eyes are drawn to the dour, dark stone of the central rounded Norman arches, scarred, pitted, cracked and age-stained so that slipped segments seem ready to crash to the ground and bring the dependent tower to ruins. This louche antiquity disdains the genteel appurtenances of later periods: the dull, smooth wood of 1910 pews and west gallery front, the brass-eagle lectern and roll-top harmonium, the pretty kneelers and scattering of marble wall-plaques. The oldest, and nearest to pure Norman church in Dorset (and only one of a dozen so complete in the

*Studland. Animal and human heads adorn the corbel tables along the nave walls.*

country) appears to begrudge the help of subsequent people and styles. The square of the tower base must be as Norman a space as there is in England, its moulded groins rising from the simple cushion capitals of the corner columns and meeting above in a canopy of whitewash. The floor below, raised a step above that of the nave, may have been the original site of the altar, with the eastern sanctuary serving as Lady Chapel at a time when the Blessed Virgin commanded fierce affection and loyalty.

There was a church here long before the Normans. (A mile inland, on the heath, the massive Agglestone may, if 'aggle' derives as it probably does from 'halig' or holy, carry local worship immeasurably far back). Signs of pre-Saxon burials have been unearthed during excavations. St Aldhelm, busy sprinkling the blessings of Christianity among the West Saxons hereabouts in the late seventh century, may have founded it. Traces of the first Saxon building survive and some can be seen, in some irregular stonework at the church's western end and more on the chancel's outer walls. Ninth century Viking raids reduced the church to its walls. It was rebuilt in the 11th century before the Normans came, and to a large extent again, much as it it now, in the 12th; though buttresses and the Early English east

window are likely to be of the thirteenth, and the gallery – bar its 1910 oak frontage – and enlarged windows in the south and west walls and the porch are all 18th century. Some original headings of the expanded windows, long plastered in, are visible. The

*Studland. Rounded Norman arches lead into the choir and chancel.*

tower is thought to have been limited to its present height because of fears that the weight of more stones – the foundations being flimsy – would sink it. As it is, massive concrete infill of 1881, together with grouting and the insertion of iron tie-bars (two visible under the arches) keep the thing in place. A small doorway high on the outside north wall of the sanctuary leads to a room or space of unknown purpose. Two lines of Norman corbels on the outside of the nave's north and south walls are adorned with a variety of animal and human heads and more puzzling symbols.

In spite of earlier precautions the tower leaned, by the late 19th century, a foot to the south. Other faults and fractures menaced other parts. Spasmodic but radical restoration over the next half-century brought the church to a stable security. Much was changed. Old box pews were replaced in the 1880s and the pitch-pine replacements themselves replaced in 1910. The gift of the organ in 1937 marked George VI's coronation. Choir stalls arrived in 1960. Traces of paintwork over the north door and western chancel arch are all that is left of original 12th century frescoes, almost entirely removed with the old plaster in 1909.

From that span of thirteen hundred years a mere handful of the thousands of parsons and parishioners, lords and vassals, knights and damsels, pirates and smugglers are commemorated in or outside the building: the Peninsular War and Waterloo veteran, Sergeant William Lawrence, and his French bride Clotilde; a 19th century bishop of Zanzibar, dead and dunked in the Indian Ocean; a rector's son, at 40 Queen's advocate for the colony of Sierra Leone, the White Man's Grave, dead at 41 'from the fatal effects of the climate' in 1872; Francis Fane 'of the Westmorland family', MP for Lyme and Dorchester, buried in the chancel. It seems the village idiot foretold his death, after which he spoke not a word but died aged 61 in 1813.

# SUTTON WALDRON
*St Bartholomew*

From a distance, buttresses flying from the four corners of the tower below give a graceful lift to the delicate spire. Closer to, in its lush graveyard behind handsome iron railings, St Bartholomew's shows off its mostly flint walls, mullioned windows, curvey Decorated tracery, roof tiles of different shades arranged in formations, gargoyles lunging from the tower top, a battery of well cut corbel heads, an overall air of good grooming – all this dating from the year 1847. Tucked into the external angle between the chancel and the vestry giving off it to the north, is the massive table-tomb of Canon Anthony Huxtable, who caused the church to be built, and of his first wife Maria, who payed the costs and played the organ. His second wife, who cared for him in his declining years, lies close by, beneath a modester cover.

East of the church, the graveyard drops steeply down to some woodland, and beyond that to the fertile undulations of the Iwerne river valley. Close to the trees the old church stood, and the little wood is populated by stooping gravestones, like friendly old people, grey and shaggy with lichens and ivy. Some stones preserve names of the 19th century dead and buried – Applin, Young, Bradley – but the crosses among them look curiously medieval, webbed by undergrowth beneath a canopy of elder, yew, laurel, larch and hazel. Even while the odd aeroplane from Compton Abbas aerodrome drones above, you can imagine some burrowing animal beckoning children to a magic subterranean world.

I suppose I should not disclose, any more than the end of a mystery story, what waits for the visitor coming into the church. When I saw it for the first time, it came as an enchanting surprise. I can only hope what I write is read during or after – and not before your visit. Anthony Huxtable's architect for the new church was George Alexander, who had done a couple of others nearby. For St Bartholomew's

*Sutton Waldron. Flying buttresses support the delicate spire, a landmark in the Iwerne Valley north of Blandford.*

*Sutton Waldron, showing the richly coloured recently restored decoration, originally the work of Owen Jones in the 1850s.*

he had a colleague, Owen Jones (1809-74), whose travels in the Mediterranean and Near East, examining Arabic and Moorish decorative arts, strengthened his belief that England was sorely in need of colour. 'Form without colour,' he wrote, 'is like a body without a soul.' He studied the use of colour and ornament in medieval churches, devised principles for their use in new structures and wrote books which thousands read and followed. He would soon be supervising the interior decoration of the halls of the Great Exhibition and the Crystal Palace. His reputation was up with those of Pugin, Ruskin and Morris. But Morris found his work too bright and formal and eventually eclipsed him with his richer, livelier, more organic and more prolific designs. What we have inside St Bartholomew's is a rare reconstruction of one of Jones's earlier and smaller works.

Twenty-five years ago the church was in a dismal state. Pevsner had had little to say of it: 'Rather ignorant tracery . . . dull interior . . .' The roof let in rain, much of Jones's

work had been painted over, and there was a proposal to whitewash everything inside. But a case for restoration was made and Jones's scheme was gradually uncovered: pale blue walls, black-lettered texts running around the top of them, mouldings of the south aisle piers picked out in dark blue and gold to alternate with stripes of bare stone. Floor tiles are nicely patterned – Pugin's design. The windows, their tinted glass decorated with stylised plants and abstract motifs, let in plenty of light. Chancel colouring is deeper, lusher and darker. The moulded chancel arch is a bit like the side of an open pattern book, blues and reds and golds overlapping each other like page edges. The walls are deep red. The east window, perhaps by William Warrington but not remarkable for draughtsmanship, is in bold colours. Colour is everywhere, and the ceiling is a blue sky with gold stars cut by beams bearing scrolled texts. Return from this intensity to the nave's cool blues can be like quenching thirst.

The simple squared stone pulpit and

*Sydling St Nicholas. The millstone headstone of Sydling's last miller is visible on the right.*

lectern, chancel piscina, and other features and fitments show the powerful influence of the Ecclesiologists, the early Victorian reformers whose mission was to return almost all churches to designs of the Decorated Gothic period. It is a model church, but with power and personality. Betjeman (though he left it out of the first edition of *English Parish Churches*) called it 'one of the best and most lovely examples of Victorian architecture'.

For Anthony Huxtable, however, aesthetics were not the first concern. Over several years, manure was. Friend of Charles Kingsley and of his neighbour, the reforming parson Sidney Godolphin Osborne, he served his parishioners, at a time of agricultural slump and growing competition from imports, by helping them keep abreast of continental and American farming techniques. He had leanings towards science, and did accurately measured and recorded experiments on different sorts of dung, introducing steam power to distribute liquid manure round his farmlands. His work on the filtration of water was a stage in the development of modern sewage management. But such unecclesiastical stuff is not recorded in his church.

## SYDLING ST NICHOLAS
*St Nicholas*

A Celtic saint worth his salt could certainly, had people been scarce, have mustered a congregation of deer and buzzards here. Sydling is as beautifully and rurally placed as any church in Dorset, at the end of a walled track, looking over the raffishly gothicised Sydling Court (its hoodmoulds 'very ignorant' rasps Pevsner), a buttressed medieval tithe barn, a sprawl of uncluttered, bumpy churchyard and a roller-coaster of woody hills beyond, in one of the county's quietest chalk-stream-and-watercress valleys. The church authorities have made a different contribution to the scene. Squashed into the corner between tower and south aisle is a modern shed, as nasty a concrete excrescence as you could imagine amid the ancient, lichened ashlar and flint of this handsome church.

Sydling is a 15th century rebuilding of an earlier church, itself a rebuilding too. Of the present building, the tower is earlier than the rest – about 1430. Nave, north porch and south aisle followed, the latter about 1500. The windows and other features are in the neat, serried style of late Perpendicular. Burly in the middle of the south aisle, like nightclub bouncers guarding the small south door, are two impressive outsize buttresses, boasting belts of quatrefoil ornament. The tower, propped by buttresses, topped by battlements and single crocketed pinnacles at the corners, with gargoyles below, contains a famous heard but not seen clock dating from 1593, the oldest of its kind in the country. In the churchyard is a huddle of fine table tombs of the Devenish family, and two others with skull and crossbones reliefs. A more recent grave, of Robert Spriggs 'the last miller of Sydling', who died in 1919, is surmounted by an inscribed millstone, about four foot across.

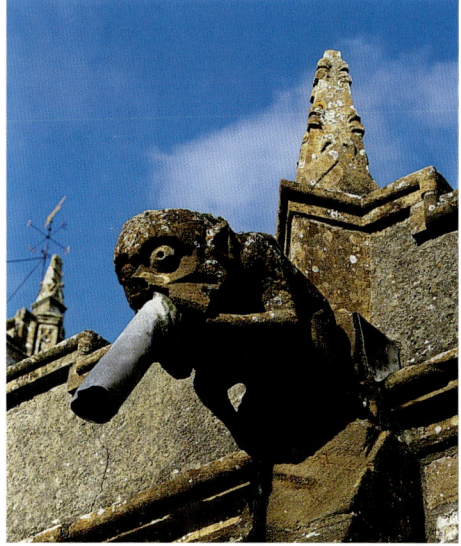

*Sydling St Nicholas. Strangely-shaped gargoyles help carry rainwater away from the roof.*

The north porch, like the south door, stands at the centre of the aisle wall. A stone bishop's mitre, probably brought from elsewhere, sits above it, and there is an original fireplace inside. A porch was once a more important space than it is now; even weddings took place there in some circumstances. To those entering the church in the morning, the sun's rays through the three-light, plain-glass east window can dazzle, especially since the chancel walls are white and the nave and aisle walls buff. (The pastoral view through the window may be due to Cromwell's men smashing the stained glass). Nave pews are ordinary, but in the south aisle 18th century box-pews of various sizes are preserved. Above are two Smith family hatchments with the motto *Semper fidelis* – 'always faithful'. The nave roof's trusses are of 1500. There is no longer a west end gallery, and under the tall arch leading into the tower, above an 18th century screen and the simply decorated 12th century font, hangs a sort of collage of fragments of old glass. The south arcade leans heavily outwards, explaining the two heavy buttresses outside. The royal arms of George I hang over the north door. Bosses at the intersections of ribs in the handsome wagon roof are original, though the paintwork is distinctly not and looks too thick. The stone head of a man, once serving as a corbel, sits in the squint. All the time you remain in the church you hear the ticking of the tower clock, and before and after the hourly strike a mechanical wheezing that sounds asthmatic.

A fine cartouche on the north nave wall commemorates Timothy Stoodly, an early 18th century vicar who died in 1724, and there is an earlier one, to Catharine Martine Gent who died in 1704, screened by the organ at the east end of the south aisle. But we may quickly forget these as we move up three steps to the broad expanse of a chancel that seems given over to ancestor worship and specifically Smith worship, its walls crammed with ornamental testimonials to a century or two of the tribe, while their earthly remains lie neatly arranged (presumably) in the family vault below. There is little room for the commemoration of non-Smiths. A couple of vicars slip in, as does the seventh earl of Guilford, perhaps on the grounds of rank, dead 'from an accident

*Sydling St Nicholas. Beyond the Georgian box pews is the chancel, its walls crammed with memorials to the Smith family.*

up conditions quite alien to modern life. There is Mary, 'mother of twelve children, three only of whom she left behind'; and Elizabeth, relict of Robert, 'whom losing early in life, she remained his widow 49 years till death reunited them'; or another Elizabeth 'taken from her lamenting Husband and Friends at the early age of 22 Years'. There is the Reverend Edmund, died in 1814, whose tribute sheds light on church matters of the early 19th century. In nearly 33 years, he 'was not absent from his parochial duties more than three months. In consequence of this conduct (well worthy of Imitation) There were not amongst his Parishioners Any who dissented from the Established Church [a serious concern of the time] and very few who ever neglected its weekly service.' Marriages of family members into the aristocracy – Duke of Roxburgh, a son of the Earl of Dunraven – are fondly recorded. As the 19th century proceeds, a formal piety and modesty enters the inscriptions. Dying in 1807, Sir John Smith's good character is entrusted to heaven, to 'the unfeigned regret of his family, numerous friends and of the

*Sydling St Nicholas. The memorial to Elizabeth Smith.*

while hunting the Sydling Hounds, 19 December 1885'. Essentially, though, this is the tabernacle of the Smiths or, as some of them became, following the Smith tendency to introduce a second barrel, the Wyldbore Smiths.

Did they simply close their ears, we might ask, those Wyldbore Smiths, when the lesson about the boasting Pharisee was read in front of them? Did they not consider the worthies of their own or a later time who might deserve some of the space they so comprehensively covered; especially since, in due course, they were to move away to other counties and even, as is the patrician way when inheritances beckon, to change their name (while hanging on to the baronetcy) to Smith-Marriott? But, ethics apart, there is visual and historical appeal in this tribal display, and a wonderful eloquence, and a sprinkling of facts and phrases that summon distressed to whom his bounty was ever directed with a willing hand', while his successor, twenty years later, 'on no presumed merits of his own, but on those only of a crucified redeemer, rested his fervent hope of salvation . . .'

These last two memorials are very large, occupying a considerable part of the chancel's south wall. They carry on, with fine artistry, an 18th century tradition of standing or kneeling mourners, urns, arches, elegant, tearless grief; and for all their eyewash they give the church a display of elegant historic sentiment others have thrown away in the interest of fair play and equality.

## TARRANT CRAWFORD
### St Mary

You might wonder what could justify the building of a church in this remote rural spot, yet at the time it happened, 800 years ago or a little less, there was not simply a village hereabouts but one of the Cistercians' wealthiest English convents. And rural seclusion was the Cistercian ideal. The church's surrounds now comprise bumpy churchyard, badger sett, trees, rookery, stream babbling along the border, and, comfortably distant, a big house – Crawford Abbey – and farm buildings. Through the care and encouragement of the farmer, flocks of lapwings may be seen. You get to the church, from east or west, by footpath. Officially redundant, it holds no regular services. With its west tower and porch of knapped flint and other local stones, its plastered nave, its tiled roof fringed with stone slates, and windows at uneven heights, it is as remote, quiet, self-effacing, singular and sleepy as a church can be.

Inside, though not grand, it is a lovely composition of greys, browns and rusty ochre. The greys are stone floor flags and the greensand arches of window frames. Browns are various woods – dark pews refashioned from 17th century box pews, wall panels, pyramidal font cover, Jacobean pulpit, altar

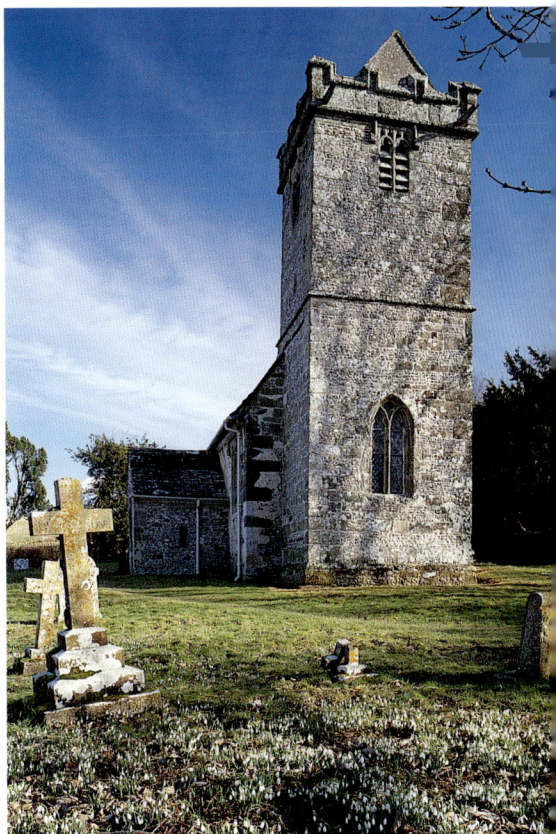

*Tarrant Crawford, now isolated at the end of a lane but once the site of one of England's wealthiest convents.*

railings, fretted modern altar-front and the paler, serried arches of the vault. The russet is from the blurred, remnant medieval murals of the south nave wall. The church does seem to preserve a trace or two of former greatness. On either side of the altar lies a coffin-lid. Because a queen (Joan, sister of Henry III, daughter of King John and childless wife of Alexander II of Scotland) and a bishop were once buried in the nearby convent church, it used to be said, wishfully, that these lids had belonged to their coffins; but they, and others found round and about, including one functioning now as window-sill to the nave's easternmost window, are more likely to have covered the remains of abbesses or lesser worthies.

*Tarrant Crawford, showing the medieval wall paintings on the wall of the nave.*

The barns and the house retain fragments of old convent buildings, though nobody is quite sure how these were arranged. They may have come right up to the south side of the church, and been a reason for inserting the main door on the north. Our church was not part of the nunnery but a private affair. The present chancel was built in the 12th century by Ralph de Kahaines, the local grandee. The thin, flat, late Norman buttress at the north-east corner, and the inside of the blocked priest's door in the chancel's south wall show that. It has been thought that Ralph also endowed a retreat for women next door: the first were three well-born sisters, young to start with, possibly dedicated by their father to God to avoid the expense of three dowries. For them a 13th century work called *The Ancren Riwle – The Anchoress's Rule* – was written by, very likely, Richard Poore, bishop of Salisbury and founder of its cathedral, who had been born here at Tarrant, was to die here in 1337, was buried here and is the bishop linked with one of the coffin lids by the altar. The ladies had servants and a cat but could only talk to visitors through a window containing a grille hung with a black curtain, and watch the conduct of holy communion through a window they shared with the church. The author of the *Rule* confidently sees their almost constant praying, meditating, confessing, and sewing clothes for the poor – on two meals a day and none on Friday – as their flight towards heaven.

Whatever the truth about Ralph's early foundation and the *Rule*, the Cistercian nunnery was built in the middle of the 13th century, with its own conventual church. Both convent and its church disappeared after the Reformation. Travelling through in 1620, John Gerard saw no trace of them. St Mary's on the other hand served the village, although this possibly stood half a mile south in order to provide the nunnery with room and – the Cistercian essential – quiet. The present nave and the windows of the chancel were made in the 13th century (reminding us once more to avoid the assumption that the date of a window is the same as that of the wall that contains it), and the wall paintings, started then, were largely accomplished in the early 14th century. Tower and porch were added around the end of the 15th century, and, as we have seen, a good deal of the wooden furniture in the 17th century.

When modern restoration came to St Mary's it came late, in two shots: in 1895-6 and 1910-11 – and sensitively, at the hands of

Charles Ponting, architect to the diocese of Salisbury. It would, it is true, have been preferable if he had left the lime plaster on all walls and refrained from sawing up the oak box pews to make panelling and standard benches, but he was not to know that the demand for seating would virtually disappear within a century.

Ponting's 1910-11 stint uncovered the wall paintings, which had probably been plastered over – easiest method of putting them out of sight – at the time of the Reformation. Full disclosure had to wait till after the Second World War. Various subjects are depicted on the nave's north wall, including (as on many north walls) St Christopher carrying Christ over a stream. In the nave's south-east corner there is an Annunciation: St Gabriel and the Virgin with a lily between them. But the main surviving paintings, faint and in many cases needing informed guesswork to interpret them, occupy two rows on the south wall. Their content is not jolly. The lower row illustrates a Flemish morality poem of the late 13th century. Out hunting, three young kings – debonair, richly dressed – come suddenly on three animated corpses, standing in their path. The dead warn the living: 'As you are so were we; as we are so shall you be'. This reminder doubtless chastened congregations by no means surfeited with merriment in the age of the Black Death. The upper row portrays, more completely than any other depiction in the country, scenes from the life of St Margaret of Antioch, whose endurance of the rack, beatings, having her bones scraped bare with iron rakes, being swallowed by a dragon, being hung up by her hair, burned and finally beheaded rather than yield her virginity to a Roman bully made her a very popular heroine. She would also intercede with God for the good health of any woman who called on her during childbirth. Only St Catherine had more churches dedicated to her. All this has alas proved too much for a more sceptical age, and Margaret was omitted from the revised official Catholic calendar of 1969.

*Tarrant Rushton, flint walls with quoins of local heathstone.*

## TARRANT RUSHTON
*St Mary*

A photograph in the folder of notes kept for reference in the church shows it and its surrounds in 1930: two or three village cottages, bare fields, wavy horizon. In the 1960s trees were planted on all sides of the rectangular grassed churchyard. The view was slowly eclipsed. Today the place is cosily bounded by a thick perimeter of beech, birch, yew and other conifers rising in some cases to a hundred feet and more, some of them draped in summer with wild roses and bramble. At the end of a little lane that goes nowhere else, Tarrant Rushton church has become a charmingly private, almost a secret place. It is a curiosity too, the shape of a cross, the nave scarcely longer than the chancel, with a stunted tower growing up from, rather than abutting on, the ridge and red tiles of the west end. The north transept is painted white outside, not so the rest. There are some puzzles within.

Walls are of flint, with courses and quoins of sandstone and heathstone. Windows show that what stands was built mainly in the Norman and Decorated periods, up to about 1350. Most of them contain plain glass,

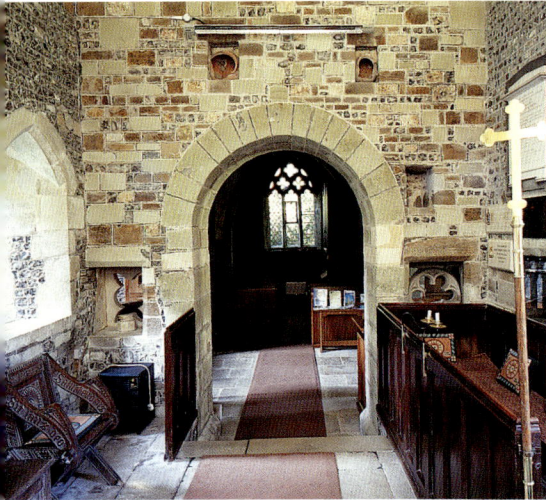

*Tarrant Rushton. Above the arch are a pair of earthenware jars for improving the acoustics by amplifying the sound from the choir. The squint is on the left.*

interesting squints, the two either side of the arch containing unusually shaped grilles. The one just within the north transept is thought to have been provided for the use of inmates of a medieval leper hospital, St Leonard's, known to have been once part of the village. The squint's line of vision runs obliquely from a lancet window in the west wall of the north transept, across to the opposite wall, through a handsome fragment of tracery, through a walled-in tunnel between chancel and north transept (its exterior visible out of doors) to the altar; allowing the diseased gathering at the window to witness altar rituals without exposing healthy worshippers to risk.

In the wall above the chancel arch on its east side are two square holes containing chipped earthenware pots. Similar jars are concealed in ancient walls all over Europe and the prevailing theory is that their purpose is to improve the quality of sound within the church – the voices of priest and choir. Experiments show they do. Walls holding up the jars seem to blot up any muddling echo.

On the north wall of the chancel is a modest memorial tablet to the Reverend Francis Smith, a Victorian rector, son of Sir John Wyldbore Smith, patron of the living, whose kith and kin carol their pieties and distinctions from the chancel walls of Sydling St Nicholas's parish church. 'Though surrounded by every thing that could render this life attractive,' we are told, 'he sought a better country' and was called to 'sleep in Jesus' in 1851. He was forty. His son Francis Alfred, also rector, followed at the age of thirty-five. A more recent departure was that of Bertie Blount, a Tarrant Rushton resident and trained scientist and German speaker buried beside his parents under a table tomb in the graveyard in 1999, whose wartime career in SOE, the Special Operations Executive, may have involved an aborted attempt to kill Hitler with anthrax. Poisons are easy, he said; it's getting them where you want them that presents the problems.

And then there are the remains and effects

allowing light into the dark interior, though this would not have been the pre-Reformation case. The south porch, in the angle of transept and nave, leads to a doorway whose height has obviously been reduced a foot or more. Inside, the probably 12th century lintel above the doorway, brutally cut to size at some stage on the underside, is crudely carved with a beast that could be almost any quadruped except for the cross-topped belt that designates it, according to expert opinion, a paschal lamb. On its left a seated man holds up a book, on the right another man holds a bird.

The general look of the church's interior is not a happy one. The walls were literally defaced by the mid-Victorian passion for 'scrape': plaster and its decorations stripped to expose a surface of harsh cold flint. Light yellowish 1960s wooden pews, lectern, pulpit, font-lid and so on and lavishly used carpeting of a later date suggest more a period furniture showroom in Tottenham Court Road than a church. Nevertheless old and fascinating features survive. The Norman chancel arch escaped Victorian enlargement and as a result retains three

of Sir Alan Cobham and his wife. He was a pioneer aviator; in his day a household name. In 1926 he flew a heroic round trip to Australia and was greeted on his return by a million cheering people and shortly afterwards a knighthood. He charted the early course of commercial aviation and developed the practice of mid-air refuelling. He lived with his wife in Bournemouth but they had a house here too and came often. They it was who – dubious benefit – paid for the present pews and pulpit and left a fund for other expenses. It was they who had the trees planted. They lie under an astonishing tomb perhaps apter for Egypt's Valley of the Kings than a quiet English rural churchyard: a vast megalithic table and casket and apse-shaped bench, all in the brightest of white stone, dominating the graveyard from the high north-east corner. It must be Dorset's most pretentious 20th century tomb.

## TOLLER FRATRUM
*St Basil*

This should be written in words of one syllable. The sweet simplicity of the place seems to call for it. But syllable is three, simplicity four. Toller Fratrum is set in one green and pleasant valley that slopes down into another, bigger one, that of the River Frome, with distant views of chalk downs. Except for a couple nearby, hardly a roof shows from three sides of the churchyard. On the fourth, the west, two fine, stone-walled barns or stables, one tiled, one thatched, hide from the churchyard the 16th century farmhouse you see on arrival, long and low, with its corkscrew chimneys and mullion windows and a monkey with a mirror perched on a corkscrew finial.

The thatched building may once have served as refectory for the *fratres*. Knights of the Order of the Hospital of St John of Jerusalem, or Hospitallers as they were known, were founded to protect and care for sick and penurious crusaders in the Holy Land. They did well, became rich and powerful, and increasingly military, owning at various times the islands of Rhodes, Cyprus and Malta and using them to fight and frustrate the infidel Turk. Nursing was left behind. Toller was no more than a remote property given to them at some time before 1300, little used by them if at all, paying a rent and forfeit at the Reformation. St Basil too seems of little relevance. There are only two dedications to him in the whole of England. In the 4th century, starting as hermit in his native Cappadocia (a large province at the eastern end of modern Turkey), he rose to bishop, turned his zeal and intellect against the Arian heresy, then in full flood and denying the full divinity of Christ, and as good as trounced it. His writings, rule and liturgy help form the bedrock of eastern Christianity. Both knights and bishop seem very alien to this rural English backwater.

The church is quickly described: a regular stone rectangle with gable ends and slate roof and little stone bellcote at the western end of the even ridge. On each of the longer sides are three lancet windows. The entrance is in the west wall: a wooden door under a pointed arch with two stone heads which would be marking the end of a hoodmould if there were a hoodmould to mark the end of. The east wall shows three lancet windows, the central one higher than the other two, all

*Toller Fratrum. Not even the age of the font is certain, whose cloaked figures, human heads and disembodied animals add to its mystery.*

sharing a hoodmould which does not end in heads. Hardly any part of the church goes back beyond a 19th century rebuild. The churchyard consists of rough, uneven grass with a scatter of tombstones and young trees. Farm sheep are occasionally introduced within the low stone perimeter wall to cut the grass. I was once butted in the side by a ram I was naively intending to stroke. Starlings and many smaller birds go about their business, and if you watched the nearest hill patiently you would surely, before long, see a strolling fox or badger.

Within, the church is as plain as any in Dorset. The floor is flagstone slabs. Pews are dark, walls whitewashed, window lights of clear glass, leaded in diamond pattern. A decorous central brass chandelier is the only ornate object. Two candles are placed in holders on north and south walls, two more on the simple pulpit and another two on the priest's reading-desk. That is the extent of the lighting, while two butane heaters on wheels are at present the only source of warmth.

A pointed arch cuts off the tiny chancel. The communion rail with its turned balusters is dated to 1730. Then, above the altar is placed one of two curious and ancient objects which, if atmosphere and setting failed to, would repay a visit. The carving on this fragment of stone is primitive, at first inscrutable and a little comical: a face, the hair round it, a foot peeking from under a floor-length gown, a hand holding the foot. As you stare at this odd job-lot, its crudity may (if you know the New Testament well) transmute. Lazarus has died. Jesus has restored him to life. The plot among priests and Pharisees to have Jesus killed is ripe. Danger is in the air. But Lazarus' sisters, Mary and Martha, give a party – the feast of Bethany. Martha is the busy one, all cheery clatter and prattle. Mary, quieter, takes their most expensive ointment, spikenard, sinks to the floor, wipes Jesus' feet with her hair and, while weak Judas censures her extravagance, anoints them. That mooning face of stone, the roll of hair, those protuberant sticks of toes – the Saxon mason's intention was that they should transmit a gesture of love, and we may feel they do.

The font is at the west end, near the door, under a conical wooden cover, possibly 12th century, possibly long before, and a mystery. Too close to the wall for an easy all-round look, it is worth some bending and squeezing. Between a carved pattern of plaited rushes and a twisted rope on top, and a line of chevrons round the base, are cloaked figures, two clutching the top rope, various human heads – not all upright and some disembodied – two lions or cats (but with rather bird-like bodies) standing on twisted columns and seeming to share a head between them. There is a cow, or cow-like animal, on its side. At the back are three figures, their right arms bent across their chests at identical angles so that you might think, if their expressions were not so lugubrious, that they were a very mature chorus line, though one of them, it is true, holds a staff with a cross on top. Explanations have of course been offered. A notice suggests a 'man-faced Lion of Judah succouring the human race . . . half-figures with heads and arms upstretched'. Another theory combines the defeat of the Amelekites by the Israelites under Moses' guidance (Exodus 17) with the worship of the golden calf (Exodus 32) and the sinner being attacked by two diabolical serpents. The jury has been out a thousand years or so. It may never come in.

## TRENT

*St Andrew*

The church today, and the buildings close to it, would, in spite of alterations, have been quite recognisable to the crowd of villagers, mostly Puritans and anti-monarchist, in their grey and dun jerkins, which assembled in Trent churchyard in October 1651 as rumours about the king's fate flew around. Charles I had been beheaded two years since. Charles II his 21-year old son, had escaped to

sanctuary in the Netherlands and recently returned with a rash resolve to recover his kingdom through a Scots alliance. At the battle of Worcester, on 3rd September, the attempt had aborted in decisive defeat. Charles escaped, hid overnight in an oak tree, and made slow, covert progress towards the Dorset coast, helped by a few brave royalists. One such was Sir Francis Wyndham, who had recently become owner of Trent Manor north of the church, through marriage to a Gerard heiress. It was four weeks since the battle. All over the south there were daily claims that the king had been seen and the reward offered for his capture earned. Now, suddenly, here in the churchyard, there was a uniformed trooper shouting at the crowd. 'I killed him, I killed him. Like this . . .' The bystanders cheered, applauded, lit bonfires. Bellringers pealed the triumphant news. And from a window in the manor where Wyndham was risking everything to try and arrange to ship his sovereign to continental refuge, King Charles II, alive, young, fit and wryly amused, looked out at the callous merry-makers he still hoped would be his subjects. 'Alas, poor people,' is all he is said to have said. When, on Oak Apple Day (29 May) nine years later, it was time to celebrate Charles's restoration, Wyndham barred the treacherous village bellringers and called in those of neighbouring Compton. To play that one annual peal, the Compton ringers have been coming ever since.

The setting remains one of Dorset's best. Modernity brings the fixing of new gravestones to the churchyard wall, a lavish new lavatory behind a Ham-stone screen, electric alarms attached to the church, and the medieval spire rebuilt only a century ago. But Trent, church and village, retains a scarcely marred inheritance of richly mellowed buildings, tall trees and broad green spaces. At the entrance to the churchyard stands the 15th century house that probably served as home to the chantry priest. Ahead, the tall spire, set on a graceful 14th century tower with early Y-tracery

ABOVE  *Trent. Only in winter is it possible to get a clear view of both church and 15th century house of the chantry priest.*

RIGHT  *Trent. A stag and hound on one of the bench-ends.*

windows – and three windows, on the south side, rather later and more complex – cuts the sky. It is set south of the nave. Close to it, from some angles, is seen the asymmetric, almost organic growth of wall and roof, ridge and gable, buttress and window, gargoyle, finial and pinnacle that makes old churches seem alive, experienced and sentient as a lined, worn Rembrandt face or old hill-folds towards sunset. There was a Norman church, and possibly a pre-Norman, but the earliest visible feature is a blocked 13th century, Early English lancet window on the west wall of the north chapel. The nave, like the tower, is 14th century. Decorated, curvy tracery, tells us that. The chancel, with more serried lines of perpendicular tracery in the windows, is 15th century. So was the chantry, which traces of an altar and a wash-bowl or piscina suggest was probably in the south chapel or transept, under the tower. This chantry was constructed for John Franks, Master of the

*Trent. The house of the chantry priest.*

Rolls under Henry VI. An extension of the nave, and a further west-end projection, planned as a baptistery and now serving as vestry, are the only significant post-Reformation additions, if we except the weathercock erected in 1698.

The interior, as we enter, is almost theatrical in its pomp and finery. Not so much the view, leftward, of the broad, light nave, though this contains a pre-Reformation Dorset treasure. Carved bench-ends of about 1500, probably saved from the destructive fury of puritan iconoclasts by being hidden in the manor house, match some of the best in Devon and Cornwall. Above, angel corbels support the ceiling ribs while holding shields painted with symbols of the apostles. Among some bench-ends are divided the constituent letters of the phrase *Ave Maria gratia plena Dominus tecum* – 'Hail Mary full of grace, the Lord be with you.' There are abstract patterns, a hart and hound, a mischievous-looking bearded human face, a tableau of four birds, the flight of Mary, Joseph and the boy Jesus into Egypt, the symbols – crown of thorns, nails, cock, whips and ladder – that mark the events leading to Christ's Passion, and what is thought to be St John the Evangelist holding a cup containing a poisonous snake which he swallowed to show faith in the healing powers of the Christian God.

A denser, richer, more shadowy vista is to our right as we enter: three arches inviting inspection of their complex and colourful contents. In the middle, under the chancel arch, a decorously ornate 15th-century rood screen, thought by some to have spent its pre-Dissolution years in Glastonbury Abbey, spreads its five wooden, traceried bays across the opening of the chancel, its gilt loft and vine-frieze supported on fan-vault springers. Left of that is a most inviting prospect, to which, though we can see much, entry is sadly denied since the area is burglar-alarmed. Under the arch is painted a text that can best be read in a mirror: *All flesh is grass and the glory of it is as the floure of the feilde.* The standard explanation – that the space within constituted the manorial family pew and ladies vain enough to check their appearance in mirrors during the sermon

*Trent. The Dutch pulpit of about 1650, and the wooden tracery rood screen, thought to have come from Glastonbury Abbey following its dissolution.*

might be alarmed by the fatalistic message – seems rickety. The north side of the arch offers another pretty curiosity. Below an inscription to Anna, wife of Thomas Gerard and daughter of Robert Coker – she died in 1633 aged 29 – two narrow columns frame a faded *trompe l'oeil* painting of a series of receding arches.

Within the chapel, around the table and chairs and funeral bier that occupy it, are arranged various effigies with village links: one 14th century, one 15th (possibly Franks of the chantry). Wall tablets include one (out of sight, on the south wall) to the Sir Francis Wyndham who sheltered the king for nearly three tense weeks. He died in 1676, honoured and rewarded by the king who, though ungrateful to almost everybody else, always remembered those who helped him elude Cromwell's toughs. More Wyndhams are commemorated on the large tablet on the north wall of the nave. The other effigy, against the chapel's west wall, is by W. Theed and much later: the Reverend William Turner, rector from 1835 to 1870, Victorian to his finger-tips, who in those thirty-five years left a stronger mark on the church's interior than anyone else. On continental travels he collected the beautiful 16th century and 17th century stained glass, squeezed scrapbook style into the great east window and the deeply carved Dutch pulpit of about 1650. He had much of the other stained glass inserted, including the 1843 apostle windows by Wailes in the chancel. He probably ordered the creation of the lectern from 17th century carved wood. He lengthened the nave, and had the nave and chancel roofed with rather fanciful rib vaulting, in which moulded plaster lines diagonally cross a star-studded background, with decorative bosses at the ends and junctions. And he cosified the chancel with deep-cut glazed flower tiles on the walls, Minton tiles over the floor and a reredos of six ogee-topped niches inscribed with the Ten Commandments, Creed, Lord's Prayer and other holy texts. His wife, who founded a set of almshouses in the village,

and died before him in 1866, is celebrated by a relief likeness of herself with children, whom she no doubt taught according to the stern instruction from the Book of Isaiah, *Precept must be upon precept, line upon line.*

It comes as no surprise that in 1962 a retiring primate of Canterbury, Lord Fisher, who was no doubt not short of options, should have chosen to accept the bishop's offer of the Trent rectory for his final years. He was here ten years and is buried in the churchyard beside his wife. His spirit lives in the south chapel, to which the font, probably Victorian, with its pre-Reformation wooden cover was brought at his suggestion. Close by, in a glass case, is a cope and mitre of Japanese silk which once covered his small, resilient frame.

## WAREHAM
*St Martin*

The church of Lady St Mary, on the south side of Wareham, goes back to the 7th century, and remained until 1840 one of the most important of its time in northern Europe. In that and subsequent years, in what some consider Dorset's worst act of ecclesiastical vandalism, it was pulled down and replaced by the present parish church which, though large and impressive, retaining extremely interesting historic artefacts, and designed by a respectable London professor of architecture, is all but starved of interior character.

St Martin's, on the other hand, situated near the site of the old north gate, is small, seldom used and mostly locked (the key kept by an obliging Gentleman's Outfitter down the road), and in spite of partial rebuildings and additions remains at its core a fascinating 11th century, pre-Conquest church – the most complete in Dorset – with several Saxon features including its essential two-cell structure.

From the green to the east, the chancel wall shows left and right the typically Saxon arrangement of quoins or corner-stones –

alternating vertical and horizontal – known as long-and-short work. Inside, the protruding round stone band above the chancel arch, originally continuing to the ground, is a Saxon feature. So possibly is the north window of the chancel; that on the south was widened in the late 13th century, when the door was inserted. But if the fabric of chancel and nave – all but the western wall – are mostly pre-Conquest, later centuries made contributions too. The north aisle is late 12th century Norman, the whole of the west wall a 15th century rebuild to add space, the east window also 15th century. The tower is early 16th century, its saddleback top rebuilt in 1712. The lower part of the tower is in fact the church porch and main entrance.

By the early 18th century, with three other churches and various chapels in action in the town, St Martin's was scarcely used. For long periods it was locked and neglected, though it served as a refuge for families whose houses were burned in the town's worst fire in 1762. A fireplace and chimney were installed for them in the chancel. The chimney remains. A hundred years ago St Martin's was bricked up and abandoned, but worthy locals fought

*Wareham, St Martin's, the most complete Saxon church in Dorset.*

for its survival and after costly repair and refurbishment it was rededicated in 1936.

There are squints either side of the chancel arch, and above the right-hand or southern one a walled-in arch, reckoned to have once been the site of a small chapel altar. The wall above the arch displays early 18th century frescoes: a massive, faded Queen Anne coat of arms dated 1713, with a sun above and on either side the Ten Commandments, stained, chipped and incomplete. The chips and gaps reveal fragments of earlier paintings. On the north wall, above the two arches leading to the north aisle, is an early 19th century text commemorating a naval surgeon, Robert Carruthers, and members of his family. His wife, it tells us, was victim of 'a Typhus Favour'.

*Wareham, St Martin's. Just visible above the chancel arch are early 18th century frescoes, including Queen Anne's coat of arms and the Ten Commandments.*

*Wareham, St Martin's. Eric Kennington's effigy of T.E. Lawrence (of Arabia).*

The fine effigy in the aisle is of T.E. Lawrence, in Arab dress, by his friend Eric Kennington, done after Lawrence's accidental death on the road close to his cottage near Bovington, in 1935. Beside the camel's saddle on which his head rests are shown the three books he kept with him on the Arab campaign: *The Morte d'Arthur, The Greek Anthology* and *The Oxford Book of Verse*. The dean of Salisbury Cathedral turned down the Lawrence family's request that the effigy should go into the cathedral. Moreton, where Lawrence is buried, might have been more appropriate.

The oldest frescoes are 12th century and in the chancel. Damaged by time, damp and the lowering of the chancel roof, they palely illustrate the moving story of St Martin, 4th century bishop of Tours, to whom the church is dedicated: how, as a young pagan soldier, seeing a naked beggar, he tore his cloak in two and gave him half. In a dream that night Christ appeared to him, wearing the cloak. Martin was converted. His popularity was highest in the Middle Ages and especially in France, where 4000 churches are still dedicated to him. The paintings tell us less than they once would have done. Lowering the chancel roof and walls removed the tops of the figures in the higher band. It is only recently that medieval murals have come to be valued highly.

# WEST STAFFORD
## St Andrew

They bypassed the village in 1992 but its main road, turning a right-angle, presses on two sides of the churchyard wall and in all directions there are houses in sight, of which only a couple were standing a lifetime ago. The churchyard is grassed, with fine tombstones of three centuries remaining in place. The cleaning of lichen-covered inscriptions displeases some but it does disclose past pieties; solace from 1898 – *Earth has lost her, heaven has found her,/ Jesus doeth all things well* – a fret from 1799 – *Affliction's rod I long endur'd/ My nights were spent with cries/ To God my prayer I did direct/ And lift my weeping eyes . . .* – and over the 1732 grave of a sister and two brothers (in which *All three Intird doth lye*), a homespun homily in which the Dorset burr is almost audible: *As we are So Shall you Be/ Prepare your selves/ Two Follow We*. The church's exterior is not over-complicated: grey stone-roofed nave and chancel in one continuous line, much restored but essentially dating from 1640, with three main exceptions. The tower, or the bulk of it, may be 16th century. An arched, Perpendicular nave window, with hood-mould that ends in worn head bosses, situated just west of the south porch, has come through from the 15th century church. The chancel was extended at the end of the 19th century.

Inside, there is something uncomfortable in the eastward view. The five yards or so of chancel, beyond the wooden screen, done over by the diocesan architect C.E. Ponting in 1897 and 1898, are loud and florid. The east window (early 20th century) has a dazzle of red and gold angels' wings and a palette of bright haloes on the frowning admirers at Christ's feet. On the walls twisting gold frames outshine dowdy paintings, and the wooden reredos contains more holy paintings. The chancel end of the continuous wagon roof has grown a pattern the nave part does not have. Much of all this east-end revision was the gift of the long-term 19th

*West Stafford, the full-size effigy of Canon Reginald Southwell Smith, rector for 60 years.*

century rector Canon Reginald Southwell Smith. His sixty-year incumbency (1836-1896) almost exactly coincides with Queen Victoria's reign (1837-1901). His full-size stone effigy adorns the north wall. His immediate predecessor, William England, was a stayer too: fifty years as curate and rector, a half-century which perhaps earned him the rewards he asked for in his last words, recorded on the nave wall : 'May I die in peace, rest in hope and rise in glory.'

If Victorian parsons sometimes opted to do very Victorian things to their churches, the ministry of Archbishop Laud's day had no choice. Puritanism and nonconformity had sprouted and spread under Queen Elizabeth and James I. Puritans had continued to clear churches of ornament, even seasonal blossoms, and some furniture – anything with a whiff of Catholic finery. Convinced that the doings of richly garbed priests at their high altars were a distraction from thoughtful worship, they had banned marble altars and insisted the wooden communion tables that replaced them should be placed longways in the nave or chancel aisle – more among the people – not crossways, remote and elevated, against the east wall.

James's son, Charles I, with no wish to restore papism (though his French wife had), was set on bringing back an Anglican middle way. In 1633, to this end, he made the efficient, thorough and fatally intolerant William Laud Archbishop of Canterbury.

Laud set about reversing the trend. He ruled that communion tables should be restored to the east wall, screens replaced, communion rails inserted (with balusters close enough together to exclude dogs from the church's holiest part), and a general beautifying take place. Provincial 'visitations' took place to make sure these things were being done, not least in Dorset which Laud knew to be obstinately Puritan. In West Stafford the happy results remain.

If, standing at the west end, you can blot the chancel out of your vision and make the wooden screen your boundary, you are in a gracefully restrained mid 17th century nave, redolent of the divine right of kings, a brewing civil war, Archbishop Laud and papaphobia; and not overwhelmed by a few anachronisms: the splash of 1920s stained glass in the big south-wall window (Christ, scarlet-robed, preaching to some singularly well-dressed prisoners), a lovely, delicate, centrally hung, brass chandelier of 1712 and showy cartouches (four 17th century

*West Stafford. The 17th century wagon roof and oak screen, with the octagonal sounding board of the pulpit on the right.*

generations of Russell on the south, a lone 17th century to 18th century Gould on the north) and brass plaques dating from before and after the period in question. But 1640 is the principal date of the nave. Apart from simply moulded ribs and pendants, the wagon roof is simple and unadorned. The tall dark-oak octagonal pulpit, with charmingly carved designs, stands under an octagonal sounding-board. There are handsome, panelled, squared-off pews with a few carved bench-end patterns, fragments of a painted creed above the south door, and the royal arms of James I on the north wall. Most conspicuous is the busily carved oak screen, with wide round arches supported by slender dividing posts above a three-tiered wainscot. These flank a low central arch without a door. Beyond, among the Victorian additions, is the faintly uneven oak altar rail. All this has come to us from the 17th century and mostly from Laud's time. Sadly, Laud was a bully, and the Puritans despised him. As the Civil War drew near, and their power grew, they impeached him for treason, and finally had him beheaded.

## WHITCHURCH CANONICORUM
*St Candida or Wite*
Set down in the valley of the little River Char, between Conegar Hill and Hardown Hill, the bulky ramparts that guard the western approach to the Marshwood Vale, St Candida's nonetheless looks lordly beside the village spreading west and south, and the green slopes close by. Its tower is tall, five stages under a battlemented top thronged with thin pinnacles. Its body – chancel, nave with south porch, north and south transepts, and 19th century vestry tucked between south transept and chancel – is impressively long. The sprawling churchyard lolls at ease over uneven ground.

There was something Roman here, and some bricks from it were used for the present north transept and chancel, but what it amounted to is not known. King Alfred founded a church on the site in the 9th century but no part of it is known to survive. In the 12th century monks from St Wandrille's monastery in Normandy, granted the site, built the first church of which anything significant remains. The wall of the south aisle, the fine, white-stone round-arched doorway by which we enter, with leafy capitals on its slender shafts, and the three central arches of the south arcade, just ahead of us, belong to what was a smaller church than the present one, with a tower at the crossing. The font, with its design of interlacing round arches between patterned bands, is also Norman. The outward lurch and lowering of one of the two round south aisle columns suggests the ground below subsided somewhat after building.

Nave, transepts and the south wall of the chancel date back to the early 13th century. So the heart of the church, with its pointed lancet windows, elaborate and varied pier capitals, and the shrine we shall shortly see, is in Early English style, not so common in predominantly Perpendicular Dorset. Tower, porch and parapet of the south aisle *are* Perpendicular, added in the early 15th century. Extra space was no doubt needed, since Whitchurch parish was one of the largest in England. But nothing very radical happened after the Reformation. The south vestry (on the site of an old chantry chapel) belongs to 1822, the insertion of quatrefoil clerestory windows to 1847-8, and much general restoration to various 18th century and 19th century dates. Characteristically, the 15th century rood loft has gone. The lone blocked doorway in the south pier of the chancel arch would once have given access to stairs leading to it. Also in character with the period, the old west-end gallery, which would have held a little local orchestra before the organ's arrival, was removed in 1832.

It is a church where, in a peculiarly guileless way, everything seems wide open to inspection. All the same, the quirks and asymmetries of the arcades; the varied capitals and mouldings of their columns, cleanly cut in white stone; the squat arches of the clerestory; the roof bosses, armorial, decorative, representative; the pointed tower arch reaching for the roof; the stone walls of the inner tower gleaming in the light that penetrates the large (Perpendicular) west window; the finely carved pulpit from (like most pulpits) the early 17th century – all these supply the nave with a rich character, redolent of the distant past and, for those inclined to read it so, a sense of holiness. This magnificent aura does not last beyond the grand sweep of the chancel arch. Without some choice ancient memorials, the chancel itself would be dull.

A 1905 brass on its south wall commemorates Admiral Sir George Somers, a local landowner who died in 1610 and whose body, less heart, is buried under the vestry. In 1605, at a time when Dorset dissenters, fishermen and adventurers were becoming increasingly familiar with North America's east coast, he led a group intending to settle at Jamestown, Virginia, but was shipwrecked on one of the Bermuda islands. This – the 'Isle of Devils' – was known but uninhabited, and thought to be wild and enchanted, but he and his companions patiently built two ships from the wreckage of their one, and in time continued their course to Virginia. Accounts of their experiences gave Shakespeare the framework of *The Tempest*, and from the islands' sinister reputation came the snarling, slavish, deformed figure of Caliban – a name cognate with 'cannibal' – who, along with his witch mother, had the run of the 'wild Bermoothes' before the Europeans were washed up on it.

On the north wall opposite is the hectically embellished tomb of Sir John Jeffery of Catherstone, three miles west of Whitchurch, who died in 1611. His effigy, showing his hair brushed up and forward, beard, stiff ruff and suit of armour, lies on a table tomb under a round arch between fluted columns topped by Corinthian capitals. Above the entablature, the topmost framing shelf of this arrangement, a complex

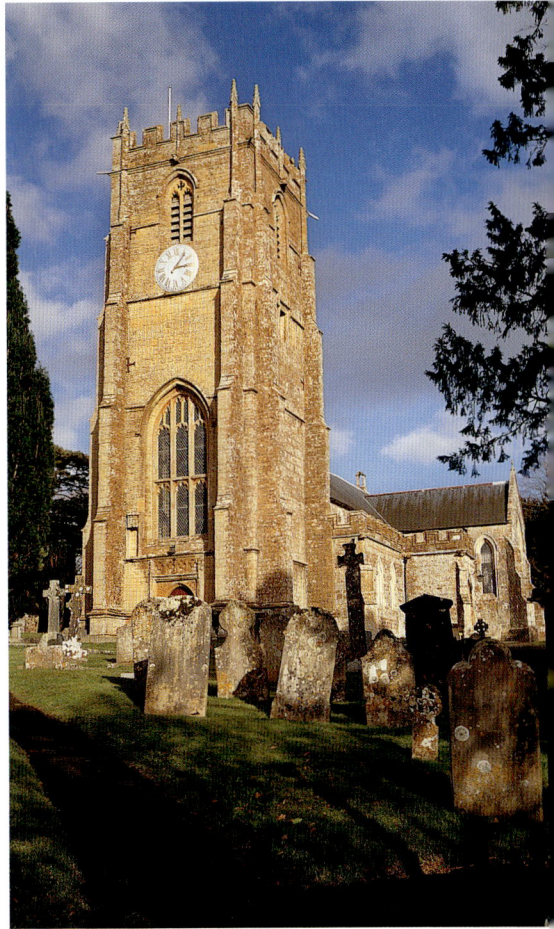

*Whitchurch Canonicorum. The first church on the site was built in the 9th century by King Alfred.*

heraldic pattern is flanked by two curious ragged figures, stunted in all but their bare breasts, one of them hampered by tiny clambering infants. The whole structure is alive with carvings, often separated by strapwork, of smiling heads and shrieking grotesques, skulls, winged angels, lions, hourglass, scythe and spade, cornucopias, bunched fruits, eagles, roses and ribbons. Some of the symbolism is easily explained. It may all be a dancing, vibrating metaphorical image of life from an age when allegory flourished; or possibly no more than the doodles of a restless sculptor.

*Whitchurch Canonicorum. The shrine of St Wite. The sick inserted the affected limbs or parts of their bodies into one of the three holes in the hope of regaining their health.*

The main reason for the church's fame and special sanctity rests on St Wite or Candida. (Wite is a Saxon word; Candida is the Latinised form). Her stone shrine stands under the north window of the north transept, about five foot high, flanked by a cluster of piers on each side, and of a simple design, pierced by three oval holes. The shrine itself is 13th century work. Bones, in a lead box inscribed in Latin 'Here rest the remains of St Wite' and contained within the upper section, were examined in 1900. The remains were reckoned to be those of a small woman of forty or so.

The 13th century was the great age of relics and shrines. They drew pilgrims, and pilgrims were religious tourists, spending money for the good of their souls and much encouraged. Shrines holding remains of the piously famous attracted countless crowds: Westminster's Edward the Confessor, Canterbury's Thomas à Becket. Lesser places had to content themselves with the remains of lesser saints and martyrs. The difficulty with St Wite is that nobody knows anything about her at all. There are theories: that she was a Breton maid who, carried by pirates to England, walked back over the sea on a miraculous path of white foam – hence her name; or that she was a local Saxon virgin living a hermit's life, murdered by Danish pirates. The evidence for each one is gapingly inadequate.

But the cult was strong, as no doubt at first was the reason for it, and the relics were soon famous for their healing powers. A person looking for a cure inserted, if possible, the affected limb or body part into one of the three holes and withdrew it healthy, or in hopes of its becoming so. Others brought a small possession of someone too ill to move, and inserted that. Some who were sound came out of awe or reverence or curiosity. Like the rich, no doubt, with their chantry chapels and canopied tombs, the poor – in spite of scriptural advice to the contrary – thought the Almighty and his saints attended best to those who brought him most. So Whitchurch grew in size and wealth till the Reformation in the 1540s banned the veneration of saints and smashed all the paraphernalia that went with it. The survival of the shrine here is probably due to its being hidden, or possibly passed off as an ordinary and inoffensive tomb. The concealment was so successful, it seems, that the true identity of the bones was lost for all time. All the same the cult did not die out altogether. To this day piles of papers and cards within the apertures, carrying new appeals and new thanks, and bits of cloth and bric-a-brac brought to represent people too ill to leave their beds continue to confirm the survival of ancient faith.

There is another grave at Whitchurch, more solemn and poignant than the others because a tragic modern crime, affecting living local people, lies behind it. Georgi Markov was a Bulgarian novelist, playwright and exile from his homeland, then governed by a totalitarian communist regime. He broadcast truths to his countrymen on Radio Free Europe. In 1978 he was murdered in broad daylight on Waterloo Bridge by a Bulgarian agent, never caught. He married a local girl, and lies here now under a flourishing Bulgarian rose.

## WHITCOMBE

*Dedication unknown*

Living in Canaan in the 5th century, young Christopher grew to be four yards tall, with the strength to go with it. So the story goes. He scorned to waste his power on ordinary or weak beings, and offered his services to a great king. The king turned out to be nervous of the devil, so Christopher offered his services to the devil. The devil turned out to be scared of Christ, so Christopher offered his services to Christ, still a child. One day he carried Christ across a river. By half way, he was staggering under the weight. 'Don't worry', the boy told him; 'When you carry me you carry the world, for I made it.' Christopher, Christian in a pagan kingdom, was persecuted, eventually arrested, tortured and finally beheaded. The king who sentenced him went blind; but dabbed some of the martyred saint's blood on his own eyes. He saw again. In time the belief grew that if you looked on an image of St Christopher no harm would come to you that day. In the middle ages, unsurprisingly, a picture of him was painted on a wall in almost every church.

*Whitcombe. The medieval wall painting of St Christopher carrying a robed child.*

*Whitcombe. The church is enclosed on three sides by a wall, and set a field away from the nearest road.*

Such was the obliteration of images of paint, wood and stone at the Reformation, that such paintings are now rarities, chipped and faded and in some details inscrutable. He must have looked fine in his 14th century heyday, painted in all the freshness of earthy ochres and umbers and vegetable dyes.

The church is deliciously set in an irregular churchyard, hemmed on three sides by a buttressed and well maintained 18th century brick wall and on the fourth, north side by a wrap of shrubs and trees. The main road is a field away. Bumps in another

*Whitcombe, the simple nave. The medieval wall paintings are on the right.*

adjacent field indicate the site of a vanished medieval village. What survives, a hundred yards off, is a little settlement of big house, thatched cottages and 17th century barn. Close to the church's south porch is the shapely 17th century table tomb of Melchisadeck Gillet with nicely carved skull and crossbones, hourglass and floral decorations. The west tower, a date high up announces, was finished in 1596, but probably begun long before. It looks bulky and masculine beside the long slender body of nave and chancel, whose roof ridge is in continuous line. The nave walls are largely Norman, with a 12th century arch either side; the north one blocked and a later arch inserted in the south doorway, underneath the original one.

The entrance is by the south porch and brings us to about sixty foot by twelve of what amounts to a very beautiful chamber. The nave floor is parquet, the chancel floor, raised a step, flags and brickwork. The walls, with an outward slant each side, are whitewashed where there are not windows or the old frescoes. The roof beams of the nave give way to the chancel's wagon roof with carved bosses. There is hardly any furniture: an altar from All Saints, Dorchester, 13th century font, wooden pulpit and lectern, a few foldable benches. Only some 15th century steps in the north wall indicate where the rood screen and loft were, and a tympanum – or high partition above the loft – on which possibly was painted the rood or cross, with the figures of the Virgin and John the Evangelist at its sides. In the blocked up Norman doorway of the north nave wall stand two rectangular stone fragments, carved with an interlace design. Found during 1912 repairs, these are the remains of 10th century crosses, and evidence of the former existence of a Saxon church. Further east is a plaque to William Barnes, in whose memory the 1912 restoration was carried out. Whitcombe was his first parish and he preached his first sermon here. He later moved to Winterborne Came, a mile away. Essentially, now, the interior is a vacant space, attractively contained, light and clean, with clear glass lancet windows in the rebuilt east wall and a large, square, clear 18th century window in the nave's south wall. You could have dances or banquets or ping-pong or lectures here. Happily, the Churches Conservation Trust maintains its fabric.

And high on the north nave wall, a large,

recognisable, bare-legged St Christopher holds on his shoulder a green-robed child who clutches in his left hand an orb with a cross rising from it. The details are by no means clear. A mermaid with tail and hand-mirror could be taken for a boat with a man in it, and what may seem like the saint's outsize shoes are in fact river-banks. No matter. You have looked on the saint, and are immune from harm till midnight.

## WIMBORNE MINSTER
### St Cuthberga

Dark brown patches of local heathstone, or pudding-stone, randomly spattered among the pale prevailing sandstone and limestone (which had to be floated miles down the River Stour) makes the minster's outside skewbald, erratic, odd. At the same time this random mottling brings a certain skittish lightness to a structure rather heavily clamped – the only Dorset church to be so – by two substantial towers: the earlier, Norman one over the transept crossing, the later, Perpendicular, mid 15th century one at the church's west end. Until 1600 further uplift was supplied by a spire on the central tower, but in that year it collapsed – in mid-service, though without human injury – and was never replaced. All the same, both inside and outside this weighty pile – bigger than most parish churches, though too small to get lost in – you are never far from levity, sometimes even whimsy. Here, for instance, on the outside of the west tower's north wall, a model redcoat soldier marks the passage of each quarter-hour by striking the two bells beside him. He began life a monk, in 1612, but changed into Guardsman's uniform during the national crisis of the Napoleonic wars. Inside we shall see an astronomical clock, two hundred years older than Copernicus, showing the sun going round the earth. We shall pass under a battery of gleaming trumpets sprouting from the massive organ, as if a squad of bandsmen were lined up behind the pipes. We shall

Wimborne Minster, the Quarterjack on the outside of the west tower.

confront an effigy with two left and no right feet, and the coffin of a man fulfilling his vow not to be buried within or without the minster's walls.

The word minster does not tightly define a church but denotes its early size and importance within a large area, later broken into several parishes. But little or no trace remains of the rigorously enclosed nunnery founded around 713 by Cuthberga, sister of Ine of Wessex, the most formidable king in northern Europe; the burial in 871 of King Ethelred (not the Unready); utter sacking by Danes in 1013; revival as a college of secular canons under Edward the Confessor in 1043. The oldest remaining part of the present church is the lower portion of the central tower, dating from the early 12th century or a bit before. There were then small Norman transepts, enlarged later. East of the crossing, the Norman building extended just beyond the present choir, as we shall see. The church's east end is 13th century. Most of the outer walls and windows go back to the middle 14th century. The west tower is 15th century and Perpendicular.

Entrance is by the 14th century north porch, which has a room above it, probably

for a priest to live in or school classes to be held. To our right, in the north aisle, wooden wall panelling indicates that here was held the medieval consistory, or bishop's, court. St Cuthberga is shown in a window, clasping in her spiny fingers a model of the present minster. There is a good 1650s marble memorial to Thomas Hanham and his wife, of Dean's Court at the town's edge, shown kneeling under a pediment. The ground floor of the west tower is the baptistery, with an octagonal Norman font. The colourful astronomical clock adorns the south wall, showing both moon and sun rotating round the earth; an apt arrangement in a religion whose main festivals (Christmas excepted) are still dated by the lunar calendar as they were at the time of Israel's pastoral tribes. Opposite is a chipped and reduced memorial stone to Isaac Gulliver, one of the most ingenious and successful Dorset smugglers of the 18th century. His personal means of law evasion included lying still in an open coffin, his face white-powdered, as excise men filed by in silent respect. Overtly he was a wine merchant. His recognition in church nicely

*Wimborne Minster, the astronomical clock, which shows both sun and moon rotating round the earth.*

suggests that crime pays in more than a worldly sense.

After the first pair of nave piers we are within the bounds of the Norman church, and move eastward under the nave's pitch-pine hammer-beam roof, with its armorial bosses, along an avenue of sturdy Norman columns. The round-arched windows above them formed the original Norman clerestory, and marks of the first roof, lower than the present one, can be seen on the tower wall. In the aisles behind the arcades are one or two 17th century and several 18th century wall memorials and colourful 19th century stained glass by Clayton and Bell. Thomas Earp's carved 1868 pulpit and the 1623 eagle lectern with mother-of-pearl eyes and a Victorian pedestal are under the tower, whose staunch rounded arches support, at the heart of the Norman church, a triforium arcade under a compartmented ceiling of nine painted panels.

The north transept has a Norman altar recess on its east side containing faded murals showing the Crucifixion, with Christ's mother raising her left forearm across her breast in a gesture full of grace. Not far away, within St George's Chapel in the north chancel aisle, is the early 17th century monument to Sir Edmund Uvedale. The knight lies, his head propped on his right arm. Above, framed by allegorical and ornamental designs characteristic of the period, is a laudatory inscription ordered by his widow. At the top are his coat of arms surmounted by a helmet. It is easy to overlook the error of a restorer in leaving Sir Edmund with two left feet. From here we can mount the steps to the choir, with its 1610 stalls, made to replace the seats destroyed by the spire's collapse ten years earlier. The scene changed again in 1855, when one of the county's nastier 'restorations' wiped away, along with much else, the Jacobean rood screen and stall canopies, simply, as Hardy observed, 'for the offence of being Jacobean'.

Eastward is the stepped three-light window (that is, with the central light higher than the

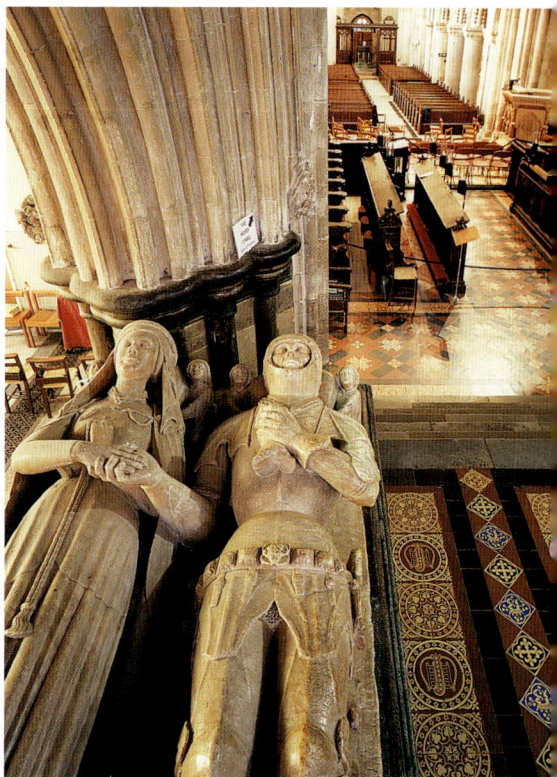

*Wimborne Minster. The effigies of John de Beaufort, Duke of Somerset, and his wife Margaret Beauchamp – their hands clasped.*

two at its sides) whose form ties it down to the Early English period; the 13th century. The middle light contains the church's oldest glass, supposedly 15th century, brought back piecemeal from Flanders by the egregious W.J. Bankes of Kingston Lacy. It aspires to show the Tree of Jesse, the descent of Christ from King David. David and Solomon can be recognised at the base, and the Virgin and Child at the top; but the latter pair are a 19th century addition and most of the glass in between is incoherent. On the south side of the presbytery are effigies of John de Beaufort, Duke of Somerset, and his wife – he in armour, their hands clasped in death. He died in 1444, possibly by his own hand after being denied high office. He was descended – but illegitimately – from John of Gaunt, and so from King Edward III. The couple's

*Wimborne Minster, the Chained Library.*

daughter Margaret married Edmund Tudor, half-brother of King Henry VI. Fortified by these two rather watery links with the royal line, Margaret's and Edmund's son won the throne from Richard III and founded the Tudor dynasty as Henry VII. But there were far stronger claims to the succession and Henry's son Henry VIII obsessively persecuted those who possessed them. Among these Henry Courtenay, Marquess of Exeter, was prominent, roused Henry's suspicions and was as a consequence beheaded in 1538. Exeter's wife Gertrude was also condemned but, less of a threat, secured a pardon. She died in her bed in 1558. Her tomb-chest is opposite the Beaufort one, on the north side. On the column to the right is a 15th century brass to King Ethelred, Alfred the Great's elder brother and predecesssor as king, buried here after his death in battle against invading Danes in 871. To the right of the Beaufort Tomb is the Moses corbel, a delightful Norman stylised portrait of the patriarch holding the tablets inscribed with the Commandments.

Below, reached by runs of steps north and south of the presbytery, is the crypt, under which is the Bankes family vault, used for the last time in 1905 though it had according to an inscription been 'for ever closed' in 1856. They owned a sizeable part of the Isle of Purbeck including Studland, much of Wimborne and their mansion at Kingston Lacy until 1981 when almost everything was handed to the National Trust. Soon after the last Bankes burial here, they commissioned Charles Ponting to build them a church at Pamphill within their park, where most of them have since been interred.

In the Holy Trinity Chapel, south of the chancel, the placing of the early 18th century tomb of Sir Anthony Ettricke is based on a form of riddle. Ettricke was Poole's Town Recorder (he had committed the rebel Duke of Monmouth for trial after the 1685 rebellion) and a crosspatch lawyer. Taking against Wimborne on personal grounds, he swore never to be buried within or without the minster, or below or above its ground. When in time he relented, he satisfied himself (as only a lawyer could) that in prescribing the present hole in the wall as his last resting-place he was fulfilling the terms of his own earlier embargo. He also foretold the year of his death and had a coffin prepared with the date on. It still lies where he wanted, with whatever remains of him inside, and with only the obvious change of date – 1693 to 1703 – showing he miffed the prophecy.

West of Holy Trinity chapel, a staircase leads to the library, one of Wimborne's great national treasures. Founded with the gift of the books by a local parson in 1686, the 240 volumes, tethered on chains that assure us pilfering from libraries is no new sport, reflect the scholarly tastes of the time. There are bibles, Greek and Latin classics, some volumes on history (a copy of Raleigh's *History of the World*), law, even gardening, and music by early English composers, but mostly these are theological works by doctors of the early church and all subsequent ages to the 17th century. It is claimed to be England's first free public library.

## WIMBORNE ST GILES

*St Giles*

The church was built in 1732, just before Blandford's St Peter and St Paul and probably by the same architects, the Bastard brothers. As at Blandford, the top level of the tower is broken by a central, elegant balustrade and surmounted at the corners by urns. You enter through the west doorway, and emerge from the shadowy low-ceilinged space under the tower into an interior made abundantly spacious – almost square in shape – by the existence of a broad north aisle, and a general loftiness. All this, though, is incised and pierced by thin lines and clean-cut shapes, pinpoints of light and fine detail of wood and metal – all very far from Georgian styles. For in 1908 much of the building burned down. Its restoration was entrusted to the Anglo-Catholic Scots architect Ninian Comper, a medievalist of independent mind ('architect, not registered' went his *Who's Who* entry), who splendidly preserved the principles of high church Victorianism into the new century. He was a pupil and disciple of G.F. Bodley, who had added a gothic dressing to the church's interior in the 1880s. The spaciousness is Comper's, achieved by moving choir, organ and ringers to the western, tower end and by the continuation of his busy open screen from the nave, under one of the broad, tall nave-arches, into the north aisle. Also Comper's are the delicacy and colours of the ornaments: the wide-winged roof angels, the long gold spire of the font-cover, the screen's apostles, the central

*Wimborne St Giles. On the left are the Sir Anthony Ashley Almshouses, founded in 1624.*

rood-cross with Christ and mourners, the pulpit and seating, the reredos figures and painted tester above – all enriching and illuminating without swamping the architectural lines. Most captivating are the stained-glass windows, all but two of which are his: done in his best phase, in deep and luminous blues, greens and crimson. Grim Pevsner saw no merit in this. 'Debased . . . preposterous . . . wilful . . . sentimental . . . anaemic' are epithets used in his pained account of St Giles's. Not so Betjeman, who loved Comper's work. 'Dazzling but subtle' he called the windows, and described as a fortunate event the fire that necessitated Comper's restorations.

Three hundred metres beyond the lodge gates, to the south of the village green, stands the huge long empty home of the Ashley Coopers, earls of Shaftesbury. Just outside the gates, and on the green, intricately fused with a long low 1624 redbrick almshouse, the church has been, though separate, (and in spite of the existence of a private chapel in the house) in some ways one more of the mansion's rooms: a large, high-ceilinged room for the family to worship, bury their dead and revere their ancestors in. Despite Comper's transformation, numerous features are preserved from before: the grandiose 1627 tomb – gaudy blend of renaissance and fairground, and surviving from the medieval church which occupied the site – of Sir

*Wimborne St Giles. The golden font cover and stained glass windows beyond the work of Ninian Comper, who restored the church after a fire in 1908.*

Anthony Ashley (who introduced from Holland the practice of growing cabbages, and founded the almshouses) and his wife, against the north window of the Lady Chapel; Rysbrack's bust of the bewigged first Earl (1621-83), Lord Chancellor and proto-Whig, on the north wall; a female figure mourning the philosopher third earl; Scheemakers' bust of the fourth earl, who 'received and diffused happiness'; many more plaques, putti and likenesses. Beside family triumph appears family grief: tablets to a

Victorian daughter 'purified in the furnace of affliction'; another dead 'after years of affliction'. The family pew spreads out on the sanctuary side of the open-work wooden screen, which excludes – by lock, key and, outside service hours, burglar alarm – the humbler majority of the congregation. Some of the contents and ritual reflect tastes and preferences of family members; most conspicuously the high-church leanings of the ninth earl, including a gold-painted wooden statue of the crowned Virgin Mary with the infant Jesus, given by the Pope in recognition of the earl's work towards the reunion of the Catholic and Anglican churches. The seventh earl of Shaftesbury (1801-85), who is buried here, was a stalwart product of the evangelical movement, which by spreading godliness and education at home and abroad in the mid 19th century supplied the British empire with much of its official high-minded morality. Shaftesbury achieved reforms in factory practice and the conditions children could work under, and founded Great Ormond Street Hospital for children. He became a kind of national godfather, and when he died it was said 'all England wept'. He had turned down an offer of burial in Westminster Abbey and his body lies here, with a modest plaque on the north wall. London did him better. Shaftesbury Avenue and the Shaftesbury Theatre are named after him, and the figure of Eros (intended to represent Christian Charity) at the centre of Piccadilly Circus, was placed there in his honour. The arrow in the figure's bow actually points to his home here.

## WINTERBORNE CAME
*St Peter*

Bearded, benign, and in a coat too big for him, the green-stained bronze figure of the Rev William Barnes (1801-1886) stands outside St Peter's parish church, Dorchester, looking down on people passing along the central and best bit of the county town's handsomest street. (Dorchester condemned the likeness of Hardy to rest his perpetual gaze on a dull and fumey off-centre highway). You can walk through development on the south of the town, and leave it by a footbridge over the bypass, cross a field, top a gentle ridge, and find that on the far side, bar the traffic's hum, modern life has

*Winterborne Came. The grave of the Dorset poet William Barnes, rector of Came for 24 years.*

hardly begun to interfere with the prime Arcadian landscape. Downs unfurl lazily to the right, while front left dairy Friesians and horses graze. Behind them, as if placed against the woods by Poussin, stand the grandly pedimented Portland stone manor house and modest rubble-stone church of Winterborne Came.

And there again is William Barnes. (You can also, of course, come by car, and if you drive from Dorchester you pass on the way – on a dangerously narrow and bendy stretch of the road – the much smartened thatched house where Barnes lived as Came's rector from 1862 until he died twenty-four years later). His grave is in the churchyard, under a white Celtic cross with what look like clever stone doodles decorating the staff. The church is late 14th or early 15th century, in Perpendicular style, except for the west-end tower top. This was added a hundred or more years later, and the church windows were changed from pointed to square-headed at about the same time.

The tower has battlements. There is the outline of a sunken doorway on the south wall. Window tracery is simple but changes from one window to another. Some 18th and early 19th century gravestones with good lettering stand against the east wall. You enter on the north, through a porch and

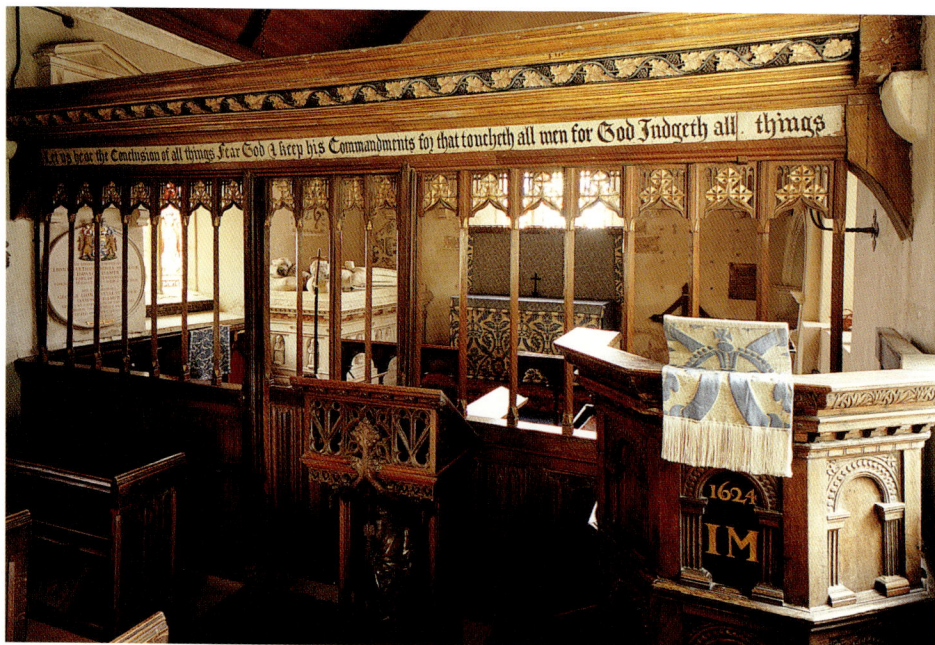

pointed doorway. Like many Dorset churches the outside of St Peter's is in itself unassuming, but by virtue of standard church-shape and delicious rural positioning a delight to the eye. And there is better inside.

The roof is a simple dark-wood barrel shape. The pews are workaday 19th century with rather dull linenfold bench-end decoration. Walls are plastered, and three Dawson-Damer hatchments hang from them. The font is of Ham-stone on a Portland stone base. Of the seven windows two are clear and five filled with unexceptional 19th century stained glass. But a glorious richness of wood and marble crams the east end, a crowded cocoon of family sanctity.

The light and graceful screen is early 16th century: a run of tracery-topped lights with linenfold panelling below, and a text and carved frieze of grape bunches and leaves above. On the the nave side of it, stand, side by side, and both of wood, an 1892 lectern, and a pulpit of lovably antique feel, its sides carved with two tiers of patterned arches and the date 1624 and initials IM – for John Meller or Miller – painted inside one of them.

*Winterborne Came. Tudor screen, Jacobean pulpit, Victorian lectern.*

It may be his father, another John Meller, lying in grand state with his wife in the chancel on the altar's left. Their feet point east, to be facing the right way at the resurrection, and they hold their hands – fingerless now – in prayer. Both are stylishly dressed. Opposite them, on the south wall, brasses above a massive altar tomb record the death in 1591 of a Meller daughter.

The name Came comes from the French

*Winterborne Came. The effigies of John Meller and his wife.*

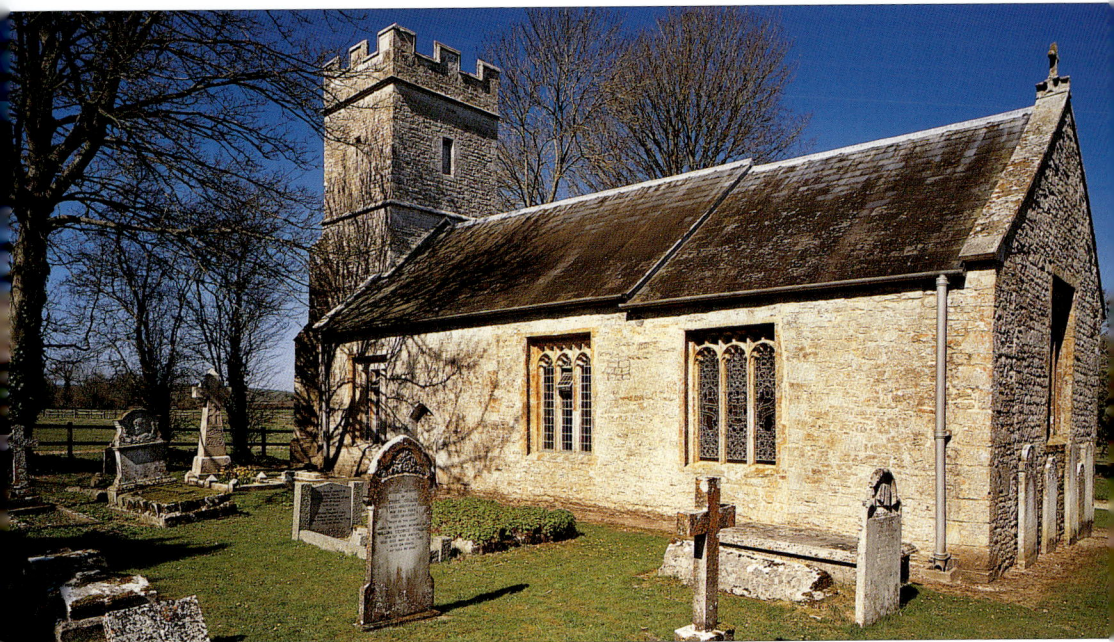

*Winterborne Came, with daffodils on William Barnes's grave in the background.*

Caen, whose abbey of St Etienne was granted the place in Norman times. The estate's first post-Reformation owners were Pembroke Herberts, based at Wilton. The Mellers bought it in 1561, kept it nearly two centuries and sold it in the early 18th century to Joseph Damer – 'miser and usurer' Swift called him. Damers already possessed estates in Dorset and Ireland, and soon (in 1752) acquired and transformed the magnificent demesne of Milton Abbas. Came, very much the junior partner, was used by younger brothers. The last of the Damers died in 1829 and left everything to Dawson cousins, earls of Portarlington, who already had one of Ireland's finer mansions, Emo Court, in county Kildare. In return for the bequest they were required to add a barrel to their name and become Dawson-Damer. They sold Milton Abbas in 1852, but Came stayed and stays in the family, though due to female inheritance the name has changed again. (Name and title continue, though, in

Australia, where the family's main line took up big-time meat-packing). Many of the tablet memorials in the chancel are linked to this sequence, with sundry connections to other West Country landowners: Montagu, earls of Sandwich, Feilding, earls of Denbigh, Seymour and so on. The most dashing description belongs to George Lionel Dawson-Damer, younger son of the first earl of Portarlington and a colonel in the army during the Napoleonic wars. He, we are told, saw the French cavalry retreat from Moscow, and at Waterloo had two horses shot from under him and was himself wounded. He survived the battle by forty years and lived during that time in Came House with his family.

All the same, after the wordy tributes to characters of wealth and title but no special note, it is nice to come across, at the other end of the church, a modester tablet put there by the Reverend Lord Sidney Osborne, dynamic reformist rector of Durweston, 'in affectionate remembrance of Harriet Voss, a servant of his family for twenty-five years: truly loved and valued.'

## WINTERBORNE TOMSON
*St Andrew*

'Do you know/ have you seen/ are you including . . . ?' Thus begin the frequent eager questions put to you when you write a book about Dorset churches. The name of the church that completes the inquiry is likely, by a majority of about five to three, to be Winterborne Tomson.

The church of St Andrew is, if ever there was one, a church for our age: stone-built, modest, free of cosmetic aids, simply handsome, with inner surfaces of plaster and bleached oakwork, fine flagstoned floor, and the apse-shaped chancel – the priest's domain – divided from the nave – the people's – by a plain and most undivisive wooden screen. Rich in the scars and character of age, the walls, due partly to the tapering of the walls, appear to lurch outwards. A slighter lean on the outside gives the curve-ended exterior some of the character of a ship's prow. St Andrew's is set unfussily beside a working farm and 17th century farmhouse in the gently uneven, hedge-chequered meadowland of the Winterborne valley. It seems to encapsulate modesty and good craftsmanship.

Taste's fluctuations are well illustrated here. In 1889, a five-minute walk away in the

*Winterborne Tomson, church and farmyard are only separated by a wall.*

tiny village of Anderson, the existence of St Andrew's was overlooked when a new church, St Michael's, in a high Victorian reproduction of Early English style, its arches and pinnacles aspiring skywards, was built on the site of the decayed old church. St Andrew's slowly rotted, becoming shelter for a motley of domestic and other animals. In time, tables turned. Ugly, perhaps, to our eyes, St Michael's is nowadays unwanted, crumbling, and locked to keep people out. Winterborne Tomson, on the other hand, was rescued from ruin. From 1929 to 1931, funded by the sale of Hardy manuscripts belonging to the Society for the Protection of Ancient Buildings, its secretary for 25 years Albert Reginald Powys, brother of the bevy of literary Powyses, supervised a full-scale restoration. Adequately maintained by the Churches Conservation Trust, St Andrew's always welcomes the wayfarer. Official redundancy seems the wrong fate for a church of such benign appeal.

It was built in the early 12th century and, though a rare single-cell survival of Norman times, no doubt resembles in main structure a large number of English churches then in use.

*Winterborne Tomson, the perfect balance between bleached oak and whitewashed walls and ceiling.*

Curved apses would soon be out of fashion (as would mannequin-thin buttresses, attached to the apse). This is the only Norman apse still in place in Dorset. Outmoded too would be round-topped windows, but one has escaped here, near the west end of the south wall. The wagon-roof and a few other changes came in either the 15th century or 16th century. The old rood-screen became the present west gallery. The bell inside the little bell-cote on the roof-ridge is dated 1668. Archbishop of Canterbury from 1716 to 1737, William Wake was responsible for the next important phase of reconstruction. An ecumenist before his time, who made moves towards a union of the Anglican with the French Catholic church, he gave the church its delightful content of bleached oak: the west door, font cover, box pews, two-decker pulpit with tester, screen with arch above the pulpit stairs to give the preacher more headroom on his way up and down, and the communion rails and table, mostly in decent condition, and, where riddled with worm holes, at least treated to halt the process. Thus, besides being almost uniquely Norman, the church matches Chalbury in the thoroughness of its 18th century character.

## WINTERBOURNE STEEPLETON
*St Michael*

It stands at the east end of a handsome stone village, opposite the gabled, Wyatt-designed, Purbeck stone manor house (now an old peoples' home) and shaded by tall beeches strewn with rookeries. On the east and south sides, the churchyard retains some crumbling early 18th century table tombs – probably of the grander local farmers – adorned with skulls, crossbones and other emblems of mortality. The fields beyond and southward rise to become the south Dorset downs. On their heights, and all around, sanctity older than Christianity is recalled by burial mounds and formations of standing stones, erected three thousand and more years ago.

*Winterbourne Steepleton, the 10th century stone carving of a winged angel*

The earliest parts of the church date from before 1066 and the Conquest, possibly from the 10th century and before. They include the nave's external corner-stones and a curious carving in the chancel. The walls of the western half of the nave went up in the 12th century, but big, three-light 15th century Perpendicular windows have been inserted into them. The tower, shortish, simple, sturdily buttressed, with a plain parapet, was added late in the 14th century. For such elegance as it possesses, it has to be grateful to the eight-sided steeple on top of it, with four plain pinnacles at its corners. This seems to be an 18th century replacement of the medieval original which gave the place its name. Inside, the whitewashed walls (above the dados) and ceilings, along with the painted gallery, built in 1708 and sporting the arms of the present Queen, have, since her Golden Jubilee of 2002, given the place a clean, rather Quakerish look. Spick, span and simple, it all holds together agreeably and with a minimum of garnish.

There are some blocked archways in the walls, one of which, on the north side, close to the pulpit and bigger than the rest, led to a chapel and, under it, the mausoleum of the Lawrence family. They acquired the manor at the Reformation and stayed two centuries, but were hardly gone before the chapel was down and their mausoleum succeeded by another, seen now as a large grassed-over hump in the ground. It is possible they were relations of the Laurences of Steeple and so distantly related to George Washington. The richly carved panels of the pulpit are 17th century, though in this case the main structure is modern. The font is late Norman, with bold three-dimensional design carving: a thick rope-work rim, above an arcade of twin round arches, every other arch resting on marble piers. On the south wall, opposite the pulpit, is a blocked aperture leading to the stone steps that until the Reformation mounted to the former rood loft.

Wispy rectangles of faint colour seem to float across the north nave wall and above the south doorway: recently revealed and restored fragments of wall paintings from as early as the 13th century and as late as the 17th century. Only a partial and faded St Christopher and the Stuart royal arms – actually half the royal arms – facing the south doorway and above a blocked alcove are remotely recognisable. We can see in the heraldry the Scottish unicorn though not the English lion, and discern the fleur-de-lys that signified, and would continue to signify well into the 18th century, English possession of France, in spite of the loss of that empire in the middle of the 15th century. A helpful framed key is in the niche below.

And there in the chancel, a wonderfully expressive, deeply discomfited winged angel lies on his back, legs twisted, head painfully crimped, one wing still outstretched, grimly stared at by a skull he holds. He could have fallen downstairs but his descent is likely to have been more cosmic. The stone carving is of the 10th century, placed now on the chancel's north wall, having been brought in from the outside to save it from weathering and worse. Its original position is as unknown as the early history of the church, but the church's dedication to St Michael may give the story away. This is Lucifer, fallen from heaven because he aspired to rise higher than God. 'Is this the man,' asks Isaiah (indirectly getting at the king of Babylon), 'that made the earth to tremble, that did shake kingdoms?' In medieval times Isaiah's

*Winterbourne Steepleton. The delicate 18th century steeple neatly mirrors the pinnacles on the corners of the tower.*

Lucifer became blended with the Satan of the Book of Revelation, that 'serpent of old', who waged war against Michael and his angels – and of course lost. In time representations of Satan became more and more gruesome, but the stark and telling simplicity of this sculpting, and others of its antiquity, are timeless.

## WYKE REGIS

*All Saints*

Roads and houses press against the boundary of the church on its hillside. But you can see and smell the sea, and perhaps the brightness of the church's white Portland stone owes something to centuries of salt spray. All Saints' attachment to the sea is strong. Its tower, boasting now a large gold-on-black clock-face, was a prominent landmark to sailors, and its graveyard accepted the corpses of hundreds of drowned seamen. John Wordsworth, the poet William's brother, was captain of the *Earl of Abergavenny* when it sank with all hands in 1805. He lies under an unmarked grave on the south side of the church. Eighty of his crew were packed together on the north.

All Saints has presented much the same lofty profile for the best part of six hundred years, ever since its rebuilding and rededication in 1455, prime time for Dorset's predominantly Perpendicular churches. Starkest in winter, the landward side loses its configuration in spring to the greenery of

*Wyke Regis. For centuries, the tall battlemented tower has been a prominent landmark for sailors.*

*Wyke Regis. The grave of Will Lewis, a smuggler 'killed by a shot from the Pigmy schooner' in 1822.*

churchyard trees and shrubs rising from among stones of all ages and conditions and a rich spread of bulbs. The list of rectors dates from 1302, but nothing but a few corbels go back to that time. There may have been a Norman church, but there is no sign of it. The tall tower has battlements and two-light belfry windows, with a bigger three-light window on the west side, while the nave parapets, as in the rest of south Dorset, are plain-topped. The south porch has empty niches above the outer entrance and the inner door.

The interior presents an impression of spaciousness. Originally this roominess would have been augmented by the absence of pews, brought in after the Reformation, but reduced by the rood screen, dividing chancel from nave, which was destroyed by it. In general over the pre-Perpendicular centuries, while the rood screen, with its loft or stage from which rose a model of Christ on the Cross, with Mary and John the Evangelist either side of it, had grown in size and significance, the arch above and beside it, dividing nave from chancel, gradually diminished until, as here, it disappeared completely. The screen and loft, very decorative, with accommodation for musicians on high, was a more than sufficient partition. To tally with Puritan phobia of ornament, however, roods and their infrastructures were done away with. The church that lacked a chancel arch became a large, rectangular, undifferentiated chamber. (The absence of one wing from each of two facing wall-angels marks the position of the beam that carried the screen). Fortunately, thanks to a mighty five-light east window, and to a nicely placed oval memorial plaque on either side, to elegant wall shafts supporting a string of moulded cornices and supported in turn by carved angels, and to a spray of wall tablets and to the tall aisle arches, Wyke Regis's east end is elegant and inviting.

The tablets, as so often, recall in quaint and sometimes outdated spellings doings and deaths of old British empire-builders: 'a Brigade Major in the Waziristan Force' who had taken part in the disastrous siege of Kut (1916, in Iraq) and endured three years in Turkish captivity; an army lieutenant, just 21,

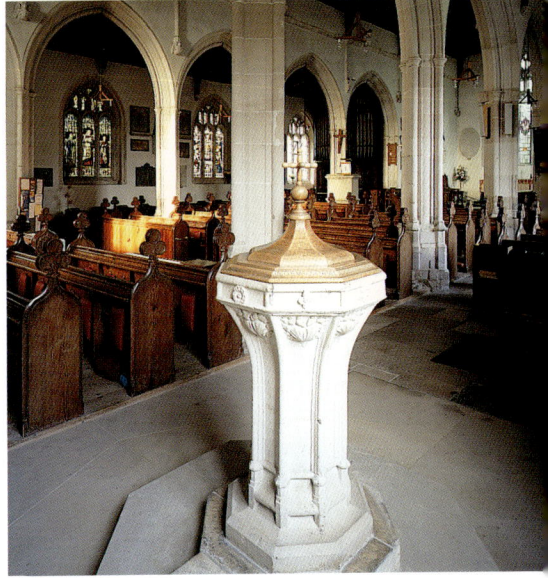

*Wyke Regis, tall aisle arches add to the roomy feel of the nave.*

dead 'from the effects of climate, at Jaccatalla, East Indies' in 1854; a scholar of New College, Oxford, killed near the village of Voormezeele in Flanders in 1916 as he tried to rescue a wounded comrade. An inscription of 1800, by a sculpted vase and female form, addresses itself to Lydia Harden aged 36: '. . . the cold convulsive grasp of death/ Seiz'd thy pale form, and check'd thy quiv'ring breath . . .' and here and there are commemorated scholarly pastors who died in their beds, old, comfortable and respected.

The head of a king and queen on the eastern pillars of, respectively, the north and south central aisle arches, are said to represent Henry VI and his spirited consort Margaret of Anjou, reigning when the present church was dedicated; an ill-matched pair, with the pious king taking his meals before a picture of Christ's five wounds while his wife was out winning battles. The church contains two royal arms. The relief version above the entrance doorway, said to have come from Sandsfoot Castle, Weymouth, is Tudor, showing the French lilies quartering the lions of England. The English claim to

France, a hundred years out of date in Tudor times, was to continue in heraldry till the 19th century. The painted version over at the west end of the north aisle is, despite appearances, from the time of George I. It shows the lions of England, the lion of Scotland, the lilies of France, the harp of Ireland and, in the bottom right-hand quarter the states the new king brought with him: the two golden lions of Brunswick, the blue lion of Lüneburg and the white horse of Hanover. The 'I' of George I was simply advanced to 'II' and then 'III' as kings of the same name succeeded.

## YETMINSTER
*St Andrew*

It is mildly astonishing. From the glowering tower, underneath the proud-tailed, gilded weathercock of 1749, every three hours on the hour, night and day; a bit flat here, then a mite sharp, and sometimes a little halting, like a persistent child at piano practice; nevertheless, bravely and unmistakably, across the dark yews and venerable table tombs of the broad churchyard, the thatched, mullion-windowed, 17th century merchant houses, farmhouses and cottages of one of Dorset's better preserved villages, and over the surrounding fields of this rich pastoral farmland; from the tower, following the striking of the hour by Thomas Bartholomew's 17th century turret clock, the bells of St Andrew's, without human agency these days, peal out the notes of the National Anthem. They have done so since 1897, the year of Queen Victoria's diamond jubilee. And it is somehow suitable that they should do so, for St Andrew's is a decent and upright church, a straight-down-the-line church, handsome, not over-complicated but with a fine framework, outside and in, and a few esteemed contents which it is touchingly keen to show you. Indeed you can see almost all its best treasures the moment you penetrate the north porch and push open the heavy wooden door.

*Yetminster. For over a century the bells have pealed out the notes of the National Anthem every three hours.*

The church's origins are obscure. The shaft of a 10th century cross, decorated with two carved holy heads emerging from a pattern of interwoven strips, and standing now on a window ledge in the chancel, suggests a Saxon church was here. What survives, though, is on the one hand an Early English chancel of around 1300, its initial character much obscured by heavy 1857 and 1890s Victorianising, and on the other a nave, aisles, porch and tower of the later 15th century. All the aisle windows are broad, four-light Perpendicular, with tracery to match. The pillars, for their part, with their dainty capitals, still, especially in the north arcade, retain more stains of dark red pigment than pillars usually do.

Taken together with the aisles, the nave is broad, almost square, and the visitor's first impression might be the airy, elevating effect of the three mighty arches on each side, and the billowing wagon roof between. But feet away, up on the west wall of the north aisle, the figure of Bridgett Minterne, wife of John Minterne, catches the eye first. She died on 19 July 1649, six months after the beheading of Charles I. Her kneeling posture, within a deep round-headed archway, is pious, her black hood and dress and white collar and cuffs are puritanical; yet the cushion is tasselled, and the adjacent paired columns, with their Corinthian capitals, under an architrave that blazons her status in the colourful language of heraldry, indicates considerable wealth. We are reminded that allegiances in the civil war and the republic that followed it did not follow class lines. Still in view, but on the opposite wall, is a slab on which are fixed the components of a brass memorial to Sir John Horsey of nearby Clifton Maybank (still a private house), who died in 1531, and his wife. These components – the figures, he in armour with a decorative breastplate and skirt of chainmail, his long locks neatly combed and hands joined in prayer, she in a long dress and flowing cloak, with a round vessel being held just off the ground at the end of her long belt, and the inscription, and little wisps of brass carrying the words 'Lady helpe' or 'Jehu mercy' as it were floating among them – were in 1890 restored and attached to their dark wall panel. The Horsey annals show well the fickleness of fortune. Soon after Sir John's death, the Reformation closed Catholic convents and his daughter, a nun, was driven from hers. A generation later, Sir John's grandson was a commissioner, acting with the spoilers and appropriators, while a nephew helped an unsuccessful plot to remove Catholic Queen Mary from the throne and substitute Elizabeth. Yetminster can recall another switch of fortune. As an agricultural recession bit into rural life in the second half of the 19th century, Lord Sydney Godolphin Osborne, Rector of Durweston, singled out the condition of Yetminster for his angry complaint : 'the cesspool' he called

*Yetminster. A 'decent and upright church, a straight-down-the-line church, handsome, not over-complicated but with a fine framework, outside and in, and a few esteemed contents . . .'*

it, 'of everything in which anything human can be recognised.' There is nothing in church or village to recall that.

Some original pews, a few with intact bench-end pommels or poppy-heads (derived not from the flower but the French *poupée*, a tied bunch of hemp or flax), stand at the back of the church. The carved screen behind them is of 1906. A millennial restoration brought this and the organ forward a bit, allowing for a glass partition to close off the tower and prevent an escape of much nave heat. Unfortunately sheets of glass, however warming, never look appropriate in this kind of arrangement.

Virtually all this is visible from close to the north door. As is the original Norman font base – the later 15th century octagonal font is attached to a south arcade pier – the

*Yetminster, the brass memorial to Sir John Horsey and his wife.*

unremarkable pulpit and lectern, some of the unobtrusive modern glass engravings, commemorating modern happenings and people, in bottom left corners of the big windows, and the two corbels on the chancel arch on which once rested the rood beam. The rood-loft is said to have been excep-

*Yetminster, the memorial to Bridgett Minterne.*

tionally grand, and the screen base evidently survived until the 1890s. Visible too are the bosses and original painted pattern of the north nave roof. Of course we move in, to take in the variant views and feel of the church, the chancel shrinking to a lesser dimension and darker shade, the old Saxon shaft it contains, and the 18th century altar rail, and the brass commemorating a young Englishman working in what was in 1912 Rhodesia – killed by a buffalo; and to appreciate the capitals on the south arcade piers. They consist of carved animals where the north has leaves and patterns. One shows a curious scene: an improvised scaffold on which a fox is being hanged on a rope whose ends are held in the beaks of two geese. The fox is said to represent the avaricious monks of the century before the Reformation, and to have given satisfaction to those many in a congregation whose tithes and offerings went to their support.

All sorts of things can depress church visitors: the lockings of doors, smothering of ancient treasures with security notices or children's scribblings and daubs, sweepings away of rood-screens, absence of brochures, failure to explain, a plethora of appeals for money, a shortage of welcome, of consideration and of Christian personality. On recent visits to St Andrew's two tiny welcome things caught my fancy. On a framed list of four benefactors who bequeathed money, between 1643 and 1811, to pay for bread for the poor, was notice of prayers in their memory to be said on the first Sunday of November every year. Gratitude that lasts suits a church. So did the reminder, written in ink on a postcard, beside electric switches in the chancel, addressed no doubt to the verger and not intended for my eyes: 'Please leave the sanctuary floodlight on when the church is unlocked,' it said; 'it makes it look more welcoming on darker days.' What surprises, I suppose, is that a simple, kind sentiment like this should seem as rare in a church as the notes of God Save the Queen resounding from the tower.

# SIGNIFICANT DATES

681 The minster at Beaminster issued with a charter.

705 King Ine founds the bishopric of Sherborne and appoints Aldhelm first bishop.

713 Cuthberga founds nunnery at Wimborne.

9th and 10th centuries Frequent Danish raids on Dorset coast.

964 Milton Abbey founded.

1043 Edward the Confessor refounds Wimborne nunnery.

1050 Approximate date for transition from Saxon to Norman or Romanesque architectural styles.

1075 Diocesan seat transferred from Sherborne to Salisbury (until 1542).

1086 Domesday Book: Dorset population 35-50,000; English population 1,200,000-1,500,000. The Church, mainly monasteries, holds about a third of Dorset's land.

1094 Building of Christchurch Priory begun (reign of William II).

1100-1175 *Very roughly*, Norman architecture.

1148 Forde Abbey built.

1150 Christchurch Priory nave complete.

1150-1200 Transitional architecture: Norman to Early English.

1200-1300 *Very roughly*, Early English architecture.

1213 Pope Innocent III imposes interdict on England, closing churches and suspending services. King John yields; accepting that England is a papal fief.

1215 Magna Carta.

1291 Dorset listed as possessing 171 churches.

1300-1400 *Very roughly*, Decorated architecture.

1300-1450 Growing resentment of slack and often French-speaking clergy.

1337-1453 Hundred Years' War: spasmodic campaigns by and against French.

1341 Dorset possesses 218 churches.

1348-1349 Black Death kills a third to a half of England's population. In Dorset 100 priests die in seven months (at Winterborne Clenston four in six months).

1380 First English bible; translated by John Wyclif. Lollards assert anti-Papal, proto-Puritanical views, foreshadowing the Reformation.

1400-1500 *Very roughly* Perpendicular architecture.

1437 Sherborne Abbey mostly destroyed by fire.

1450 Jack Cade's Rebellion in London. Bishop Ayscough of Salisbury, landlord of Sherborne, murdered.

1475 Bere Regis wooden roof built.

1485 Battle of Bosworth. Henry VII, first Tudor monarch, crowned; appoints Dorset-born John Morton Archbishop of Canterbury and Chancellor.

1500-1600 *Very roughly* Tudor architecture (but few churches built after 1540).

1534 Henry VIII Supreme Head of Church in England.

1535 234 churches in Dorset.

1536 English Bible placed in every church in England.

1539 Dissolution of the Monasteries. Seven in Dorset closed in ten days.

1542 Dorset incorporated in new Bristol diocese till 1836.

1545-1547 Suppression of chantries and their funds.

1547-1553 Reign of Edward VI. Reformation warms up. Services in English,

English prayer book compulsory, clergy may marry, images, screens and stained glass smashed, plate and other valuables confiscated.

1553-1558 Reign of Catholic Queen Mary. 300 Protestants burned at stake.

1558-1603 Reign of Queen Elizabeth I.

1559 Acts of Supremacy and Uniformity restore Protestantism as English religion.

1570 Pope excommunicates Queen Elizabeth and orders her to be deposed.

1581 Reconciling or being reconciled to Rome made high treason.

1581-1600 Fifteen Dorset RC priests and laymen executed.

1588 Spanish Armada defeated.

1600-1700 *Very roughly* Jacobean and Renaissance architecture.

1605 Gunpowder Plot.

1605 John White rector of Holy Trinity and St Peter's, Dorchester.

1623 John White's Dorchester Company sends Puritans to found New Dorchester, Massachussets.

1633-1640 William Laud, Archbishop of Canterbury, suppresses Puritan practices and imposes his High Church reforms.

1642 Denzil Holles of Dorchester, maverick Parliamentarian, is one of five urging Puritan measures whom Charles I fails to arrest in Parliament. The episode helps set off the Civil War.

1642-1645 Civil War. Defence of Corfe Castle by Lady Bankes and its destruction by Parliamentarians. Two sieges of Sherborne. Most Dorset towns change hands more than once.

1645 Clubmen try to disrupt the war; Cromwell arrests many on Hambledon Hill and locks them in Shroton church.

1649 Execution of Charles I. Plain Puritan styles adopted in church furniture and services.

1653 Cromwell Lord Protector.

1660 Restoration of Charles II. The Clarendon Code (1661-1665) and other measures re-establish Anglicanism and Nonconformity.

1685 Death of Charles II. His RC brother succeeds as James II. Monmouth Rebellion, starting at Lyme, tries to oust him in favour of Protestant Monmouth, and is ferociously suppressed by Judge Jeffreys, sitting in Dorchester. James begins to restore Catholicism.

1688 William III ousts James in the 'Glorious Revolution' and affirms England as Protestant. Various acts relieve Nonconformists but not Catholics.

1732 Rebuilding of Blandford Forum and its church after fire.

1786-1787 First free-standing Catholic church in England since Reformation built at Lulworth.

1800 and after Evangelicals preach brotherhood of man and an end to slavery.

1831 Reform Bill riots lead to burning down of Bristol Bishop's Palace and library and loss of mass of records.

1833 Launch of the high church Oxford Movement aiming for more ritual, spirituality and beauty of service and building.

1836 Dorset restored to Salisbury diocese.

1836 A.W.Pugin inspires revival of the Gothic style for new churches. His influence is huge and accompanies a resurgence of ceremonial and ritual.

1837-1854 Great revival of church building in the Salisbury diocese under Bishops Denniston and Kerr Hamilton.

1850 Catholic hierarchy re-established in England and Wales.

1877 William Morris founds the Society for the Protection of Ancient Buildings.

1959 Founding of Dorset Historic Churches Trust.

1969 Founding of Redundant Churches Trust, now Churches Conservation Trust.

# GLOSSARY

**altar tomb:** see **table tomb**

**ambulatory:** passage running behind sanctuary and altar, usually within an east end apse.

**apse:** semi-circular, often vaulted, east end of a generally Norman chancel or side-chapel.

**arabesque:** decorative pattern of curved lines.

**arch:** Norman doorway and window arches were round and narrow, within very thick walls. Early English were narrow, pointed 'lancets'. Ogee arches arrived around 1300.Much wider and shallower arches were typical of the 15th and 16th centuries.

**architrave:** the moulding framing a doorway or window; a horizontal main beam resting on column capitals in the entablature.

**Arts and Crafts Movement:** a movement of the second half of the 19th century, inspired by Ruskin and Morris; resolved to return to traditional, individual skills and handwork.

**ashlar:** smooth-faced blocks of squared masonry, used to form neat wall surfaces, concealing rougher stone.

**aumbry:** small cupboard or recess in which communion vessels are kept.

**baluster:** one of the curve-shaped posts supporting the railing of a balustrade.

**baptistery:** the part of a church containing the font and used for baptisms; usually at the west end, to signify the arrival of a newcomer in the body of the church.

**barrel vault:** see **vault**

**bellcote:** simple turret usually on a towerless church's west gable, incorporating an arch or arches in which bell or bells are hung.

**bell-window:** window in upper part of a tower, often part-blocked by louvres or tracery to soften the sound of bells.

**bier:** a stand, usually wheeled, on which a coffin was brought to the church.

**buttress:** a projecting external support for a wall. Norman buttresses were simple and slight. The thinner walls, bigger windows and increasingly heavy vaults of Gothic styles necessitated ever stronger buttressing. Built in stages that grew smaller from base to top, buttresses became conspicuously decorative. *Angle buttresses,* used from the 13th century onwards, were built in pairs, at right-angles to the wall and adjacent to corners. *Setback* buttresses were placed a short distance away from corners. *Clasping buttresses* are square, clamping the building's entire corners. *Diagonal buttresses,* a 14th century introduction, also clamp the corner but are set diagonally to it. *Flying buttresses,* generally of the 15th century, are set away from the building and linked to it, high up, by half-arches.

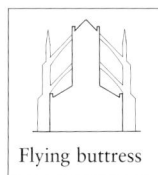

Flying buttress

**capital:** a pillar, pilaster or column usually has a masonry capping. Earlier Norman capitals tend to be plainly shaped in the *cushion, scallop* and other pattern designs. Later came various leaf designs, and by the late 12th century the prominent, stylised *stiff-leaf.* More lifelike leaves and fruits appeared in the 13th century, but in the 14th century plainer designs return, with or without bands of naturalistic leaves. Much 15th century Perpendicular work is characterised by octagonal capitals on circular pillars. In fact simply *moulded* capitals, undecorated, occur throughout the Gothic period.

**carillon:** a set of church bells, or one of the

---

*Buttresses*

Angle    Diagonal    Setback    Clasping

---

*Capitals*

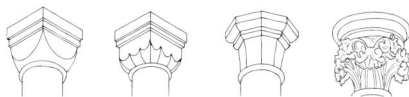

Cushion    Scallop    Moulded    Stiff-leaf

peals, tunes or changes played on it.

**cartouche:** a wall memorial tablet with a curvily ornate frame.

**chamfer:** the surface resulting from cutting away a square angle, eg. of a window or door frame, to make it oblique or splayed.

**chantry:** a late medieval chapel, usually within a church, often enclosed by tracery, intended for services for the soul of the founder.

**charnel house:** see **ossuary**

**cherub:** winged angel, as opposed to the unwinged putto, a small boy

**chevron:** zigzag moulding, mainly Norman.

**chi rho emblem:** symbol denoting Christ, formed of the Greek letters that start his name: chi (written X) and rho (written P).

**churching:** historically, a ceremony to readmit a woman to church life after childbirth.

**cinquefoil, quatrefoil, trefoil:** five-, four- or three-'foiled' or lobed apertures; particularly the tops of Gothic window-lights and other apertures, each lobe being separated from its neighbours by pointed cusps.

**clerestory or clearstory:** the upper part of nave or choir walls, above the aisle roofs, containing a line of windows.

**column, pier, pillar:** columns are usually round, slender and sometimes tapering, consisting of base, shaft and capital, and supporting an entablature, arch or simply a statue. A pillar is usually rectangular and bulkier and may lack separate base and capital. A pier is a more massive pillar supporting a heavier load. But the three terms tend to be used interchangeably.

**coping:** the sloping, protective top course of a wall.

**corbel:** bracket projecting from a wall, often decorative but essentially supporting an arch or ornament.

**corbel table:** a line of corbels supporting a stone course or cornice high on a wall.

**Corinthian:** see **order**

**cornice:** a (usually) moulded, continuous projection along the top of a wall or arch.

**course:** continuous horizontal line of masonry along an external wall.

**crenellated:** battlemented.

**cusp:** the point formed by the adjacency of two foils or lobes in Gothic tracery.

**Decorated:** see **vault**

**diaper:** decorative pattern of simple shapes like squares or lozenges all over a flat surface.

**dogtooth:** little pyramid-shaped ornament set diagonally on a moulding in a Norman or Early English archway.

**doom painting:** medieval wall painting or stained glass design showing Christ committing the damned to painful perdition on his left and the good to paradise.

**Doric:** see **order**

**dripstone:** see **hoodmould**

**Early English:** see **vault**

**Easter sepulchre:** a recess, generally in the north chancel wall, and containing a tomb, in which an effigy of Christ was concealed from Good Friday to Easter Sunday.

**Ecclesiology:** one of the early Victorian movements aimed at restoring pre-Reformation church design and decoration, stressing the sacred, the sacramental and the ritual; now applied more generally to the study of churches.

**encaustic tile:** tiles with patterns of yellow and dark red baked into them, common in both Gothic and Gothic Revival churches.

**entablature:** collective term for the architrave (or lintel), frieze and cornice arranged horizontally on columns or dividing wall from ceiling in classical architecture.

**Geometrical style:** see **window**

**Gothic:** architecture characterised by the pointed window and arch, pointed rib-vault, complex tracery and a variety of buttresses, prevailing in England from the late twelfth to the early sixteenth century, with later recurrences.

**Green Man:** a sculptured male head sprouting vegetation from its orifices, signifying fertility and surviving as a common medieval ornament from pre-Christian times.

**hammer beam:** short horizontal beam, sometimes very ornate, projecting from the base of a medieval timber roof and supporting the main braces.

**hatchment:** diamond-shaped wooden panel painted with a dead person's shield of arms, hung on his house, later in church.

**hood-mould:** projecting moulding above a window or doorway to keep off rain; also known as a **dripstone** or **label.**

**iconoclast:** one of the mainly post-Reformation Puritans who smashed religious images – statues, stained glass and so on.

**Ionic:** see **order**

**journeyman:** in the middle ages, an artisan who travelled about hiring out his skills.

**keystone:** wedge-shaped stone placed centrally in an arch to make the structure fast.

**knapped flint:** flint chipped to make it square and smooth for wall-building.

**label:** see **hood-mould**

**label-stop:** the termination of a hood-mould, often made into a decorative feature.

**lancet:** tall narrow window with a pointed top, characteristic of the Early English style.

**lierne:** see **vault**

**linenfold:** wooden panelling carved to represent linen neatly folded in vertical curves.

**long-and-short work:** arrangement of Saxon quoins, or stones at the corners of buildings, in which horizontal stones alternate with vertical ones.

**lych gate:** covered gate at the churchyard entrance where, during a funeral, the coffin was set down to await the clergyman's arrival.

**minster:** originally signifying a monastery or its church, the word came to mean a church, occasionally a cathedral, with a large staff and within a parish containing several smaller churches

**misericord:** small shelf or bracket on the underside of a choir-stall's hinged seat to support a monk standing for long periods; often carved with decorative scenes or figures, often comical.

**moulding:** projecting or recessed strip, with a contoured cross-section, enriching and emphasising a wall, pier, doorway or other architectural feature.

**mullion:** vertical bar separating lights in a Gothic window.

**narthex:** a vestibule or lobby extending right across a church's main entrance.

**ogee:** a double curve, similar to but with a shallower sweep than a letter S or reverse S. One of each kind, joined at the top, often formed the head of a Gothic door or window.

**order:** any one of the five main classical styles of architecture: three Greek – Doric, Ionic, Corinthian – and two Roman – Tuscan and Composite. They are most easily identified by their shafts and capitals. The *Doric* shaft is fluted, without a base and with a plain capital. The *Ionic* has a base, a fluted shaft and curved volutes either side of its capital. The *Corinthian* shaft is fluted and its capital is a large round bundle of acanthus leaves. *Tuscan* is the most massive style, plain and with an unfluted shaft. The *Composite* style unites in its capital the leaf arrangement of Corinthian with Ionic volutes. The entablature and other features of each style are also distinctive.

**ossuary** or **charnel-house:** part of a church, or a separate building, in which bones lifted from the churchyard to make way for new burials were stored.

**Oxford Movement:** influential movement from 1833 to 1845, formed to revive and strengthen High Church Anglican principles, liturgy and architecture and revive select Gothic church designs; led by Keble, Newman and Pusey.

**pardoner:** before the Reformation, a church official licensed to sell indulgences, by which divine punishment was remitted.

**Perpendicular:** see **windows**

**pier:** see **column**

**piscina:** a basin, usually in a canopied niche in the wall south of the altar, in which communion vessels are washed.

**pillar:** see **column**

**poppy head:** ornamental finial on a bench end, probably derived ultimately from the Latin puppis meaning prow or figurehead, and having no real floral connection.

**presbytery:** the sanctuary: the raised part of a chancel to the east of the choir and traditionally containing the high altar.

**pulpit, two- and three-decker:** the two-decker provided a lower desk for reading the gospel and a higher for preaching the sermon. The three-decker allowed seat and desk at the bottom for the clerk.

**purlin:** roof timber fixed along the length of a roof, and helping to support the rafters.

**putto:** see **cherub**

**pyx:** vessel used to contain the bread and wine reserved for communion: or the vessel used to carry them to the homes of the sick.

**quatrefoil:** see **cinquefoil**

**quoin:** dressed stone at the external corner or angle formed by two walls meeting.

**rafter:** sloping beam supporting a wooden roof and running from the wall-plate to the central ridge.

rebus: a visual riddle, expressing the name of a
person not by letters but by carved images;
like the mill and tun (or barrel) representing
Bishop Milton in Milton Abbey.

reredos: screen of wood or stone, often
containing ornamental carvings, rising
behind the altar.

respond: half-pier or pillar set against the wall,
usually at the end of an arcade, and
supporting the last arch.

reveal: the surface cut into a wall to make the
opening for a door or window, especially
when the surface is at right angles, and not
diagonal to, the wall's main face.

rib: moulding raised on the surface of a vault to
mark the lines between its compartments or
simply as ornamentation

Ritualist: one who in the nineteenth century
tried to revive medieval church forms,
vestments and ceremony

rood: a rood was a cross; until the
Reformation, one stood in the rood loft of
every church. This rood loft was built on the
rood screen, which divided and still
occasionally does divide nave from chancel.

roundel: round window, panel or niche; the
latter often containing a bust.

sanctuary: the part of the chancel around the
high altar, east of the choir.

sedilia: row of seats, usually three, set in the
chancel's south wall, often under Gothic
canopies, for clergymen's use.

shaft: the part of a column, pillar or pier
between its base and its capital.

soffit: the underside of an architectural feature,
eg. arch or beam.

spandrel: the roughly triangular wall-space
marked by one side of an arch, a line drawn
vertically up from its springer and a line
drawn horizontally from its apex; or the
triangle between two arches and a line
joining both their apexes.

springer: the point from which an arch rises
from corbel, capital or other support.

squint or hagioscope: opening cut obliquely
through a wall to enable a priest conducting
a service at a side chapel to see and keep time
with a priest at the high altar.

stair turret: the turret attached to the outside of
a main church tower and containing the
stairs which lead from the ground floor to
the belfry and roof.

Stations of the Cross: fourteen scenes from
Christ's condemnation by Pontius Pilate
to his burial. They are painted or carved and
arranged around the church

stoup: dish containing holy water and placed
near the church's entrance.

strapwork: long bands or straps of carved stone
ornamentally arranged with twists, turns and
interlacing among other adornments on
Tudor and later tombs.

string course: horizontal, usually moulded band
running along the surface of an external wall.

tabernacle: ornamental canopied shrine
containing the wafer of bread representing
Christ's sacrifice.

table tomb: mainly 17th or 18th century
churchyard stone tomb of a well-off family
or individual, shaped like a solid altar.

tester: sounding-board, set above a pulpit to
amplify the preacher's voice.

tie beam: transverse beam of a timber roof,
connecting the bases of two rafters.

tierceron: see vault

tracery: see windows

Tractarians: early members of the Oxford
Movement who produced the *Tracts for Our
Times* from 1833 to 1841, promoting High
Church principles.

transept: the extension of a church to north and
south at the east end of the nave, making the
church cross-shaped.

transom: horizontal bar separating lights in a
Gothic window.

trefoil: see cinquefoil

triforium: arcaded passage above the nave
arcade and below the clerestory.

truss: triangular wooden framework supporting
a timber roof.

Tuscan: see order

tympanum: space between the lintel of a
doorway and the arch above it, sometimes
applied to the wall-space between chancel
arch and ceiling.

vault: the arched ceiling, or inner covering, of
part or all of a building, as opposed to the
roof, or topmost covering. Normans built
semi-cylindrical stone *barrel* or *wagon* vaults
over their church aisles, but not over wider
spaces such as naves, which were often
covered with flat timbers or by the outer roof
alone. The arches of arcades marking off
aisles and the outer windows opposite them

called for semi-cylindrical cuts, as it were, being made across the aisle vaults. The resulting intersections are *groins*, crossing the vaults diagonally and often marked by lines of stones. Each bay – the division of an aisle formed by one arch and the corresponding window – was marked off from its neighbours by a transverse *rib*. The arrival of the Gothic pointed arch at the end of the twelfth century allowed more scope for variety and greater size of vaults. From then on they could be built over naves and chancels. In the fourteenth century rib arrangements grew more complicated, with sprays of ribs rising from corner capitals and decorative bosses were often placed where ribs intersected. By the late Decorated period (late fourteenth century) rib patterns are being elaborated by smaller ribs known as *tiercerons*, which link side capitals with the central ridge rib, and *liernes*, running between the main ribs. The fifteenth century Perpendicular style brought in *fan-vaulting*, (actually first used with stone in mid fifteenth century) the sumptuous climax of vault development and a wholly English style, in which, all over the ceiling, sprays and wheels of ribs radiate from side capitals, or from massive pendants and other hubs on the vault's surface, in swirls of delicate tracery.

**vestry:** the room, sometimes an interior chapel or part of an aisle, in which vestments and some other movable church property is kept

**wagon roof: see vault**

**windows:** Due to the expense of glass, or fear of attack or robbery, or the need to keep the cold out, Norman windows were narrow and round-headed. When the Gothic style came to England, during the late twelfth century, the thin window gained a Gothic pointed top and is known as a *lancet*. Over the next century lancets grew taller and were often made in groups of two or more with pointed arches moulded above them. The space between the window tops and the arch was sometimes pierced by circular, quatrefoil or other decorative shapes. Such cut-out work is known as *plate tracery*. The thirteenth century Early English period introduced a marked refinement known as *bar tracery*. Where in plate tracery solid stone pierced with patterns had occupied the space within

*Window Tracery*

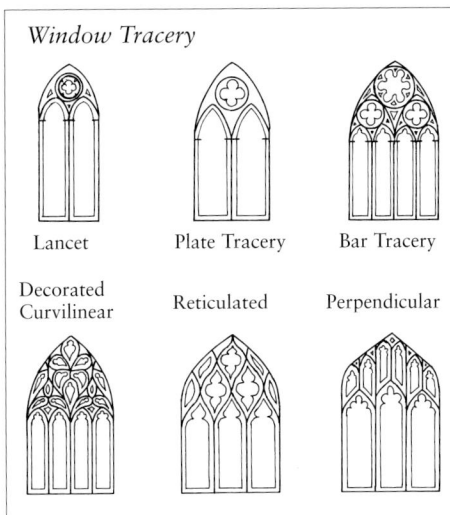

Lancet — Plate Tracery — Bar Tracery

Decorated Curvilinear — Reticulated — Perpendicular

the window arch, decorative patterns were now formed by sculptured stone bars. At first, till the start of the fourteenth century, the patterns were *Geometrical*, involving a large central circle or other shape with smaller shapes arranged around, or *Y-tracery*, in which a vertical mullion would divide into two towards the top, forming a Y shape. The main, lower part of the window would now be divided into separate lights by mullions, with cusped heads. In the fourteenth century, the Decorated period, the ogee arch was introduced, and the rich variety of tracery became more flowing and curving, or *Curvilinear*. *Reticulated*, or 'net-like' design, a regular mesh made from tracery curves and double curves, often within a square-headed window, now makes an appearance. The momentum of the Curvilinear style was much reduced, though not stopped, by the outbreak of Black Death in 1348-9. The *Perpendicular* style, the final major phase of medieval Gothic, dominated the fifteenth and early sixteenth centuries. Windows had grown in size, occupying whole bays between buttresses, and requiring the support of many mullions, which normally reached right up to the dripstone. The arches heading windows were shallower than before and, towards the end of the period, flat. Decorated's sumptuous curviness gives way to busy series of vertical lines and compartments: far less ornate, but a good setting for stained glass.

# FURTHER READING

Addleshaw, G.W.O and Etchells, F: *Architectural Setting of Anglican Worship.* Faber, 1948

Anderson, M.D: *History and Imagery in British Churches.* Murray, 1971

Bettey, J.H: *Church and Parish.* Batsford, 1987

Braun, H: *Parish Churches: their architectural development in England.* Faber, 1970

Briggs, M.S: *Goths and Vandals.* Constable, 1952

Brocklebank, J: *Victorian Stone Carvers in Dorset Churches.* Dovecote Press, 1979

Clarke, B.F.L: *Church Builders of the Nineteenth Century.* SPCK, 1938

Clifton-Taylor, A: *English Parish Churches as Works of Art.* Batsford, 1974

Coldstream, N: *Medieval Architecture.* OUP, 2002

Colvin, H.M: *Biographical Dictionary of English Architects.* Murray, 1954

Cox, J.C: and Ford, C.B: *Parish Churches of England,* 5th edition. Batsford, 1946

Cross, F.L (editor): *Oxford Dictionary of the Christian Church.* OUP, 1957

Crossley, F.H: *English Church Craftsmanship.* Batsford, 1941

Cullingford, C.N: *History of Dorset.* Phillimore, 1980

Cunningham, C: *Stones of Witness.* Sutton Publishing, 1999

Cunnington, P: *How Old is that Church?* Marston House, 1990

Curl, J.S: *Oxford Dictionary of Architecture.* OUP, 1999

Curl, J.S: *Piety Proclaimed.* Historical Publications, 2002

Draper, J: *Dorset, the Complete Guide.* Dovecote Press, 1992

Fleming, J, Honour, H, Pevsner, N: *Penguin Dictionary of Architecture,* 1999

Fowler, J: *Medieval Sherborne.* 1951

Friar, S: *Companion to the English Parish Church.* Sutton Publishing, 1996

Gardner, S: *Guide to English Gothic Architecture.* Cambridge U.P. 1925

Goodhart-Rendell, H.S: *English Architecture since the Regency.* Constable, 1953

Gray, A.S: *Edwardian Architecture.* Wordsworth, 1988

Hall, J: *Dictionary of Subjects and Symbols in Art.* Murray, 1974

Harris, J and Lever, J: *Illustrated Glossary of Architecture,* 850-1830. Faber, 1969

Harvey, J: *Gothic England.* Batsford, 1947

Hutchins, J: *History and Antiquities of Dorset.* 3rd edition, Nichols & Sons, 1861

Jenkins, S: *England's Thousand Best Churches.* Penguin, 2000

Johnson, Paul: *A History of Christianity.* Atheneum, New York, 1977

Jones, A: *A Thousand Years of the English Parish.* Cassell, 2002

*Kelly's Directory of Dorsetshire.* Kelly's Directories, 1939

Kerr, N (reviser): Sir John Betjeman's *Guide to English Parish Churches.* HarperCollins, 1993

Little, B: *Catholic Churches since 1623.* Hale, 1966

Livingstone, E.A: *Concise Oxford Dictionary of the Christian Church.* OUP, 2000

Long, E.T: *Introduction to Dorset Church Architecture.* Journal of the British Archaeological Association, 4, 1939

Miller, A: *Monasteries of Dorset*. Albemarle Books, 1999

Morris, R: *Churches in the Landscape*. Dent, 1989

Newman, J and Pevsner, N: *Dorset (Buildings of England)*. Penguin, 1972

Pitfield, F.P: *Dorset Parish Churches A-D*. Dorset Publishing Co, 1981

Pitt-Rivers, M: *Shell Guide to Dorset*. Faber, 1966

Platt, C: *Parish Churches of Medieval England*. Secker & Warburg, 1981

*Proceedings of the Dorset Natural History and Antiquarian Field Club*. Various articles, by E. T. Long and others

*Proceedings of the Dorset Natural History and Archaeological Society*. Various articles

Randall, G: *Church Furnishing and Decoration*. Batsford, 1980

Randall, G: *The English Parish Church*. Batsford, 1982

Royal Commission on Historical Monuments: *County of Dorset* (8 vols). 1952-1976

Service, Alastair: *Buildings of Britain* (6 volumes) Barrie and Jenkins, 1982

Summerson, J: *Architecture in Britain*, 1530-1830. Penguin, 1953

Taylor, C: *Dorset (Making of the English Landscape)*. Hodder and Stoughton, 1970

Thompson, A.H: *Ground-Plan of the English Parish Church*. Cambridge UP, 1911

Thompson, A.H: *Historical Growth of the English Parish Church*. Cambridge UP, 1911

Underdown, D: *Fire from Heaven*. Pimlico, 2003

*Victoria County History: Dorset*. Constable, 1908

Whiffen, M: *Stuart and Georgian Churches*. Batsford, 1947

Yates, N: *Buildings, Faith and Worship*. OUP, 1991

# INDEX